COTTON WAS KING

The Mill Girl by Winslow Homer. Courtesy of Merrimack Valley Textile Museum.

COTTON WAS KING

A History of Lowell, Massachusetts

Arthur L. Eno, Jr.
Editor

New Hampshire Publishing Company
in collaboration with the
Lowell Historical Society
1976

Permission to quote from the following
is gratefully acknowledged:

Columbia University Press for John P. Coolidge,
Mill and Mansion

Harvard University Press for John B. Pickard,
The Letters of John Greenleaf Whittier

Hannah Josephson for
The Golden Threads

CONTENTS

ILLUSTRATIONS

APPENDICES

Preface

It has been more than fifty years since the last general history of Lowell was published. Since Frederick W. Coburn wrote his three-volume study in 1920, a new technique of writing local history has emerged, stressing causes and effects rather than local lore and genealogy. During the same period there has been a great deal of scholarly investigation of Lowell as an industrial and cultural phenomenon. The technological basis of the Lowell Experiment has been measured and explored in depth; labor controversies have been outlined and analyzed; and the place of Lowell's female mill operatives in the history of American women has been recognized and much discussed.

After such activity, it is surprising that there is no modern general history of Lowell. To fill this void and to celebrate the sesquicentennial year of the incorporation of Lowell as a town in 1826, the Lowell Historical Society offers this new narrative of the highlights of the history of Lowell from Indian camp to modern city. This work is intended to stir the imagination of the young people of Lowell by retelling the accomplishments of the past. We also hope it will enable the student and scholar from beyond Lowell's boundaries to read, in one place, the background of the story as a prelude to their definitive analysis of the causes for the city's growth and decline. Finally, like Lowell's first historian, Charles Cowley, we hope that it "may tend to awaken that due sense of local pride, that patriotic public spirit, the absence of which, among us, has so often been the subject of criticism, both from strangers and residents, heretofore."

To produce this history, the Lowell Historical Society has drawn upon the multitude of talent in the community and the University of Lowell. A dozen different historians were asked to prepare individual chapters, each in an individual field of interest. The coordination of the chapters was left to an editorial committee of the Society, which was charged with making the style of writing consistent, avoiding gaps and overlapping material, and generally putting together the book. The result is this volume.

          *   *   *

The Society is grateful to many people for their cooperation in the production of this book: first of all, the authors for their time, patience and learning; Mildred E. Wahlgren for preparing the index; Martha Mayo, special collections librarian at the University of Lowell, for her courtesy and assistance throughout the preparation of this book, and particularly for preparing the bibliography; and, most of all, the editorial committee, consisting of Peter F. Blewett, Arthur L. Eno, Jr., Linda M. Frawley and Nancy Zaroulis, for their thoughtful editing and careful guiding of this book through publication.

Mary H. Blewett
President
Lowell Historical Society

September, 1976

Introduction

In man's four million year career he has revolutionized his economy only twice. The first time was about seven thousand years ago when man learned to domesticate wild cereal grasses. He went from being a hunter to being a farmer. This "agricultural revolution" began on the uplands of Iran, but reached its earliest full development in the Tigris and Euphrates river valleys. The food energy in the seed grains of emmer wheat and barley made possible the first great urban civilizations of Mesopotamia, Egypt, Greece and Rome.

In the mid-eighteenth century the second economic revolution introduced factory production of textile goods on a large scale using machines powered by energy derived from water-wheels. It began in the small river valleys of Lancashire, England. In America the first large factories rose beside the Pawtucket Falls on the Merrimack River in northeastern Massachusetts. What had been an underdeveloped section of the rural town of Chelmsford quickly became in the early nineteenth century America's first industrial city. It was named Lowell after the amateur industrial spy who memorized the design of the English power loom and later duplicated it for the American factories. The "industrial revolution" began in America at Lowell, and the new city became the prototype for a reorganization of American life.

The area which later became Lowell has had a long history of human occupation. American Indians of the Pennacook Confederacy fished the river and farmed the land near the Pawtucket

Falls for centuries. English colonial farmers gradually displaced them in the seventeenth century; after the Indians were gone their lands became part of Chelmsford, Massachusetts. Their surviving legacy in Lowell is meager: occasionally discovered caches of arrowheads, and a few street and mill names.

Lowell remained part of Chelmsford until 1826. The town's history in the colonial period rehearsed in detail the experience of the Massachusetts Bay Colony at large. In the seventeenth century Chelmsford had problems with church organization, Indians, the poor quality of the land, frontier wars, and overpopulation. After 1700 there were still more wars and considerable religious dissidence. Towards the end of the eighteenth century the agrarian economy changed. Taking advantage of the water power of both the Concord and Merrimack rivers, individual entrepreneurs opened small factories, sawmills, and woolentextile mills. Most of this activity centered on East Chelmsford near the place where the two rivers joined—the future site of Lowell.

Around the turn of the nineteenth century economic activity in East Chelmsford increased. Some merchants from Newburyport at the mouth of the Merrimack River tried to open the New Hampshire hinterland to commerce. They financed the building of the Pawtucket Canal which would allow barges to skirt the great falls of the Merrimack river at East Chelmsford. Within a short time a competing canal opened. Boston merchants constructed the Middlesex Canal which connected the Merrimack River above the Pawtucket Falls with Charlestown at Boston Harbor. It strangled the Pawtucket Canal's business. A failure as a transportation canal, the Pawtucket was available to become the nucleus of Lowell's system of power canals.

In 1821 the industrial revolution came to quiet, rural East Chelmsford. The site fulfilled the prerequisites for the development of factories. The water flowing over Pawtucket Falls provided the energy to power the machines; land was cheap and available; the Middlesex Canal gave access to Boston; rural New England could supply the young women who would work the textile machinery. By 1830 a considerable industrial town of red-brick factories and boarding houses had risen where only farms and a few small mills had existed ten years earlier. In 1826 it had broken away from Chelmsford to become Lowell; by 1840 it would be Massachusetts' second largest city.

For its first quarter century Lowell was the model industrial city. Its work force of young women was advertised to the world as well housed, well fed, and intellectually alive. Publicists failed to notice the shanty-town slum of the Irish who were the city's laborers. The visitors traipsing through Lowell on an itinerary provided by the mill management came away convinced that an industrial city did not have to be a hellish slum like Manchester, England. After 1845, beginning with the Irish, immigrants replaced the native women in the mills. The owners' paternalism ended, and with it Lowell's "golden age."

During the Civil War the cotton industry in Lowell closed down. After the war ended, the city's textile pre-eminence did not return. Throughout the remainder of the nineteenth century the industry's decline accelerated. In other areas of the city's life there were other changes. By 1900 the native population had given up political control of Lowell to the Irish, who were the largest of a number of foreign immigrant groups living in the city. The biggest of these ethnic groups have in turn challenged the Irish in politics. During the 1920s and 1930s the great textile mills closed. Depression, unemployment, and economic dislocation have dogged the city ever since. In the 1970s Lowell's unique position as the place where the industrial revolution started in America has been recognized. It is the basis of a projected revival of the city, now that cotton is no longer king.

Part One

I

Passaconaway's Kingdom

By J. Frederic Burtt

On a brilliant autumn day in 1660, an old man revered for his wisdom and his power to predict the future bade farewell to his people. They had gathered at the Amoskeag Falls, in what is now southern New Hampshire, to hear him.

"Take heed how you quarrel with the English," he said. "The white men are the sons of the morning. Never make war with them. Sure as you light the fires, the breath of heaven will turn the flame upon you, and destroy you. Listen to my advice. It is the last I shall be allowed to give you. Remember it and live."

The man who spoke was Passaconaway, "child of the Bear," sachem of the Pennacook Confederacy.* Passaconaway came to power about 1620. He was an excellent leader, a medicine man, a sorcerer and conjurer, a famous "powwow."

Before the European incursions of the early seventeenth century, the confederacy controlled all the territory from the northern Massachusetts coast to the White Mountains, and west to the Connecticut River. It was made up of several tribes: Pennacooks, Pawtuckets, Wamesits, Nashobas, Souhegans. They spoke an Algonquian dialect which is classed with those of the Cree, Montagnais, and Micmac of Canada.

*There is considerable confusion about the names of the Indian tribes. The settlers, following the lead of Gookin, appear to have applied the term "Pawtucket" to all the Indians north of the Merrimack River, and not only to the tribe which frequented the Pawtucket Falls.

Each spring, many Pennacooks gathered for the fishing season at the Pawtucket Falls in what is now Lowell. For this annual event tribes of the neighboring Massachusetts Confederacy joined them. During the day they caught the salmon, shad, sturgeon, alewives, and eels which then filled the river. These they cleaned, smoked, and cured. In the evenings they attended to tribal business: treaties, declarations of war, religious ceremonies, and the arrangement of marriages. After the fish had passed the falls, the Indians folded their wiciups (tents), gathered their possessions, and moved on to their planting grounds.

In cleared fields along the Merrimack and Concord, and on Robins Hill to the southwest of what was to become Chelmsford Center, the Indian women planted beans, squash, and pumpkins amidst hills of corn. They worked all summer long with their crude clamshell hoes to keep down weeds; they picked beans in August and harvested the squash and pumpkins before frost. The corn remained on the stalks as long as the kernels on the short, nubbly ears continued to grow. After the ears were gathered, the kernels were cut from the cob, boiled, and then beaten to make bread or porridge. Quantities of corn were stored underground in woven baskets to provide nourishment throughout the winter.

This way of life which had served the Pennacooks for hundreds of years began to come to an end early in the seventeenth century. They engaged in a disastrous war with a tribe from Maine, the Tarrantines. They were further weakened by a fatal disease—smallpox, or perhaps a form of plague—which spread rapidly and within a few years killed thousands of Pennacooks.

When the settlers of the Massachusetts Bay Colony began to move inland, they traded regularly with the local tribes. Blankets, hatchets, kettles, and trinkets were bartered for fish, baskets, and, especially, furs. Inevitably the white men coveted the Indians' lands. In 1629 Passaconaway made his mark on a deed which conveyed to one Reverend John Wheelwright all the land between the Piscataqua and Merrimack rivers.

Passaconaway tried to maintain good relations with the English. In 1632 he captured and delivered to Governor Winthrop for punishment an Indian who had killed an English trader. In 1642 the colonial authorities, alarmed by reports of Indian massacres of white settlers in Connecticut, sent a party of forty armed men to disarm Passaconaway and his tribe. They failed to find the sachem, but came upon his son, Wannalancit. They arrested him along with his wife and child.

Wannalancit escaped; shortly afterwards, when the other prisoners were returned by the authorities, Passaconaway accepted the whites' apologies and delivered all his guns to the colonial governor.

In 1644 Passaconaway signed another document drawn up by the English: a treaty whereby he submitted himself and his tribes to the authority of the Massachusetts Bay Colony, to be "governed and protected by them, according to their Just Lawes." The treaty further committed the Indians "from tyme to tyme to give speedy notice of any conspiracie . . . which we shall know or heare of against the same" and "from tyme to tyme to be instructed in the knowledge and worship of God."

The major missionary to the Indians was a remarkable man named John Eliot, minister of the Church at Roxbury. He began preaching to the natives at Nonantum (now Newton Corner) on the Charles River about ten miles west of Boston. He was a dedicated, zealous preacher who became known as the "Apostle to the Indians." He spoke fluently to the Indians in their language and translated the Bible for them.

In the spring of 1647 John Eliot visited the gathering of the tribes at Pawtucket Falls. Passaconaway, remembering the wrongs done to him and his family by the white man, refused to see him. The sachem wanted nothing to do with a religion which tolerated such injustices; further, he claimed that he was afraid the English would kill him. Eliot returned in 1648 and remained for many days, preaching and conversing. This time Passaconaway was more willing to listen; at the end of Eliot's stay he announced his conversion to the "God of the English." In 1649, on the occasion of Eliot's third visit, Passaconaway begged him to stay permanently. "My heart much yearneth toward them," commented Eliot, but he refused the invitation.

In 1653, at Eliot's instigation, the land which now comprises downtown Lowell—the triangle between the Merrimack and Concord rivers—was reserved by colonial authorities for the sole use of the Indians. It was called Wamesit, and it was one of Eliot's seven "Praying Villages" or Christian Indian towns. Every May, Eliot came to Wamesit to hold church services. The colony's superintendent (or magistrate) of the Indians, Daniel Gookin, accompanied him to hold court as justice of the peace.

John Eliot, 1604-1690. Courtesy of Roxbury Latin School.

Major General Daniel Gookin was as remarkable a man as John Eliot. He wrote two histories of the New England Indians which have been valuable sources for historians. He spent much of his life attempting to improve the condition of the increasingly dispossessed natives. He was charged by the authorities with the responsibility of overseeing every aspect of the Indians' lives and of attempting to educate them in the ways of the colonists. He served in this office for more than thirty years. When he died impoverished in 1687, Gookin was genuinely mourned by the people he had tried to help.

In 1660, Passaconaway abdicated in favor of his son. Wannalancit was slow to abandon his traditional deities—in part, said Gookin, because he feared that many of his "chief men and relatives" would turn against him if he converted to Christianity.

But in 1674, when Gookin and Eliot were at Wamesit during their annual visit, after Eliot had preached on the parable of the wedding of the King's son, Wannalancit announced his conversion to the Christian God. He was prepared "to enter into a new canoe," as he put it. He took up residence on an island just above the Pawtucket Falls. It was then called Wickassee, later Tyng's Island. This beautiful and fertile island had been sold by Wannalancit, with the permission of the colonial authorities, to bail his brother out of debtor's prison. Later, the purchaser, John Evered (alias Webb) was granted five hundred acres north of the Merrimack in return for releasing the island to Wannalancit.

King Philip's War broke out in 1675. Wannalancit, determined to remain neutral as his father had counseled, retreated to the north. Many of the residents of Wamesit Village accompanied him. The "praying Indians" who remained suffered at the hands of both Philip and the colonials. They were killed indiscriminately by both sides; they were confined to their village; many were interned on Deer Island in Boston Harbor.

The remaining Indians at Wamesit fled to join Wannalancit at the head of the Connecticut River in what is now northern Vermont. They suffered greatly that winter; many died. A few, too old or sick to travel, had been left behind. They were burned to death in their homes by Chelmsford men, who later took over their land. Despite these and other atrocities, Wannalancit continued to serve the colonists by informing them of imminent attacks by King Philip's troops.

After the war, a few Pennacook survivors returned to Wickassee Island where they were placed under the protection of

Colonel Jonathan Tyng. On his return, Wannalancit called upon the Reverend Mr. Fiske of Chelmsford and inquired how the town had fared during the war. Mr. Fiske replied that they had been highly favored, for which he desired to thank God. "Me next," replied Wannalancit, claiming his share of the credit for the whites' survival.

Soon Wannalancit and his people returned to the north, to the St. Francis River at Odanak, Canada, to unite with the St. Francis Indians. In 1686 they came south again and deeded to the English all the lands still remaining in their name. Homeless, they wandered back to Canada. In 1692, King William's War again threatened the colonists with attacks by hostile Indians. The residents of the Pawtucket Falls area, remembering Wannalancit's past friendship, requested him to return in the belief that his presence would make them more secure. Wannalancit came back and lived out the last four years of his life in Colonel Jonathan Tyng's house in Tyngsborough overlooking the Merrimack River. In 1696 he died. He was buried in the Tyng family cemetery. Colonel Tyng was rewarded for his generosity with a twenty-pound grant from the General Court, given to him after he petitioned for financial assistance for "the care and comfort of Wannalancit, last Sachem of the Merrimack Valley Indians and giving him a decent Christian burial."

A few remaining members of the original tribes continued to visit the Pawtucket Falls area well into the nineteenth century. In 1904 Judge Samuel Hadley of Lowell recalled that sixty years earlier he had visited the Indians who taught him to handle the bow and arrow. Lucy Larcom, in her reminiscences of her girlhood in Lowell, recalled seeing a fleet of canoes gliding up the Merrimack, carrying "grotesque relics of aboriginal forest life"—Penobscot Indians dressed in "loose gowns, stove-pipe hats, and moccasins." On August 18, 1834, Mary Hall, a weaver at the Merrimack Corporation, noted in her diary: "On Saturday evening went down to see some Indians about fifty in number who had pitched their tents on the banks of the Merrimack back of the Lawrence corporation." The natives, who had first been sought after for their trading goods, and later feared as a dangerous enemy and held in derision after their defeat by the whites, were now merely objects of curiosity. There is a local legend of the last surviving Indians in the area being placed on a train about 1842 and sent to the Penobscot Reservation at Old Town, Maine.

Arrowheads and other Indian artifacts can still be found occa-

sionally on the banks of the Concord and Merrimack rivers—
small relics of a well ordered, socialistic society depending upon
cooperative labor, a society antithetical to the driving, capitalist,
laissez faire industrialism of the successors to Passaconaway's
kingdom.

II

The First White Settlement: The Seventeenth Century

By Charles F. Carroll

During the 1630s, twenty thousand adventurers left the gently rolling, treeless English countryside and the narrow, winding London streets, crossed three thousand miles of ocean in frail wooden ships, and entered the dark and wild virgin forests of New England. Most of these pioneers were Puritans who believed that religious reforms, such as the abolition of the bishops and their courts and the election of church officials by members of individual congregations, were no longer possible under the Stuart king, Charles I. Some even believed that God was about to punish England for this perceived neglect of the Christian religion. They saw New England as a wilderness refuge, a new land of Canaan, where those who kept the faith might find protection from the wrath of the Lord.

The Puritan settlements of the early 1630s were along the coast of Massachusetts Bay, but as the Great Migration from England continued, many were forced to search for agricultural land in the interior. Farmers often settled on lands first explored and surveyed by men who roamed the wilderness in search of beaver skins for the European market. In 1635 Simon Willard, a fur trader at Cambridge, led a group of colonists through dense swamps and woodlands to the grassy river plain in the Musketaquid Valley at Concord. By 1640 Englishmen were settling the broad meadows of Sudbury. By 1644 Woburn and Reading were established. These were the earliest frontier towns in the eastern section of Massachusetts Bay. But by the early 1650s the frontier was moving again. By 1653 there were enough settlers at the fur trading post at Lancaster to form a town, and other farmers and traders were about to complete a new frontier line by founding Groton, Billerica, and Chelmsford.

Once these towns were established, the frontier in eastern Massachusetts did not advance for more than half a century. A few miles west of Chelmsford and Groton lay uplands cut by valleys and ravines, a land where overland transportation was extremely difficult. Although decimated by diseases contracted from European fishermen and explorers very early in the seventeenth century, the Indians were still numerous enough to keep Englishmen from encroaching on all of their lands. There were also some among the English who believed that there was sufficient room for all, and that Puritan and Indian could live side by side—provided the latter realized the awesome power of English firearms and gradually accepted Puritan attitudes towards nature, society, and religion.

Nowhere on the Massachusetts frontier did groups of Englishmen and Indians live in closer proximity than in the region around the confluence of the Merrimack and Concord rivers. It was the annual concentration of the Indians that first attracted the Englishmen. During the 1640s Simon Willard and his associates were dealing with the Indian fur trappers in this region, and Willard explored the Merrimack as far north as Lake Winnipesaukee. At the same time, John Eliot, the minister at Roxbury, began the study of the Algonquian language in order to spread the gospel among the Indian tribes. Eliot, unlike most of his fellow ministers, believed that the Indians were descendants of the Lost Tribe of Israel and that their conversion would hasten the Second Coming of Christ. As early as 1647 Eliot preached to the Indians on the banks of the Merrimack and established a small Christian community there. Willard and Eliot apparently worked in harmony. Willard, combining shrewd political and business practices with religious ideals, believed that Christianization would make the Indians more ambitious and honest in their dealings with the English. Indians who gave up their semi-nomadic way of life would also be better credit risks. Eliot wanted his native converts to settle permanently in one place, reject all customs and practices that conflicted with the Bible or traditional English values, learn to read and write, engage in agriculture, and learn carpentry, blacksmithing, and other trades. And if some of the older Indians were slow to learn English ways in such a "praying town," there was hope for the children who, more thoroughly anglicized, would transcend their "savage" state and discover that there were material as well as spiritual rewards to be gained from the Puritan ethic of industry and thrift.

But if the desire for Indian trade and conversions brought the first Englishmen to the Merrimack, it was land that attracted the Puritans who followed. In 1653 twenty-nine male residents of Woburn and Concord, some of whom owned no land at all, noted that the land near the Indian fishing grounds on the Merrimack was "a very comfortable place to accommodate a company of God's people." On May 18 of that year the Massachusetts General Court granted these Englishmen a large rectangular tract called Chelmsford, extending from the area near the present Groton-Westford border northeastward across Westford to a designated point (Pautuxet Stake) on the Concord River. In addition to the present Westford, the grant seems to have included a large portion of what is now Littleton and Carlisle. However, because of John Eliot's desire to protect his Indian community at Wamesit, the fields and meadows along the Merrimack and along the western bank of the Concord, an area of about fifteen hundred acres, were not included within the English grant. Thus, most of what became Lowell in the nineteenth century was set aside as Indian territory in 1653. The General Court also granted the Indians the right to retain their planting grounds on Robins Hill until the settlers opened an equivalent amount of land for the Indians' use within the Wamesit grant.

The English named their new settlement Chelmsford. About fifteen families began to erect the first hewn oak-framed houses at Center Village. They chose this site, in the northeast corner of their grant, because the brooks and a tract without trees or thick bushes allowed them to till the land and plant essential crops. In the beginning there was no organized Congregational church and no meeting house. Civil and religious meetings were held in the homes of leading men. It was at one such meeting in the late summer of 1654 that the town authorized four men, Robert and William Fletcher, Thomas Adams, and William Buttrick, to write a letter inviting the Reverend John Fiske and his small congregation at Wenham to settle in Chelmsford. After consultation with his congregation, Fiske and a number of Wenham settlers journeyed to Chelmsford to view the land, negotiate accommodations, and settle upon terms for the maintenance of the new minister. On October 10, 1654, Fiske and six men representing the majority of the Wenham Church agreed to migrate to Chelmsford the following year, and some began to sell their lands and houses. A number of the Wenham residents had second thoughts about the move during the winter of 1654–55. There may have been opposition from those they were leaving behind, but the persuasive rhetoric of Isaac Lernet, the agent for Chelmsford at Wenham, and a recommendation in favor of the move by Governor John Endicott and five leading men of Massachusetts Bay led to a final agreement. The migration probably took place after the fall harvest in 1655. On November 13 of that year Fiske and his small Wenham congregation of six members met at Chelmsford, inspected the letters of dismissal that seven Chelmsford inhabitants had received from their churches at Concord, Woburn, and Cambridge, and unanimously voted to receive these seven into the fold. The Chelmsford church was now organized, and as its first official act it voted to admit fourteen additional members. By the following summer at least sixteen more Chelmsford residents were voted into full fellowship, and by this time Fiske had baptized many of the children of church members. In 1660 the town levied a rate for a meeting house which by 1663 had been completed.

Aside from the account by John Fiske concerning the formation of the church at Chelmsford there are almost no sources for the daily life of the town during the early years of settlement. It does appear, however, that, unlike Andover, Sudbury, and many other New England towns, Chelmsford began its development mainly under a "closed-field" system of land tenure. Although the early inhabitants of nearby Andover received strips of land in a number of large "open-fields" that had to be protected by a common fence, and, in most cases, had to be exploited collectively, the settlers at Chelmsford received relatively consolidated farms that were enclosed by fences constructed by the individual owners. The only evidence of an exception to this system of land tenure during the early years was the development of Newfield, a 214-acre tract bordering the Merrimack north of Stony Brook in what is now North Chelmsford. Here twenty-two proprietors held lots of various sizes within the field, and they built sections of a common fence around the entire field under the supervision of fence viewers appointed by the selectmen of the town.

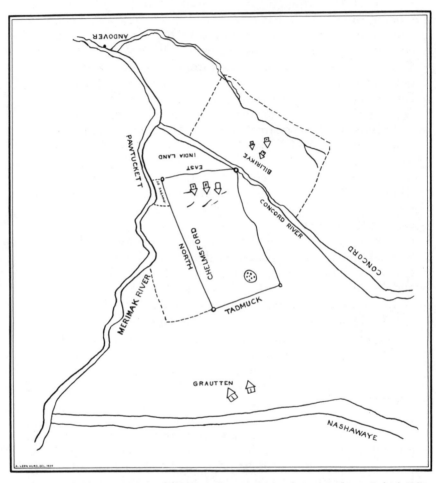

Early map of Chelmsford, 1653-1656. Original map in Massachusetts Archives. Robin's Hill is the circle containing dots in the center of the map. Middlesex Village is approximately where "Jo Sagamo" appears. (Lowell Historical Society)

Under the closed-field system the individually owned family farms in Chelmsford varied in size, the grants determined by both the need and social status of the individual recipient. Men with large families and those who were considered to be better than the majority received the largest amounts of land. It is doubtful, however, that the initial grants of land were very large. In other New England towns operating under the closed-field system the initial grants varied between two to twenty acres for a houselot with its vegetable garden. Additional acreage was granted for meadow and cropland a distance away from the houselot. Most of the land was not distributed at all in the initial phase of settlement; rather, it was set aside as town commons. The commons could be used for grazing and wood cutting by most inhabitants of the town, and was reserved for distribution to the inhabitants and their heirs, and sometimes newcomers, when the need arose.

The widespread use of the English closed-field system at Chelmsford was one of the most important factors influencing the physical development of the town. In the open-field villages of seventeenth century England and America the inhabitants tended to live side by side along the streets of a village. Only later in the colonial period did these "nuclear" towns begin to change. But where the closed-field system prevailed the inhabitants tended to disperse very quickly to a number of sections or neighborhoods. Many of the settlers met together to attend church and conduct government business, but they did not all see each other on a day-to-day basis. In Chelmsford, the meadows of Beaver Brook to the west of the town center were developed relatively early, and the Robins Hill area was quickly exploited. Some settlers also moved onto the lands at the northeast corner of the town, in the Black Brook area (which eventually became Lowell), almost immediately after the initial settlement.* Many of these pioneers must have coveted the fertile lands reserved for the Indians at Wamesit.

For the farmers at Chelmsford did not prosper. They found much of the soil sour, rocky, poor in nutriments, and porous in structure. Even where manure was used, the yield per acre probably decreased during the first years of settlement. And although the native New England grass sometimes grew as high as a man's shoulders, it did not prove nutritious for cattle. The

*The Jerathmell Bowers house, the oldest house still standing in Lowell, was built in 1671.

hay barely kept small numbers of cattle alive over the long winter season, and it was often in short supply. As early as 1656 some settlers complained that settlement toward the northeast was impossible because there was "no outlet for our Cattell to feed on" within the boundaries set out by the General Court.

What the settlers desired was a portion of the Indian lands on the grassy Merrimack plain, and in May, 1656, after negotiations with John Eliot, the Indians, and the General Court, the representatives of the Chelmsford farmers partially achieved their goal. The General Court granted the Indians Neahambeak, a mile-long tract extending from Black Brook in Middlesex Village westward to North Chelmsford Center. This tract, known as the "Joe Sagamore Grant," prevented the Chelmsford inhabitants from expanding towards the river. However, a much larger tract upriver, bordering the Indian grant and the Merrimack, and taking in most of what is now North Chelmsford, the northern section of Westford, and a small portion of Tyngsborough opposite Tyng's Island, was granted to Chelmsford and the Indians jointly. Because of constant conflict between the English and the Indians, there were further negotiations and adjustments in 1660. In that year the Indians agreed to give up all control over the larger tract in exchange for exclusive ownership of a small section of land on the northeast side of the original Chelmsford grant. However, the Indians still retained their lands around the area of Chelmsford Neck within the present city of Lowell. In 1665 committees from Chelmsford, Billerica, and Wamesit village met and established clear lines around the Indian reservation.

If the settlers steadily encroached on Indian land during the early years of settlement there is little evidence that they intended to destroy the Indians in the villages and drive them into the interior. At least some settlers believed that friendly Indians on the borders of their land would give warnings of attacks by the French or by hostile Indians. A number of English farmers supplemented their meager incomes by exchanging produce for Indian furs and using the furs to buy essential English manufactured goods at Boston. In 1657 the General Court granted the exclusive right to trade with the Indians on the Merrimack to Simon Willard (who had moved from Concord to Chelmsford) and three partners. The following year thirty-three Chelmsford settlers complained that the Indian trade was their "Lawfull Libertie" and essential for the support of their families in "this Remoat Corner of the wilderness."

But despite the interdependence of Englishmen and Indians during the 1650s the underlying cultural conflict was very great. The Indians lived in close harmony with both the living and nonliving components of their environment. To them, all beings possessed a mysterious force that interacted with the human spirit or soul. All of their activities were bound up with this spiritual or magical relationship with nature. The plants they grew or gathered, the animals they hunted, the tools they made, the very land on which they trod were all "fellows" intimately tied to them in some mysterious way. They maintained contact with these magical forces through dreams and through the medicine men who invoked a great variety of spirits in attempts to increase the food supply, heal the sick, and predict events.

The English settlers, on the other hand, were inheritors of a Christian civilization. Although most believed that a man should control no more land than he and his heirs could cultivate or develop, they had a strong concept of the right to private property and the right to exploit that property for the purpose of accumulating wealth. The settlers also had particularly strong views on eternal salvation. Unable to get along with their fellow Christians in the state church in England, the New England Puritans, believing that they were the new Israelites, God's specially chosen people, had devised a system for separating the eternally saved from the eternally damned in this life. Full membership in the church at Chelmsford, including voting rights and the right to participate in the Lord's Supper, was open only to those baptized Christians who had been able to demonstrate to a church congregation that they had undergone an internal "conversion experience" leading to the possession of "saving grace." (Only adult males who had undergone such an experience were allowed to vote in Massachusetts Bay elections.) In 1656 the Chelmsford church members emphasized that all new members must be tested "concerning their life and conversation," that the test would be conducted by a church officer, and that any male or female church members had liberty "to be present at the first Tryall." Power in the society was generally controlled by the "saints" who, despite constant protestations that no person could be absolutely sure of salvation, could not help but experience a feeling of confidence and self-assurance and display an air of superiority towards those who were outside the fold. The Puritans, therefore, were predisposed to direct the full force of their strength and authority against any individual or group opposed to their ideals.

Because of these great cultural differences, and the racial differences, it was inevitable that Anglo-Indian relations would deteriorate. As the supply of fur-bearing animals diminished, the settlers saw less need for economic cooperation with their Indian neighbors and absolutely no need for the preservation of Indian culture. By the 1660s the praying-Indian town at the confluence of the Concord and the Merrimack, like the others in Massachusetts, was looked upon by the government of the colony as a reservation that helped to prevent conflict between settlers and Indians over land and acted as a buffer between the English frontier settlements and the Indian warriors to the north and west. Although some Indians were still baptized and even went through some sort of conversion experience, the Christian Indians were only a small minority and there was never any thought of assimilating them into English society. The original land grant to Chelmsford and the boundary adjustments of 1656 and 1660 convinced most Indians that Christianity meant surrender of all land that was not used for farming and grazing. Those who accepted baptism and gave up their old way of life found themselves living suspended between the English and the Indian societies. And they were fast becoming the victims of a foreign governmental and legal system over which they never would have any influence or control. The Indians of Massachusetts really had no place to go. There was no escape from the advance of the English. Even a retreat into the interior was denied them, for the hostile Mohawks, one of the Five Nations of the powerful Iroquois Confederacy, controlled the lands beyond the Hudson River.

By the 1660s the English population in Massachusetts was surpassing that of the Indians and most Puritans considered themselves masters of the land. Nevertheless the population of the frontier towns was still small. Chelmsford, with a population of about 200 in 1660, had only about 260 souls by 1670. If the Indians were to organize and conduct a surprise attack, either under the leadership of their own sachems or of the French in Canada, frontier towns like Chelmsford still could be completely destroyed. For this reason New Englanders developed a system of universal military training based on the old militia system of the mother country. In theory almost every able-bodied man was a member of a local militia company and was trained, under elected officers, in European military tactics. The scattered militia companies were organized into regiments under the command of a major. Although members of a town militia company could be used to defend their own community, contingency plans were also formulated to make up roving companies of militia from volunteers or conscripts drawn out of the local companies by a system of town quotas. The towns used their tax powers to raise funds for the purchase of ammunition and shot for the militia. For example, as early as 1660 Chelmsford raised £13.6s. "for a toune stock of ammunition."

There were war scares in southern New England in 1666, 1667, and 1669, and many people reported that they had seen the Indians making weapons, repairing guns, and attending mysterious powwows. Although Philip, the Wampanoag sachem, surrendered his weapons to Plymouth Colony authorities in 1671, fear of an uprising of all New England Indians was prevalent in all of the frontier towns. In July, 1670, the Chelmsford town meeting ordered all male residents over fifteen years of age to provide a five-foot club with a knob on the end. The clubs were to be left at the meeting house "untill ocation fore use." Militia training was also conducted in the European manner, and in May, 1672, the town hired Abraham Parker to keep down the brush in the training field so that drills could be conducted. In 1673 the town built a small house measuring eighteen by sixteen feet on Robins Hill. The house was probably designed as a garrison and lookout for the residents in this section of the town. On the same day the contract for the house was let out the town ordered that every male between twelve and sixty spend one day each year "for the Clearing of Robbins Hill," presumably to prevent a sneak attack by the Indians. In the following year the town sold gunpowder to sixty male inhabitants, and it is likely that other garrison houses were readied and stocked with supplies.

Towards the end of June, 1675, Chelmsford inhabitants must have heard of the Indian attack at Swansea in which nine Englishmen were killed. Whether this was meant to be the first phase of a well coordinated conspiracy organized by King Philip against the English is uncertain. But Massachusetts mobilized against the Indians, and by July the war had spread to Rehoboth, Taunton, Middleborough, Mendon, Dartmouth, and Providence. At the beginning of August, Brookfield, the isolated village in central Massachusetts, was under siege, and it was finally abandoned. And in the same month Indian warriors were seen south of the Merrimack River and the towns of Marlborough, Lancaster, Dunstable, Groton, and Chelmsford were endangered.

As panic and hysteria spread in Chelmsford and the surrounding communities, the Massachusetts Bay Colony government sent two companies of militia into the Merrimack Valley region. One company was under the command of Captain Samuel Moseley, a Puritan who hated all Indians with a passion. When a group of unidentified Indians killed seven settlers at Lancaster on August 22, Moseley and his men invaded the Indian village at Marlborough, put ropes around the necks of fifteen suspects, and marched them to Boston where they were nearly lynched by angry mobs. The Indians of the Merrimack Valley were now in fear of their lives. The village of Wamesit was nearly abandoned, and Wannalancit, sachem of the Pennacooks, led his tribe north to avoid interracial warfare. Nevertheless, in September Moseley and his men burned a village deep in Pennacook territory. The Indians knew that if they were caught by such roving bands of uncontrollable militia they faced death or slavery in the sugar plantations of the West Indies.

John Eliot as well as many of the officials of the Bay Colony government urged a policy of moderation towards friendly and Christian Indians and argued that the heavy-handed tactics of men like Moseley would prolong the war. The official policy, set forth September 8, 1675, was to garrison the towns of Lancaster, Chelmsford, Groton, and Dunstable with militia from the less vulnerable communities. And, while the garrisons kept watch and patrolled the towns, the officers were ordered to "compose & quiet matters respecting the indians our neighbors, particularly those that live at Wamesit, Nashubah, & Marlborough." Wannalancit was to be encouraged "to com[e] in againe [and] live at Wamesit quietly and pecabley," provided that he "deliver for a hostage to the english his sonne who shalbe wel[l] used by us."

Apparently a number of Indians, probably those who were members of the Christian Church, had remained at Wamesit or returned there, for on September 21, 1675, the governor and council of Massachusetts ordered that the Indians at Wamesit be allowed to gather their harvest. Wannalancit, however, knew that the government officials could not control the outraged Puritan settlers, and most of the Pennacooks remained deep in the wilderness.

On October 18, 1675, when a party of hostile Indians set fire to the haystack of James Richardson at Chelmsford, hatred of all Indians consumed the citizens of Massachusetts Bay. Because of popular clamor the Massachusetts General Court ordered that all the Christian Indians at Wamesit be rounded up and marched to Boston. One hundred and forty-five men, women, and children began the forced march, but as the Governor's Council could not provide accommodations for such a large number all but thirty-three able-bodied Indians were ordered returned to their village. A few days later the moderate forces within the Massachusetts government prevailed and all but three Indians were returned to their village in Wamesit.

Shortly after, however, a barn fire of mysterious origin in Chelmsford so aroused a group of Puritans that they invaded Wamesit and called to the natives to come out of their wigwams. When the Indians emerged John Largin and George Robbins opened fire and killed one boy and wounded a number of women. Largin and Robbins were arrested, but no jury would convict them, and they were finally released from prison. "It is to be feared that there is guilt upon the land in respect of the Indians," Increase Mather wrote in Boston "yea Guilt of blood in respect of the Indians so treacherously murdered at Chelmsford. I am affraid God will viset for that grief."

The Indians at Wamesit again sought safety in the wilderness, but there they encountered hostile Indians, and they were without food and essential supplies. In December, 1675, they again returned to Wamesit, and while the Chelmsford inhabitants complained of the "dangerous conditions that we are in, in reffereance to our lives and estate by reason of the retourne of the Wamasack Indians Emongst us," the Governor's Council promised that all groups would live in safety. The Indians, however, suffered miserably from cold and hunger, and they knew that many Puritans were extremely mistrustful and were conspiring to kill them and some of their white protectors. In February, 1676, the Indians pleaded with the government to remove them to a safer location. There was no response; the majority abandoned Wamesit and fled north to join Wannalancit and his followers. They left some half dozen of their aged and blind behind. It was hoped that no harm would come to the helpless, but the English invaded the village, set fire to the wigwams, and burned to death all who remained inside.

The retreat of the Christian Indians into the forest aroused the suspicion of many Chelmsford inhabitants who believed that the withdrawal was associated with a general Indian plan for a surprise winter attack. As early as January 24, 1676, two Christian Indian spies had told the English of an Indian plan to destroy Lancaster and raid Groton, Marlborough, Sudbury, and Medfield. It appeared that this plan was being put into effect when, on February 10, four hundred Indians burned most of the deserted homes and outbuildings in Lancaster, killed or wounded fifty inhabitants, and took more than twenty prisoners. The town was soon abandoned. On February 15 Joseph Parker and his son were fired upon by Indians lying in ambush four miles from the meeting house at Chelmsford. The Parkers urged their horses onward and escaped, but the young man was wounded in the shoulder by a musket bullet and his clothes were torn in several places by pistol shots. On February 21 several hundred Indians crept by night into Medfield—a town garrisoned by one hundred colonial soldiers. At dawn, as the sleepy soldiers and farmers stepped out of doors, the Indians shot them and then set on fire more than forty houses and barns. Groton, under siege for many weeks, was attacked on March 13 by four hundred Nipmuck warriors under the command of One-Eyed John. The Indians burned the meeting house and a large number of dwellings. Most of the garrison houses withstood the attack, but the town had to be abandoned, and most residents took refuge in Chelmsford and Concord. Forty Indians burned a number of the houses belonging to Chelmsford citizens on the north side of the Merrimack on March 18, and they killed two sons of Samuel Varnum who were crossing the river to look after their cattle. "I humbly intreat you to pray the Council," Dr. David Middleton, a military surgeon, wrote from Chelmsford on March 20, "to grant us a stronger guard for wee shall be all cutt off." Six days later a large section of Marlborough was destroyed, and except for the garrison, the town was abandoned.

By the beginning of April, 1676, Dunstable and Chelmsford were the only inhabited towns west of the Concord River. Almost the entire outer ring of the eastern frontier of Massachusetts Bay had been destroyed, and there was serious talk of building an eight-foot palisade from the head of navigation on the Charles River at Watertown north to the Concord River and even to the Merrimack. Many believed that only such a drastic measure would prevent the English from being driven back to the sea.

On April 15 the Indians again raided Chelmsford and burned at least fourteen houses. By this time morale among the settlers had reached its lowest point, for the planting season was coming and many militia-men were needed in the fields. Some Chelmsford men had been pressed into the roving militia companies and their families were unable to provide for themselves. Those men who remained in Chelmsford feared that they would meet death either from Indian bullets or from starvation if they could not plant their crops. Because of close confinement in the garrison houses epidemic diseases were also prevalent. Many could not help believing that such calamities were part of a divine plan to punish them for their sins. However, almost no one believed that the punishment might be due to previous mistreatment of the Indians.

Garrisoned towns such as Chelmsford were required to provide food not only for themselves but for soldiers who came from other communities to protect the garrison. To ease the burden on the Chelmsford farmers the Massachusetts government allowed the soldiers in Lieutenant Thomas Hinchman's garrison near the Merrimack to plow the Indian lands at Wamesit and Neahambeak in the hope that one thousand bushels of corn could be provided.

The Indians were also suffering from disease and hunger, and they were even less able than the English to prepare their grounds properly for spring planting. Also, because of the war, many of the falls of the rivers, such as those on the Concord and the Merrimack, were unavailable for fishing. Thus, in the spring of 1676, many demoralized Indians began to fight among themselves and to blame their leaders for their plight. As disorganization spread the fearsome Mohawks in the west launched a series of raids against their Indian enemies in New England. The colonial soldiers concentrated their efforts on destroying Indian crops and caches, and many small groups of hungry and war-weary Indians began surrendering to the English authorities. In early June Wannalancit and a group of Pennacooks who had remained neutral all during the war came to Dover, New Hampshire. There, on July 3, they signed an agreement pledging fidelity to the English.

During the hot, dry midsummer days the crops of the settlers wilted in the fields. The Indians, however, were too weak to launch even small raids. Larger and larger numbers surrendered or moved westward to the Housatonic and Hudson to take their chances among the Mohawks. On August 12 King Philip and many of his warriors were killed in the Great Swamp at Mount

Hope, Rhode Island. By this time the militia bands were sweep-
ing the woods, rounding up hundreds of starving and bewildered
Indians, many of whom were eventually sold into slavery in the
West Indies. By October of 1676 the Massachusetts General
Court proclaimed that there remained scarcely one Indian family
in their former habitations. Most were "either slayne, captivated,
or fled into remote parts of this wildernes, or lye hid, dispayring
of their first intentions against us, at least in these parts."

King Philip's War was the most devastating conflict in Massachusetts history. The Indians suffered untold losses. At least
thirteen English frontier villages were totally destroyed;
Chelmsford and five other towns were partially burned. Ten
percent of the five thousand males of military age in the Massachusetts militia companies were killed or captured. Families
were broken up; farm animals, fences, and buildings were destroyed. The work of several decades of wilderness labor lay in
ashes, and fields were abandoned to tree seedlings and weeds.
For many Chelmsford residents the war did not end completely
in 1676: north of the Merrimack, in New Hampshire and Maine,
the Abnaki Indians, encouraged by the French in Canada, continued to fight, and Massachusetts Bay was forced to send soldiers into that sparsely populated region. In June, 1677, Lieutenant James Richardson and his militia company at Chelmsford
were ordered "to scout and range the woods between Merrimack
and Piscataqua River & endeavor to kill and sease the Lurking
enemy in those parts." The party was to receive twenty shillings
for every Indian scalp collected and forty shillings for each pris-
oner. The company was then ordered to march to Blackpoint on
the Maine coast for garrison duty. A similar military expedition
was sent from Salem on July 4 of the same year and it included
James Parker of Chelmsford who was subsequently wounded in
the shoulder. In the fight at Blackpoint on July 29, Richardson
was killed soon after the first attack.

The war in Massachusetts, however, was over. The few Indians who remained in the region were under constant observa-
tion and the four "praying towns" that remained after the war
were nothing but reservations where all the Indians were to live
under close supervision. Wamesit was set aside by the Massachusetts government as one of the reservation towns, but the
Chelmsford inhabitants who had suffered so much during the
war coveted this land. Some of the Wamesit Indians returned.
However, Wannalancit did not trust the English, for many of his

followers had been sold into slavery. On September 22, 1677, Increase Mather recorded in his diary that the Indians at Chelmsford again had withdrawn. King Philip's War had been a war of extermination between two very different cultures and the English had emerged supreme. The land was now theirs, and the few Indians who wandered back would quickly become poor tenant farmers or hired servants and farmworkers.

The Englishmen at Chelmsford paid the Indians for their lands. On November 18, 1685, Thomas Hinchman, whose land bordered the Indian plantation on the west, purchased Wanna-lancit's thirty-acre planting field. In the following year Hinchman and Johnathan Tyng of Dunstable conducted successful negotiations for the purchase of the remainder of the Wamesit lands. The Indians formally conveyed their lands to these two men who, in turn, for the sum of £199 sold their rights to fifty New Englanders, most of whom were Chelmsford residents. The fifty men became the proprietors of the "Wamesit Purchase," a tract of about twenty-five hundred acres on both sides of the Merrimack that encompassed about the same area that later was incorporated as Lowell. In 1687 the proprietors, meeting separately from the Chelmsford town meeting, divided a portion of this land equally among themselves according to lot. They laid out ways, built fences, and began to exploit the earth that the Indians had cherished and nurtured for many hundreds of years.

III

Church and State in Early Chelmsford

By Charles F. Carroll

For Chelmsford, the decades following King Philip's War were a time of internal expansion, renewed warfare, migration, and sectional, political, and religious crises. The war had taken a great toll in lives and property. Although many of the homesteads could be rebuilt, numerous families would never be reconstituted. A number of impoverished widows and children were forced to rely on private charity. However, peace allowed the further development of the lands within the community. By the 1680s there were at least five distinct neighborhoods within the town: the Center; the "North End," which included the Black Brook area, Middlesex Village, and the Wamesit Lands beyond (now part of Lowell); the "West End," which included Robins Hill, the Beaver Brook Meadows, and South Chelmsford; the Stony Brook Valley and the region around the center of the present town of Westford; and the Great Brook area, which is now in Carlisle. In addition, the movement north across the Merrimack River that had begun during the 1660s continued after the war. This movement raised serious problems because the territory was outside the Chelmsford grant.

The town developed greatly in the decades after the war, but not everyone had access to good agricultural land. Even as early as the 1660s the town had begun to grant land to individuals without granting them rights to future divisions of the town commons. For example, John Webb received twenty acres of land in November, 1661 "without any towne privelidges saveing the Kepeing A beast or two" on the commons. It was probably for this reason that he soon crossed the Merrimack and began to develop the public lands of the colony. By the 1670s it is evident that some of the sons of the original settlers were not receiving portions of their fathers' lands, but only houselots of a few acres from the town. Some probably did not receive any land at all.

The shortage of good land together with the renewed danger of attacks by the Indian allies of the French after 1689 led to the migration of at least ten Chelmsford families to a more peaceful region of New England. In 1690, while most Chelmsfordites were preparing their weapons, barricading their houses, scouting the woods, and watching the fords of the Merrimack and the bridge to Billerica over the Concord, this minority sold their houses and lands, and together with settlers from Woburn, Concord, Ipswich, Haverhill, and Stow, founded Plainfield and Canterbury in eastern Connecticut. The hostilities, known in America as King William's War, ended in 1697. Chelmsford, unlike Haverhill and some communities in northern New England, had suffered no serious casualties or damage. Nevertheless those who left for Connecticut did not return.

Migration during King William's War, the first of the international colonial wars between Britain and France, helped ease the pressure of the population on the land. Queen Anne's War (1702–13), America's second intercolonial war, again created dangers and hardships in Chelmsford, and again there was some migration. The town seems to have been a staging area for colonial troops in this war, but it was not a prime target for Indian attack.

After 1713 New England troops and Indians occasionally skirmished in the wilderness and some Chelmsford men were involved in the fighting. Relative peace along the frontier lasted until King George's War (1743–48), however; by that time many new communities had been formed to the west and north of Chelmsford so that the town was no longer on the frontier.

During Queen Anne's War the Chelmsford town meeting began to prepare for the final divisions of the common lands. In 1707 it elected a committee to search the book of land grants to determine which men held rights to the commons by direct grant or inheritance. There also were men who had received such rights as gifts or had purchased them and held deeds of sale.

After the book was examined the common lands were surveyed, and between 1710 and 1712 the first division was carried out. Three more divisions followed in 1716–20, 1720–22, and 1722–25. After the last division all the land was in private hands except the small portion reserved for public purposes.

Many fathers were able to divide portions of their newly acquired lands among their sons. However, much of the land in the eighteenth century divisions was not suitable for farming or grazing, and migration was the only solution for many families who wished to become independent. Those who had previously migrated to Connecticut had been escaping the terrors of war. Now, in the 1720s, settlers from Chelmsford and surrounding towns were moving in search of economic opportunity. One group from Chelmsford and Billerica moved north into Litchfield, New Hampshire (north of Nashua on the Merrimack), and another group founded Amherst a short distance to the northwest. In 1735 sixty men, many of them Chelmsford residents, were grantees of Tyngstown, which included the greater part of what is now Manchester, New Hampshire. When this grant was revoked in 1741 they received land at Wilton, Maine. In the 1740s and 1750s many Chelmsfordites moved into Maine, and by the 1760s many were living in the twelve townships east of the Penobscot River. By this time some with family connections in Chelmsford also were beginning to move into Vermont.

Those families who remained in Chelmsford experienced substantial political and religious changes during the late seventeenth and early eighteenth centuries. As the population dispersed more and more into areas remote from the center of the village, residents found the distances that they were forced to travel to hear the word of God or to conduct civil affairs much too great. Distance was destroying the sense of a single community and leading to the development of closer relationships among families located in remote regions. This, in turn, led to petitions to the General Court for independent churches and townships.

Although the families situated on the northern side of the Merrimack were not located within the precincts of any town, they had always attended town meetings in Chelmsford, and they paid taxes, participated in the militia, and held church membership in the town. But there were no bridges across the Merrimack, and travel to the center was particularly difficult in winter and spring. Thus, the General Court allowed these settlers to incorporate the new town of Dracut in 1702. They were unable to obtain a minister, however, and the Court required them to help maintain the ministry in Chelmsford until their own church was established in 1721.

The establishment of an iron works by Captain Jonas Prescott on the Stony Brook at Forge Pond and the exploitation of agricultural land in this region also led to the formation of another distinct community by the early eighteenth century. The sense of uniqueness felt by the settlers in this area encouraged them to petition the General Court which ordered Chelmsford to pay £100 to this "West Parish" for the construction of a meeting house for public worship. Although the town meeting of Chelmsford opposed petitions for complete independence for many years, the General Court conferred the status of "Precinct" upon this region in 1724. The inhabitants of Littleton hoped that the Forge Pond region would be annexed to their community but in 1729 the General Court granted the region independence and the town of Westford was incorporated.

There were also sectional crises involving the Blood Farms and the Wamesit Purchase. In 1693 Robert Blood purchased a one-thousand-acre tract from the Indians south of the Wamesit Purchase in a region claimed by Chelmsford, Billerica, and Concord. After some controversy, a committee composed of representatives of the three towns was appointed to run the boundary lines and Billerica gained a sizable portion of land west of the Concord River.

The controversy involving the Wamesit Purchase was much more serious, but ultimately it benefited Chelmsford. Even though the neck of land between the Merrimack and the Concord was owned chiefly by Chelmsford citizens, it was settled by tenant farmers and was not annexed to the town. However, the settlers on this land considered themselves residents of Chelmsford; they paid taxes and participated in town affairs. It was not until 1725 that this lack of attention to colonial law led to a crisis. In that year the Chelmsford town meeting elected Stephen Pierce, an inhabitant of the Wamesit lands, to represent them in the Massachusetts General Court. But the Court refused to seat Pierce on the grounds that he was not a resident of Chelmsford. When Pierce returned home the Wamesit inhabitants angrily declared that they would no longer pay taxes to Chelmsford. The other inhabitants of the town were fearful that they would lose a good deal of revenue, and the proprietors of Wamesit who lived in Chelmsford feared that their tenants might secede and form an independent community. Therefore, Chelmsford selectmen petitioned Lieutenant Governor William Dummer asking him to force the Wamesit inhabitants to pay their taxes. They also requested that these lands be annexed to the town. The Governor's Council set a date for a hearing on the matter for June, 1726, but in the meantime the General Court passed an order making Wamesit part of Chelmsford. In April, 1729, the Wamesit inhabitants were given permission to form a precinct within Chelmsford provided they built a "suitable house for public worship" and hire and support their own minister. However, Chelmsford protested this move towards independence and Wamesit remained part of the town until it was incorporated as part of Lowell in 1826.

Controversies over control of the various sections of Chelmsford were aggravated by other serious quarrels among the settlers. As early as 1656 Richard Hildreth moved to Chelmsford from Cambridge and complained that the Reverend John Fiske was a poor minister. In 1661 three families moved to Groton because "uncomfortable differences ... pressed upon their spirits as in reference to Church Administration." And five years later Joshua Fletcher was publicly admonished by a vote of the church members after they received reports that he had been "at Road Island among the Quakers." However, consensus in religious affairs seems to have been the rule among the early settlers. In 1657 the Reverend John Fiske published *The Watering of the Olive Plant in Christs Garden or a Short Catechism for the First Entrance of our Chelmsford Children*. Written "in the midst of many wilderness-discouragements," the little volume was used to indoctrinate the children of the town who gathered monthly at Fiske's residence. The Reverend Thomas Clarke continued this work after Fiske died in January, 1677. But by the early eighteenth century the childrens' schooling for reception into full church membership was sporadic. In 1710, during Queen Anne's War, the town requested that its children be exempted from the Massachusetts school law because of the dangers of Indian attack. "Our habitations are very scattering & distant one from another," the townsmen wrote, "so that altho a school were placed in the Centre it would be very remote from the greater part of our Inhabitants, & our Children in passing too & from the same would be so greatly exposed to the snares of our Lurking Enemy, that very few would Venture to send them to school in such danger." Chelmsford was one of a number of Middlesex

County towns cited for the lack of school facilities during the early decades of the eighteenth century.

By the eighteenth century the Congregational Churches of New England, and the members within the congregations, were held together by a number of rules and formulas drawn up in the previous century. These rules, derived from argument and compromise, had allowed the majority of Christians in Massachusetts to develop the wilderness without harassment from those intent on instituting their own highly individualistic religious practices. Although the Puritans required a demonstrable conversion experience prior to full church membership, after 1662, under an agreement known as the Half-Way Covenant, they baptized the children of the unconverted and made them "half-way" members. They admonished those who refused to present their children for baptism because infant baptism was to be found nowhere in the Scripture. They exiled those who claimed to have had direct revelations from the Holy Spirit. In order to prevent the congregations in the towns from becoming too autonomous, the General Court of Massachusetts passed laws regulating their initial organization, their control over their ministers, and their relationships with other Congregational churches.

Rigid rules and a growing formalism within the congregations helped maintain religious peace during the critical times of initial land development and during King Philip's War. But rigidity and formalism stifled emotional religious experiences, and piety waned. By the eighteenth century sermons were rarely preached with feeling, and they no longer evoked an emotional response from the listeners. In addition, frontier wars, relative prosperity, geographic dispersal, pressure of population on the land, migration, and increasing awareness of activities in other parts of the world all placed internal strains on society. These forces prevented ministers and elders from exercising tight control and rigid discipline over their flocks. Conflicts and tensions were developing in society, and there was bound to be an explosion.

However, when the Reverend Ebenezer Bridge arrived in Chelmsford in 1740 to take up his position as the new minister, he could scarcely have anticipated what was about to occur. The son of a Boston blacksmith, only four years out of Harvard, he told his new congregation of his "delight & satisfaction in ye peace, love & unanimity subsisting among you." Yet a year later, all the suppressed guilt over the successful development of the wilderness and over the feeling that society had abandoned the

The fourth Unitarian Meeting House in Chelmsford, 1843. Courtesy of First Congregational Society, Unitarian, of Chelmsford.

religious goals of the founding fathers, all the pent-up religious emotions, and all the tensions created by social dislocations burst forth in Chelmsford and in most of the other New England towns. Uneasily searching for new sources of authority, new principles of action, and new foundations for hope, large numbers of New Englanders, stirred up initially by itinerant preachers, took part in a great emotional upheaval. They claimed that they experienced, in a very direct and intimate way, the grace of God working on their souls. This outburst of emotional religious fervor is known as the Great Awakening.

The itinerant preachers, both educated ministers and unlettered laymen, who conducted revivals in the New England countryside emphasized that God would damn all those who had not experienced conversion. They suggested that the converted saints had special powers enabling them to distinguish the saved from the damned here on earth. Many preachers told their terrified audiences that most ministers and most church members were unconverted and did not "experimentally know Christ." In the highly charged emotional atmosphere of the revivals the fear of damnation encouraged thousands to pound on the doors of heaven in search of assurances of salvation. Many claimed that they felt the hand of God touching their hearts in a very special way. They became sure of salvation and eternal life. The new converts then separated from their "unconverted" brethren and conducted services only for the elect. Those who separated became known as Separates or New Lights. Moreover, having once experienced saving grace, a number of New Lights felt an inescapable compulsion to become proselytizers of the new reformation. They joined the host of lay preachers already roaming through the towns defying many of the old laws designed to prevent disorder among churches and within congregations.

One such itinerant preacher was Elisha Paine, a lawyer from Canterbury, Connecticut, who quit the courts when he became convinced that he was "called of God" to preach the gospel. He became the Moses of the Separates in Windham County, Connecticut, and his fame spread as he travelled throughout New England preaching his message of the absolute need for the converted to separate themselves from the unconverted and their "unspiritual shepherds" and to establish their own "pure" churches. In 1743 John Burge and Gershom Proctor, members of two well established families, invited Paine to Chelmsford. He preached his message in their house under protest from the Reverend Bridge and the majority of his congregation who were apparently strong "Old Lights." In November, 1743, the Chelmsford church charged that such preaching was a "great disturbance of Towns & Churches and to ye breach of Christian Communion," and asserted that "this Town and Church have been sorely disturbed by ye Conduct of such persons coming among us, & preaching & exhorting in private houses. . . ." Such preaching, they claimed, offended "the greatest part of ye Church." Therefore, Burge and Proctor were called before the whole congregation to explain their actions and "they gave the Church Satisfaction by Saying They were Sorry that They had so done, and designed not To do so Again."

However, the repentance of Burge and Proctor did not heal the schism that was developing in the church, for their wives, Sarah Burge and Rebecca Proctor, together with Sarah Proctor, Mary and Elizabeth Barrett, Thankful Foster, and Sarah Burge's daughter-in-law, Sarah, had followed Paine to Westford where they participated in a New Light meeting. When these women were brought before the Chelmsford church, Elizabeth Barrett and Sarah Proctor apologized, but the other women attempted to justify their conduct "in a Very Audacious manner." After argument failed "to bring em To a sense Of their Mis-conduct" the church excommunicated them and refused to admit them to the Lord's Table "until they would give satisfaction." A week later, all admitted their errors, promised to be watchful in the future, and were again admitted to full communion. However, a number of these women, together with their husbands, continued to be attracted to New Light preachers.

The Reverend Bridge and the Old Lights of the Chelmsford congregation prevented the formation of a Separatist church in their community, but they could not prevent their fellow townspeople from attending New Light services in other towns. Concord apparently provided an outlet for Chelmsford revivalists, for the pastor of the established church there, Daniel Bliss, was a New Light preacher who encouraged itinerant and lay preachers. In February, 1746, when the Chelmsford Church demanded to know why Job and Lydia Spaulding were attending the church at Concord, they answered that they were "better Edified & Enlightened into Gospel Truths by hearing Mr. Bliss than by hearing Mr. Bridge." When they approached the Lord's Table in the Chelmsford Church they were excommunicated.

The Chelmsford Church was also unable to prevent townspeople from wilfully withdrawing from their communion. In 1747 Mary Stedman claimed that the Reverend Bridge and the majority of church members looked upon revivalists as "Deceivers," and their work "a piece of delusion." This attack on the "Glorious Work" of the revivalists brought "great grief" to her soul. Concluding that Bridge's preaching was "much wanting, because he delivers his discourses promiscuously, not Dividing the Word aright," she found a "Necessity to Separate." Two years later, Daniel Locke, whom the Reverend Bridge considered "a most violent Newlight," refused to invite the Chelmsford minister to the funeral of his child.

During the 1750s the small group of New Lights who separated from the Church at Chelmsford came under the influence of a number of preachers. Samuel Hyde, originally from Canterbury, Connecticut, preached a pure separatist doctrine in the homes of a number of residents of South Chelmsford. In 1754 the Reverend Bridge asked Sarah Burge to withdraw from the meeting house, "she being one of the followers of Hyde, the Separatist speaker." The minister also refused to baptize the child of Israel Proctor because of Proctor's association with Hyde. During the following year Bridge records that he refrained from going to a meeting of ministers so that he could attend Israel Proctor's funeral. He was perhaps intent on bringing about a reconciliation. But when he arrived at the meeting house he learned that Hyde had already conducted a burial service at Proctor's home. Bridge, therefore, refused to pray with the mourners in the meeting house and claimed that he was "treated ill" by them.

It was in this same year that the Chelmsford town meeting voted to allow settlers in the "South End" to join with others from Billerica, Acton, Concord, and Westford to form the District of Carlisle. According to the Reverend Bridge most of the Chelmsford residents to be included in this new district "were Separates under Hyde, the lay exhorter, and tho' not under a formal censure by the vote of the [Chelmsford] Church, were debarred of enjoyment of special ordinances while they continue in a state of separation." In 1757 the group in the District of Carlisle, citing the great distance between them and the nearest meeting houses, petitioned the General Court for incorporation as a new town. The Court refused, and this district was not made independent until 1780. Apparently a Separatist church was not erected in Carlisle, for in 1759, after Hyde left for Madbury, New Hampshire, a number of "Hydes hearers" who lived in that area, including Gershom Proctor and Job and Lydia Spaulding, successfully petitioned for reconciliation with the Chelmsford Church.

The reconciled New Lights apparently believed that the old church could be reformed from within, for it is probable that there were some moderate New Lights who always remained within the Chelmsford Church and who aided in the reconciliation of the Separates. But after the reconciliation of 1759 a small group of radical Chelmsford pietists remained outside the fold. Some in this group may have been under the influence of Shadrach Ireland who had begun to preach at Harvard, Massachusetts, in 1753. The Reverend Bridge found Ireland "grossly ignorant & enthusiastick" for he and his followers claimed that their conversion experience had brought about such a change in both soul and body that they had become perfect and immortal and that they were no longer subject to illness or death.

Other unreconciled Separatists were attracted to antipedobaptism, the belief that there is no scriptural authority for baptizing infants. For example, as early as 1758 the Reverend Bridge met with John Spaulding, Jr., "about his turning to ye antipedo baptists & his being about to be re-baptized. . . ." Bridge's arguments were to no avail. Spalding was rebaptized by plunging, and he attracted other Chelmsfordites to his new sect.

The members of the Baptist Church in New England had not been enthusiastic supporters of the Great Awakening in the 1740s. Almost all of the revivalists were Congregationalists, the denomination that had persecuted Baptists for many years. Most revivalists also had advocated infant baptism, but gradually as pedobaptist New Lights (revivalists who believed in infant baptism) reconciled themselves with their old churches, many unreconciled Separatist New Lights such as John Spaulding, Jr., became antipedobaptists and began to think of reconstituting themselves by forming Baptist churches. At first, Spaulding and others did not look upon their activities in denominational terms; rather, they believed that they were reforming Christianity so that its practices would conform to the original teachings of Jesus. As time went on, the combination of their practices and beliefs—antipedobaptism, immersion, evangelistic zeal, and the voluntary support of the ministry—tended to set them apart as a denomination. And, although the cynics were probably incorrect when they claimed that antipedobaptists were immersed in the river to wash away taxes owed to the established Congregational church, many revivalists did find that, by becoming Baptists, they could obtain under Massachusetts law an exemption from taxes owed to the established Congregational church.

Despite Massachusetts law, tax exemptions for Baptists were not easily won in strong Congregational towns such as Chelmsford. The law did not clearly establish how a group was to be recognized as "Baptist," and there was much room for harassment by bigoted Congregationalists. As early as 1761 there was a warrant presented to the Chelmsford town meeting demanding that Baptists in the community pay taxes for the support of the established church. At this time the Baptist group was still meeting in private homes, and apparently did not have a permanent pastor. However, the Reverend Hezekiah Smith, the pastor of the Baptist Church in Haverhill, sometimes travelled to Chelmsford and immersed new members, at least some of whom were recruited from the Congregational church. In November, 1770, the Reverend Bridge recorded that one of his parishoners, Nathan Crosby, "turned baptist, and was baptized by plunging, when one of their preachers preached at John Spauldings."

It was not until October 22, 1771, however, that the Chelmsford Baptists, together with some residents of surrounding towns, formally organized a church. On that date twenty-four persons met at the home of Daniel Locke in South Chelmsford and reconstituted themselves as Baptists. A number of others soon joined, and the church appointed John Spaulding and two other members to hand out documents certifying membership in the new organization. Under Massachusetts law, Baptists who handed in certificates of membership to the town assessors could obtain tax exemptions.

However, when Gershom Proctor, Henry Proctor, and Nathan Crosby turned in their exemption certificates to the Chelmsford assessor, Oliver Barrows, the certificates were ignored. When these Baptists, in turn, refused to pay their taxes for the upkeep of the Chelmsford Congregational Church they were arrested by Constable John Robbins in January, 1773, and taken to the Concord jail. The Proctors remained in jail for nine months. Crosby paid his tax and was released in four days. He then hired a Congregational lawyer, Jonathan Sewall, who advised him to sue both Barrows and Robbins. The case against Robbins was dismissed in the lower court but Crosby won against Barrows. Barrows appealed, however, and, although Crosby won again in Superior Court in April, 1774, he was awarded only £3 damages. This was raised by the town by a tax that all, including Baptists, were required to pay.

The injustices surrounding the arrest of the Chelmsford Baptists and the incompetence displayed by Crosby's Congregational lawyer in court became a cause célèbre among all Baptists in New England. The Baptist leader, Isaac Backus, declared in 1773 that "liberty of conscience, the great and most important article of liberty, is evidently not allowed as it ought to be in this country, not even by the very men who are now making loud complaints of encroachments upon their own liberties [by Parliament]." The only solution, many Baptists agreed, was the adoption of a policy of massive civil disobedience aimed at the severance of all connections between church and state. If all Baptists stood united, and, like Gershom Proctor, Henry Proctor, and

Nathan Crosby, refused to pay religious taxes, and even to hand
in exemption certificates to the assessors, then full religious
liberty could be achieved. Other Baptists, however, believed
that civil disobedience was too radical and too dangerous a step.
Despite the continuing pressure of the Baptist lobby before the
Congress, in the Massachusetts legislature, at the Massachusetts
constitutional conventions, and in the courts, full religious liberty did not come about in the Commonwealth until long after
the founding of Lowell and the emergence of the industrial
revolution in America.

Paradoxically, while Chelmsfordites quarreled over political,
economic, and religious issues at home, they were taking major
steps leading them towards the formation of an American union.
They were forced to counter the build-up of French military
power on the frontier by joining with residents of other towns
and colonies in common cause against the French and Indian
armies. In 1741, while many New Englanders were waiting for
the hand of God to touch their souls, two Chelmsford residents,
Oliver Spaulding and Ephraim Fletcher, went off to fight
France's ally, Spain, in the West Indies. When the West Indian
War of Jenkins' Ear spread to the Continent as King George's
War (1743–1748), a number of Chelmsford residents went off
with Governor William Shirley's forces to Nova Scotia. There
they participated in the siege and conquest of Louisbourg, the
strongest French fort in America. Others ranged the woods in
search of the Indian allies of the French. A number, including
Joseph Richardson and Zacheus Blodget, never returned. Henry
Stevens was captured by Indians at Fort Dummer in June, 1748.
Carried to Quebec and then placed aboard a French man-of-war
destined for Cape Breton, he became sick with fever and "suffered great Hardships and Distresses" before arriving home in
Chelmsford in November, 1748.

The culmination of the struggle between the French and the
English in America was the French and Indian War (1754–63). In
this war the whole of American society was militarized, and
almost all able-bodied male Chelmsford residents saw service in
distant places. "Such Vast preparation & armaments upon this
Continent & these northern seas," the Reverend Bridge told his
congregation, "had never bin known before." In 1755 more than
two dozen Chelmsford men served Governor Shirley's companies in Nova Scotia. In the same year another two dozen
Chelmsfordites served in Colonel Eleazer Tyng's regiment during the unsuccessful expedition against the French at Crown

Point, the gateway to Lake Champlain. Chelmsford residents also volunteered or were pressed into service for campaigns on the Maine frontier, at Fort William Henry on Lake George, and at Fort Niagara between Lake Erie and Lake Ontario. Several joined Major Robert Rogers' Rangers. On April 6, 1759, there was a "muster of militia to raise men . . . against Canada," and a week later the Reverend Bridge preached from the Book of Kings "on occasion of Soldiers going off to the war." Numerous Chelmsford citizens took part in the successful attack on Quebec, the victory that insured the successful outcome of the war for the English. On October 25, 1759, Bridge held a "Thanksgiving day on account of the Reduction of Quebec," and his brother John, returned from the war, fired off a dozen skyrockets that he had obtained in Boston.

Chelmsfordites who remained at home celebrated the English victories, but they were also adversely affected by the great war which seriously disrupted and sometimes destroyed their lives. During the war, French refugees from Nova Scotia, Acadians forcibly evicted from their lands by English armies, were herded into Chelmsford and other New England towns and settled in private homes. The refugees were supported by expenditures granted to the selectmen from the colonial treasury, but the census taken by the selectmen in Chelmsford reveals their sad plight. Charles and Tithorne Trawhorn along with their five children were among seventeen Acadian refugees living in the town in 1757. Charles was listed as "Sickly & not able to Labour." His four-year-old son, Joseph, was also "sickly." Sixty-year-old Maudlin Landrie was "labouring under the misfortune of a broken arm." Charles Landrie, age twenty, was "sickly & not able to Labour." After the war ended the refugees who survived quickly left for Canada or Louisiana.

The war also left in its wake dead and maimed men and grief-stricken widows and parents. On June 18, 1755, the Reverend Bridge visited with Jonathan Barron who was "going off in the Expedition to Crown Point tomorrow, and is made a Lieutenant in the Army." On September 25 of the same year Bridge visited Barron's wife "upon a flying report of her husband being killed in the battle against the enemy on the way to Crown Point." Soon news arrived that Jacob Parker and James Emery had also been killed. On December 4, 1755, Benjamin Adams, Jr., returned home to Chelmsford after serving as a guard for wagoners at Lake George. Adams was so ill that he stopped at

Peter Proctor's home three miles from his own. His fever increased, and he never left Proctor's house. He died there on December 18. Adams was not the only man who returned home to Chelmsford to die. In the eighteenth century epidemics killed more men than did enemy armies.

Americans, mobilized for warfare for almost a decade, radiated a feeling of self-confidence after their victory over the French. And this confidence did not bode well for the continuation of British power in America. Prior to 1763 the British had maintained their power without resorting to heavy-handed tactics precisely because the French had been America's major enemy. The French were hated especially by the New England Puritans. Because most of the French were Catholics, it was believed that they were in league with the devil. The French, the Reverend Bridge told his Chelmsford congregation in July, 1755, were the cause of all of their misery. "Base born miscreants," "dupes to Arbitrary power and Tyranny—blind adherers to the Doct[rine]s of passive obedience and non resistance . . . Nourished and brot up, upon the breasts of the great Whore, the Mother of Harlots" [the Catholic Church], they were the "mortal Enemies To our liberties as English men and Christians."

In the Great Awakening, which continued even during the French and Indian War, many Puritans rejected the old sources of authority; they lost respect for old traditions and customs. They claimed to possess direct revelations from heaven. Thus, a new source of authority was emerging: the individual believer who derived his authority directly from God. Now that the French Catholic power had been destroyed in America, and the British had begun to tighten up imperial control over the colonies by maintaining troops and legislating taxation, the old hatreds were channeled in a new direction: against British tax collectors, customs commissioners, members of Parliament, and eventually the King himself. Americans, feeling an incipient nationalism, accustomed to military victories, suffering from a serious post-war depression, and preparing for western expansion, were in no mood to bow down to rulers whom they could not choose and who lived so far across the sea.

measures may be taken, and Remonstrances made to the King and Parliament, as may obtain a Speedy Repeal of the aforesaid act."

However, there is no indication that a majority of Chelmsford-ites approved of the destructive Stamp Act riots in Boston. For the Reverend Bridge such audacious conduct was unjustified. "Every day," he wrote on August 30, 1765, "we hear news of the mobish doings [there]. . . They hanged Secretary Oliver in effigy, and then burnt the Stamp-Office and rifled his dwelling house." In May, 1767, Bridge, in his election sermon to the General Court, gave no indication of any desire for independence. The British colonists in North America were happy, he claimed, "in the enjoyment of the same liberties and privileges, as our brethe-ren in our mother country; what a lasting foundation is hereby laid for continual union and harmony, and a mutual dependence between the parent and her children!"

Even as late as 1773—after the Boston Committee of Cor-respondence pamphlet, *The Votes and Proceedings of the Freeholders and other Inhabitants of the Town of Boston In Town Meeting assembled, According to Law* (1772), had ar-rived in Chelmsford–most Chelmsford residents were not ready to take radical action. The pamphlet set forth a long list of British infringements and violations of colonial rights: unconstitutional taxation, occupation by a standing army, trials without jury, the unconstitutional appropriation of funds. It then appealed directly to the citizens in the towns to take some form of direct action against British tyranny before all Americans were made slaves. Chelmsfordites met to consider the Boston pamphlet on January 11, 1773, and appointed a committee of five to study the work more fully. The committee reported that at least some of the inhabitants' basic rights and liberties were in danger and that a protest should be made. However, "all Rash, Unmeaning, pas-sionate Proceeduers" were "by no means Justifiable in So Deli-cate a Crisis." The community, they argued, must be cautious and avoid "Turbulance and Tumults," and must remain loyal to the English government. "Greevancies we at present Labour under: But we can by no means think the Resolves of a Single Town Can be any Removeal." The only acceptable form of pro-test would be a formal petition to England by the members of the Massachusetts General Court. And, of course, the Court should reflect good manners and proper decorum. Simeon Spaulding, Chelmsford's representative, was instructed "not to trample on

Majesty, while you are firmly but decently Pleading the Liberties of the Subject." He was to avoid participation in "any Rash, Passionate Plan of Action," for such activity would result in "the utter Destruction of the cause we pretend to support."

The majority of Chelmsford residents did not favor radical action until the news arrived that Parliament had closed the port of Boston in retaliation for the Boston Tea Party. The British ministry also was on the verge of restricting the calling of town meetings, thus virtually annulling the Massachusetts Charter of 1692. At the request of the Boston Committee of Correspondence the town met on May 30, 1774, to consider an appropriate response to these drastic new policies. The townsmen now agreed that all legal protests had been ignored and that their basic rights and liberties were in immediate danger. The "Iron hand of Despotism and oppression" was upon them, and the true intentions of the British government were now openly revealed. The British, they believed, intended to make Americans slaves. "We justly fear as Compleat a System of Slavery is forming for this province, as any people unhappily experienced." The question now was "whether we submit to the arbitrary, lawless, tyrannical will of a minister, or by using those Powers given us by the God of nature, and which it were sacrilege to surrender, prevent so awful a Catastrophe." Chelmsford could no longer be "cajoled on the one hand nor Intimidated on the other." Liberties, purchased by their ancestors "at the expense of so much Blood and Treasure," would not be wrenched from them. They were, they concluded, "the guardians of unborn millions," and the prevailing sentiment was: "IN FREEDOM WE'RE BORN AND IN FREEDOM WE'LL DIE."

In the summer of 1774, in the absence of a provincial assembly, the county conventions emerged briefly as the primary extra-legal organs for coordinating and directing political activity in Massachusetts. At least five Chelmsford residents attended the Middlesex County Convention in Concord at the end of August. The Reverend Bridge's son, Ebenezer, was chosen clerk of the convention. Although his father had been a strong Tory and a friend of the royal governor, Thomas Hutchinson, both father and son were now on the revolutionary side. Twenty-three-year-old Jonathan Williams Austin, chairman of the Chelmsford Committee of Correspondence, still fresh from his apprenticeship in the legal office of John Adams, was chosen chairman of the county convention's committee on resolutions.

His committee issued the Middlesex Resolves, which called for raising an armed force.

In October, 1774, when General Thomas Gage dissolved the Massachusetts General Court he had called to meet at Salem, Chelmsford chose Jonathan Austin and Samuel Perham delegates to the extra-legal Provincial Congress held at Concord and Cambridge. The congress requested that the tax collectors stop payments of money to the treasurer of the colony and instead send their collections to a receiver-general elected by the congress. Chelmsford apparently followed this resolve, for in March of the following year the town voted to protect the constables and assessors for not obeying the colonial treasurer's warrant for the taxes. The money collected by the revolutionary receiver-general was used to buy field pieces, mortars, bombs, powder, lead, muskets, and flints. The congress also appointed a committee of safety with powers to call out the militia when needed and to provide them with supplies.

The first Massachusetts Provincial Congress dissolved itself in December, 1774, amidst rumors that some members wished to call out the militia immediately and attack the British forces. A second Provincial Congress was called for February 1, 1775, perhaps with the hope that the delegates would return with instructions to take more radical steps. When the congress opened in Cambridge Simeon Spaulding was the Chelmsford representative. The congress did little except debate, but towards the end of February, 1775, a few days after the congress adjourned, its committee of safety and supply voted to buy enough military supplies to field an army of 15,000 men. It also established military supply depots and drafted letters ordering the commanders of the local militia companies to make preparations for assembling at least one-fourth of their men. This order was implemented in Chelmsford on March 6, 1775, when the town voted that "the Alarm list should be equipt with fire arms and ammunition, and to raise fifty minutemen, including officers: that they be disciplined one half day in a week for eight weeks ensuing." The minutemen were to be the elite force, prepared to march at the shortest notice. They were to be paid eight pence for each half day they trained over and above the required days set aside for the training of the whole militia company.

When the Massachusetts Provincial Congress reassembled on March 27, 1775, it voted that no militia should be mustered unless the British troops at Boston marched into the countryside with baggage and artillery. There was great fear, even on the part of extreme radicals, that a war might begin before military preparations were completed. However, on April 3, the delegates heard that Parliament had adopted an address to the king declaring Massachusetts to be in a state of rebellion. Four regiments of British troops were to be sent from Ireland, and Lord North had proposed a bill blocking New England's access to the Newfoundland fisheries and placing additional limitations on its trade.

On April 8 the Massachusetts Provincial Congress voted to make preparations for raising a permanent army and sent delegates to the other New England colonies asking for their cooperation. Then, on April 15, the congress adjourned until May 10. Although General Gage's spies had been suggesting that a sudden military strike at the colonials would destroy all radical plans, Gage was fearful of starting hostilities without direct orders from England. Those definitive orders arrived in Boston on April 16. Lord Dartmouth ordered Gage to use the army to enforce the Coercive Acts of 1774. Gage organized a secret expedition to seize the military stores at Concord. With the aid of his spy, Dr. Benjamin Church, he provided the leader of the expedition, Colonel Francis Smith, with a detailed description of the stores and a map showing the houses and barns where they could be found.

Colonel Smith's "secret expedition" did not remain secret for long. Paul Revere and others had been watching the British army in Boston for days, and when the redcoats set out across the Charles River on the evening of April 18, 1775, Revere and William Dawes warned the countryside. As the British marched to Lexington on the night of April 18-19 they could hear the firing of alarm guns, the beating of drums, and the tolling of church bells. At dawn, on the green at Lexington, they killed eight minutemen before continuing on to Concord.

By this time the minutemen of Chelmsford, nine miles north of Concord, were receiving the alarm. It was a warm spring morning and many were already plowing their fields. Some men gathered at what later became known as the revolutionary memorial boulder in the village center, but those on the south side of the town probably headed directly for Concord. Benjamin Pierce, the father of President Franklin Pierce, was plowing a field in what is now the Highlands section of Lowell when he heard the signal. He chained his oxen to a tree and "the plow was in mid-furrow stayed." He grabbed his uncle's gun and equipment and went off on foot.

The number of Chelmsford residents who reached Concord in time to join the Concord, Bedford, and Acton militia companies in the mid-morning fight at the North Bridge is uncertain. It is probable that only those Chelmsfordites who had horses or who ran all the way arrived in time to take part in the fray. Later the family of William Fletcher claimed that he said: "I was one of those who stepped over the body of the first British soldier killed at Concord Bridge."

The British, however, tarried in Concord center until noon before beginning their retreat through Concord and on towards Lexington and Boston. Thus the redcoats gave most of the 104 men organized in Chelmsford's two militia companies time to reach the scene of action. Some Chelmsford residents engaged the British in the skirmish at Merriam's Corner, and the Reverend Bridge reported that the British "were followed by our men down to Cambridge before night." During the almost continuous clashes with the British troops, Captain Oliver Barron, the leader of one of the Chelmsford militia companies, was wounded, as was Aaron Chamberlain, a member of Moses Parker's company. Sergeant John Ford, who ran a mill in what is now Lowell and who was later to take command of Barron's company, killed five British soldiers before the end of the day. On the following day, most residents of Chelmsford got their first look at the enemy. A number of captured British officers were locked up in the town after residents of other communities, fearing reprisals from the British army, refused to hold them. Some in Chelmsford also were "much frightened" by the presence of the captives, but the committee of safety permitted the officers to remain provided they were well guarded by the militia.

"The Civil War was begun at Concord this morning!" the Reverend Bridge recorded in his diary. He, like other Chelmsford residents, and like most people in America, did not immediately consider the initial engagements a war between two independent foreign states. Not favoring independence, they believed that they were fighting a civil war to defend their rights as Englishmen. "The Lord direct all things for his glory, the good of his Church and people, and the preservation of the British Colonies, and to the Shame and Confusion of our Oppressors."

Most agreed, however, that things were in a "terrible state" after April 19. They were now in a conflict of which "the Lord only knows what will be the issue." In the days that followed, Chelmsford residents saw "a constant marching of soldiers" through their town towards Boston. On the Lord's Day, April 23, Bridge found only "a small assembly" in the meeting house. "Tis a Very destressing day," he wrote, "Soldiers a-passing all day & all night." By this time even revolutionary leaders could do little to prevent the spontaneous siege of the British base at Boston.

As the militia from the various towns gathered around the capital city many feared that another clash with the British was inevitable. The situation became even more alarming after May 25, 1775, when three British major generals, William Howe, Henry Clinton, and John Burgoyne, arrived in Boston eager for action and glory. They had orders for General Gage that all those guilty of treason and rebellion were to be arrested and jailed. This news, together with the occupation of Dorchester Heights by the British troops, increased the already significant flow of refugees from Boston and Charlestown. Even before April 19 Ebenezer Symmes and his family had fled to Chelmsford "to secure a place of retreat, etc., in the present troublesome season." Now many more refugees were arriving to take up residence with other families in town. On May 28 they heard "news at noon of a fight, begun yesterday, between the regulars & our Soldiers at Chelsea, Noddle's Island [East Boston], etc., & yet going on."

The clashes at Chelsea Creek and on the harbor islands were minor affairs, however, compared to what was to follow. On June 12, 1775, General Gage, after receiving additional reinforcements, decided to occupy the hills of the Charlestown peninsula north of Boston. The Massachusetts Committee of Safety, learning that an occupation was imminent, ordered General Artemas Ward, whose headquarters were at Cambridge, to fortify Bunker Hill. Ward, in turn, sent John Ford, now captain of one of the militia companies of Chelmsford, with these orders to Colonel William Prescott of Pepperell. On the evening of June 16, after Ford returned to his company at Cambridge, Prescott, together with General Israel Putnam of Connecticut, and Colonel Richard Gridley, the Bay Colony's chief military engineer, decided to fortify the more advanced and exposed Breed's Hill rather than Bunker Hill.

Among the men who climbed the sixty-seven-foot-high hill under cover of darkness on June 16 was Colonel Ebenezer Bridge, Jr., of Billerica, the son of the Reverend Bridge. The

younger Bridge was the commander of a newly organized and
still incomplete regiment in the new Massachusetts army. His
appointment as colonel reflected political rather than military
prestige, but he was accompanied by his lieutenant-colonel,
Moses Parker of Chelmsford, who had served with valor in the
French and Indian War. Both Bridge and Parker helped supervise the nine hundred men—a few of whom were from
Chelmsford—who worked through the night fortifying the circu-
lar summit with ditches, dirt walls, dirt-filled barrels, and
wooden firing platforms. On the following morning, as the hill
came under British cannon fire, it was Bridge and Parker who
pleaded with Colonel Prescott to relieve the weary men who had
been digging all through the night. But Prescott ordered that the
men who built the breastworks were the ones best able to defend
them.

During the late morning of June 17, while the British forces
were crossing from Boston to Charlestown to dislodge the
Americans from Breed's Hill, Captain Benjamin Walker of
Chelmsford distributed his men, a number of whom were also
from Chelmsford, in the abandoned houses of Charlestown village on the right side of the American line close to the shore.
Meanwhile, Captain Ford was preparing to lead his Chelmsford
company from Cambridge to the scene of the impending battle.

The men stationed in the houses of Charlestown village were
the first to fire on the British, and young Joseph Spaulding of
Chelmsford claimed to have fired before the order was given. "I
fired ahead of time," he later said, "and [General Israel] Putnam
rushed up and struck at me for violating orders. I suppose I
deserved it, but I was anxious to get another good shot at Gage's
men ever since our affair at Concord." The British marines re-
taliated by charging into the village, and a bloody house-to-house
struggle began. The American companies were broken up and
the men scattered, but Walker collected a group of adventurers
from a number of companies and led a series of daring counterat-
tacks. Even after the British gunners poured "hot shot" into the
town, setting most buildings on fire, Walker fought amidst the
flames until only one man, Jacob Frost of Tewksbury, remained
with him.

By the time Ford's company arrived at Charlestown the British
were advancing in force. Crossing the narrow peninsula in the
midst of cannon fire from British batteries in the harbor, Ford
and his soldiers headed for the front. General Putnam ordered

Ford and some of his men to take two abandoned four-pound pieces and place them on the left side of the American line at the bottom of Breed's Hill. Most men in Ford's company, along with the members of other units, were placed along the stone and rail fence that ran for two hundred yards in the grassy plain between Breed's Hill and the Mystic River. The maintenance of this line was necessary to prevent the British from encircling Breed's Hill and trapping the Americans who were maintaining the breastworks at the summit.

In one of the bloodiest frontal assaults in the history of warfare 450 of 750 British soldiers were killed or wounded by the Americans who fired from behind the fence and from behind the makeshift barricade constructed on the beach by the Mystic River. It was because of the failure of the British to break this line that General Howe ordered a series of bloody assaults on the breastworks on the hill. At the end of the day, after suffering extremely heavy casualties, the British finally stormed into the fort. Colonel Bridge, who already had been wounded, was hacked on the head and neck by a British sword during the final British assault. As the defenders of the fort were making their final stands while retreating down the hill, Lieutenant Colonel Parker fell with a shattered thigh bone. In the confusion he was left in agony on the field of battle. Near him lay Joseph Warren, president of the Massachusetts Provincial Congress, killed by a musket ball that smashed into his head. A short distance away lay Captain Walker, his leg also shattered. Walker, together with Jacob Frost, who had remained with him in the burning village of Charlestown, had crossed the whole line and had joined Ford and his Chelmsford men along the fence between the hill and the Mystic River.

Both Parker and Walker spent the night of June 17 amidst the other dead and wounded on Breed's Hill. On the following day they were picked up by the British, carried to the fort for medical treatment, and then transported across the harbor to the second floor of the Boston jail. In British eyes they were rebels rather than prisoners of war. On June 22 Parker told his wife he was "as well treated as I can desire and attended with great care and tenderness by Doc Whitworth, as are the rest of the prisoners." We are "well & sufficiently supply'd with all Necessaries but Fresh Provision," Parker and Walker wrote on July 3. In reality, they were subjected to harsh treatment. Both had their legs amputated in the squalor of the jail. Parker died on July 4;

Walker lingered on until August 15. Both paid the harsh penalty for courage. Many Americans at Bunker Hill had run away under fire.

Chelmsford learned of the Battle of Bunker Hill from express riders on the afternoon of June 17. That evening they could see the fires still burning in Charlestown village thirty miles away. Because of the heavy American casualties—140 dead, 271 wounded, and 30 other badly wounded prisoners taken by the British—most looked upon the battle as a serious defeat. The reports of mass desertions during the battle reinforced the pessimism. It was a time "big with distress & trouble," the Reverend Bridge recorded in his diary. He still believed that he was witnessing a civil war. "The Lord suffers it to be so, that our Enemies are they who were our brethren—Of the same Nation, & Subjects of the Same King." The blood of his badly wounded son was shed, he believed, because of the "Vengeance of a Wicked & Corrupt Ministry a deluded—A Devilish Venal parliament." It is significant that King George III was not yet the object of Bridge's wrath.

The Battle of Bunker Hill convinced many Americans that the British ministers and a majority in Parliament were prepared to wage an all-out war to enforce their policies. It convinced the members of the Continental Congress at Philadelphia to support a continental army. In England, the news of the loss of 226 British soldiers killed and 828 wounded—almost fifty percent of the attacking force—convinced both the king and his ministers that Lexington and Concord had not been accidental skirmishes. The war in America, Lord North declared, had to be "treated as a foreign war," and the English government began taking a series of drastic measures that made any hope of reconciliation impossible. By the end of 1775 the English government had hired Hessian mercenaries to quell the rebellion, Parliament had passed the American Prohibitory Act that declared all vessels and cargoes belonging to Americans forfeited to the Crown, and George III had denounced the colonists for engaging in a general rebellion "carried on for the purpose of establishing an independent empire."

Such policies convinced many Americans that they must break completely not only with the English government but even with the king. As early as May 13, 1776, Chelmsford voted to support a declaration for an independent state. Such a resolution was introduced in the Continental Congress on June 7, 1776, and three days later Congress selected a committee to draw up a declaration of independence. Congress voted for independence on July 2 and accepted Thomas Jefferson's Declaration of Independence on July 4. Chelmsford residents first read the Declaration in the newspapers, and in August the Massachusetts Council ordered that it be read in all the churches of the Commonwealth. On the afternoon of September 1, 1776, the Reverend Bridge "read the declaration of independence of the United States of America in the pub[lic] congregation." And when he was finished he added: "Zion heard and was glad and the Daughters of Juda rejoiced because of thy Judgements, O Lord."

During the summer and fall of 1776 residents watched events similar to those witnessed by their ancestors during the Indian wars. In June, 1776, a group of prisoners—royal marines and members of the Seventy-first Regiment of Foot, Highlanders— were captured by Massachusetts privateers and sent inland by the government for safe-keeping. "A number of highland soldiers are brot in among us as prisoners," the Reverend Bridge wrote on June 25, "and a numbr [are] sent off this morng. to Dunstable." "The town again in confusion," Bridge wrote on July 3, "Companies mett to draw out men for Canada." On July 23 Captain John Ford and his company marched off to Fort Ticonderoga to reinforce the American army that was retreating from Quebec. Ford and his men remained on Lake Champlain until December, 1776 and then returned home by way of Albany. But one Dracut resident remained with the Northern Army a little longer. Barzillai Lew, a free black cooper who had served as the fifer in Ford's company both at Bunker Hill and Ticonderoga, did not return with his fellow townsmen. He was discharged from the service at Albany on January 1, 1777. Despite his patriotism Lew had been serving illegally, for a Massachusetts law of January, 1776, specifically forbade all Negroes, Indians, and mulattoes from joining the militia.*

While Captain John Ford's company was strengthening the Northern Army, other Chelmsford residents were fighting in George Washington's army to the south. British general William Howe, planning to use New York City as a base of operations, moved thousands of troops onto Staten Island in July, 1776. On August 22 he began landing twenty thousand troops on Long Island in preparation for an attack on the American lines. On August 24, just two days before Howe's attack, Nathaniel Foster

*This law was repealed in 1777.

wrote home to Chelmsford that from his station at Red Hook, South Brooklyn, New York, he could see between 250 and 300 British ships. The American tents were exposed to British fire, and he expected "to be Kild or taken if We Dont beat them for there is no Room to Retreat for the Water is all Round us When the tid[e] is up." Despite very heavy American casualties, the main body of Washington's forces escaped capture. More than twenty Chelmsford men escaped from Long Island to Manhattan; then they crossed the Harlem River to White Plains and finally retreated west of the Hudson into New Jersey.

During the spring and summer of 1777 at least sixteen Chelmsford residents were serving in the American forces in Rhode Island. But during that year the important encounter involving Chelmsford soldiers was in northern New York. On September 30 Captain John Ford with more than fifty Chelmsford men marched to Saratoga to reinforce the army of Horatio Gates and block the movement of General John Burgoyne's forces down the Hudson River valley. Although Noah Foster of Chelmsford fought and died on October 7 in the Battle of Bemis Heights—the decisive encounter that ensured the American victory—most Chelmsford men were still moving with their pack-horses through the wilderness during that engagement. They arrived only in time for Burgoyne's surrender on October 17, but they were entrusted with forty or fifty prisoners, part of the fifty-seven hundred man British contingent that Burgoyne had promised to ship back to England as part of the terms of surrender.

The American victory at Saratoga led to the formal Franco-American alliance of 1778, an alliance that eventually brought about the complete defeat of the British. Yet even before the formal alliance French aid had been arriving in America. As early as 1776 Marie Louis Amand Ansart De Marisquelles had arrived in Boston. "Glowing with ardor" for the Revolution, he called attention to his association with the cannon manufacturing industry of France. His father and his uncle were the suppliers of cannon for the King of France, and Ansart had been trained as a metallurgist and military engineer. On December 9, 1776, he told the members of the Massachusetts General Court that he had particular methods for softening iron by a mixture of ores and minerals, and that he could cast solid cannon and then bore and polish a cylinder. Cannons made with boring machines would be much stronger than those cast as cylinders, and production time would be cut to twenty-four hours for pieces firing twenty-four pound shot.

Colonel Lewis Ansart, 1742-1804. Courtesy of Dracut Historical Society.

The General Court, extremely short of artillery, gave Ansart everything he requested. They appointed him Colonel of Artillery and Inspector General of the Foundries of Massachusetts at a salary of one thousand dollars a year for the duration of the war and two-thirds of that amount for life after the war. They paid for the foundry and boring machines located at Bridgewater, Massachusetts, and his project was immediately underway. As early as February 1777 Lieutenant Colonel Paul Revere was ordered to Bridgewater to inspect Ansart's work. He was to observe the testing of the cannon and to move the cannon that passed inspection to Boston. Revere learned a good deal about metallurgy from Ansart. This knowledge was later of great value when Revere started his foundry for the manufacture of bells.

During July and August, 1778, Ansart served as aide-de-camp to General John Sullivan, the commander of the American forces that were planning to drive the British from Newport, Rhode Island, with the aid of the French fleet commanded by Comte d'Estaing. When d'Estaing's fleet was disabled in a storm and sailed to Boston for repairs Ansart supervised the construction of fortifications in Boston harbor.

It was at Newport in 1778 that Ansart met General James Mitchell Varnum. The Varnum family had come to Chelmsford shortly after its founding, and they were one of the first families to cross to the north side of the Merrimack and develop land in what became Dracut in the eighteenth century and part of Lowell in the nineteenth. Although General Varnum made his home in East Greenwich, Connecticut, he had been born in Dracut and members of his family owned extensive lands in that town. It was probably because of his association with Varnum that Ansart decided to make his home in Dracut after the war. On February 22, 1785, the Reverend Bridge, who thirty years before had told his congregation that the French were their "mortal Enemies" and the cause of all their miseries, entered in his diary: "Col. Mareschall,* a French Gentlemen, now of Dracut, and his wife at my house."

A French nobleman at Dracut was only one of many changes witnessed by Chelmsford residents during the revolutionary era. New constitutional governments, migrations to the north and

---

*The Colonel's correct name, "de Marisquelles," was apparently too difficult for Yankee tongues, which corrupted it to "Mareschall." After the war, by act of the Massachusetts General Court, the name was legally changed to simply "Lewis Ansart."

west, epidemics, shortages of essential supplies, and severe inflation were characteristic of this era. But in the midst of these changes the basic economy of the town did not change. Most of those who lived in Chelmsford had been farmers and cattle raisers, and farming and cattle raising had not changed much in over 125 years. The land was poor and the hardships many. Despite political and social upheaval the basic economy would not change until the coming of the Industrial Revolution.

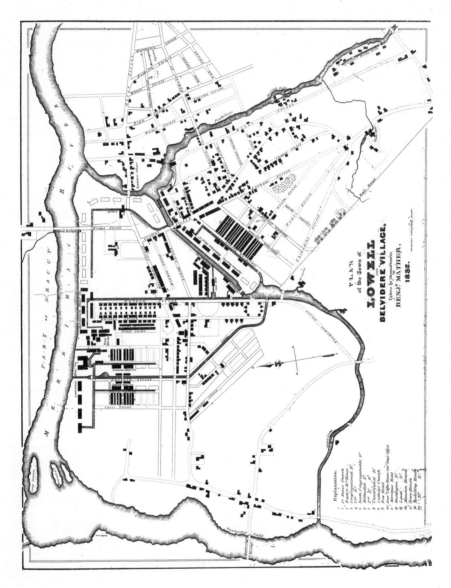

Map of Belvidere Village by Benjamin Mather, 1832. (Lowell Historical Society)

V

Villages at Wamesit Neck

By John A. Goodwin

For more than a century before the first large cotton factories were built along the Merrimack River at Lowell, the inhabitants of the area had used the waterpower of the Merrimack and Concord rivers in a limited way to cut lumber, to grind grains, and to produce cotton and woolen yarn for home weaving. They lived as Thomas Jefferson hoped most people in the United States would live: in a slow-paced, rural, agrarian world, where men's lives were attuned to the seasons and every household was more or less independent of every other. The new era arrived almost overnight and transformed the place forever. It exemplified Alexander Hamilton's view that the United States would become a great and prosperous nation only if its citizens turned to large scale manufacture and trade. Early in the nineteenth century, in the peaceful land surrounding the Concord and Merrimack rivers, no one could foresee the consequences of that swift and irrevocable transformation.

The story of organized white settlement of the Great Neck between the Merrimack and Concord rivers begins with the Wamesit purchase in 1686. The Indians deeded to Jonathan Tyng and Major Thomas Hinchman all of the Wamesit praying Indian village lying on the west side of the Concord River, except for a small Indian field along the Concord River.* Tyng

---

*Also excepted was the "Margaret Winthrop grant," which consisted of 3000 acres on the south side of the Merrimack River, most of it east of the Concord River, granted by the legislature in 1640 to the widow of Governor John Winthrop.

and Hinchman immediately conveyed their respective half-interests to fifty proprietors.

These men organized and recorded in the "Proprietors' Book" all their real estate transactions, including the division of the land into individual parcels assigned by lot to each proprietor. Among these were Jerihmeel Bowers and Benjamin Parker, whose descendants still own and occupy a part of their original lot; the ancestors of President Franklin Pierce; and Major Thomas Hinchman, a friend of the Indians. During King Philip's War Hinchman built a garrison house on the north bank of the Merrimack River for the defense of that area.

In retrospect, an entry in the Proprietors' Book on April 11, 1697, was a significant one:

aparell the: 11: 97.

land layd out for the incoregdment of bilding a mill
at wamasite this land is twenty aceres moer or lese
bounded south and southarly by the riuer medo riuer
and north and noreast and norweast by marked tres: one
whight ocke one red ocke on the nor weste part: on the
north and noreast part: thre black ocke tres marcked:
one acere of sayd land lys on the south syd of sayd
riuer by the mill place.

> Solloman Keyes, senier
> Sameuell foster, Junier
> Andrew Spolding, Senier
> Committee

The informal affiliation of the Wamesit, or Chelmsford Neck, residents with the Town of Chelmsford continued satisfactorily until 1725 when Stephen Pierce, a resident of the Neck, was elected to the Massachusetts legislature. When the House refused to seat Pierce (because he was not a legal resident of the town of Chelmsford), the residents of the Neck refused to pay taxes to the town. Chelmsford promptly secured an act of the legislature officially annexing Wamesit to the town.

The population of the Neck was concentrated in three centers. The first was Middlesex Village, about a mile above the Pawtucket Falls. Here Jerihmeel (or Jerathmell) Bowers in 1671 built the house which still stands today. He had a legal still and was duly licensed by the selectmen to produce alcoholic beverages.

Nearer the river was Colonel Jonas Clark's tavern, opened before 1739, which later became the Middlesex Tavern, for many years the preferred place for visitors to Middlesex Village to stay. Clark was the great-uncle of John Hancock.

Middlesex Village and the tavern's custom both grew with the construction of the Middlesex Canal. During the "canal fever" after the Revolution, a group of Boston entrepreneurs conceived the idea of connecting the port of Boston with the interior of New Hampshire. In 1793 a charter was obtained by these proprietors of the Middlesex Canal to dig a canal from Charlestown Mill Pond to the Merrimack River at Middlesex Village. They chose this terminus because the Merrimack River here, just before it turns toward the sea, lies closest to Boston. The construction work was supervised by Colonel Loammi Baldwin of Woburn, later the Superintendent of the Canal. The canal was opened for business in 1803 and immediately diverted most of the trade away from Newburyport . Its source of water was the Concord River at North Billerica, which is 24½ feet above the level of the Merrimack River at Middlesex Village, and 104 feet above the Charles River at Charlestown. The Middlesex Canal, 27¼ miles long, was the first major traction canal to be built in the United States. Horses or oxen pulled the packet boats, barges, and rafts of timber through the canal's 20 locks and over its 8 aqueducts. The packet boat *Governor Sullivan* (named for one of the original proprietors of the canal) left the head of the canal at Middlesex Village at 8:00 A.M. on Monday, Wednesday, and Friday, and returned on alternate days. Stages left Lowell (after its settlement) and Boston to connect with the boat at Middlesex and Charlestown.

The barges were flat-bottomed, 40 to 70 feet long and 9 to 9½ feet wide. On the canal, two men, a driver and a steersman, usually made up the crew. Most of the boats were owned by private operators who paid tolls for whatever merchandise they were carrying, but the canal corporation owned the packet boats, *Governor Sullivan* and *George Washington*.

Firewood and lumber from the Merrimack Valley, granite from Tyngsborough and agricultural products from New Hampshire were shipped down the canal to Boston. Much of the brick used in the first buildings of the Merrimack Corporation in Lowell was transported from Charlestown over the canal. When the mills started operations, the canal was a convenient way of shipping the raw cotton and the finished cotton cloth. The canal was a factor in the decision to build the textile factories in East

Lock and Tollhouse on Middlesex Canal. Painting by Joseph Payro. Courtesy of Middlesex Canal Association.

Chelmsford, and the mills' business greatly added to the canal's income.

After the digging of several canals around the falls of the Merrimack River in New Hampshire, the Middlesex Canal provided access by water to that state's interior. The steamboat was developed on the canal for navigation on the river. Eventually the Boston & Concord Boating Company made a regular run between those cities.

Night travel on the canal was prohibited to prevent damage to the banks; Sunday travel was prohibited for religious reasons. Travel was suspended also during the winter months when the canal froze, making it an unreliable method of transport. When the Boston & Lowell Railroad opened in 1835, therefore, its year-round service immediately took over a great deal of the canal's business and ultimately forced its closing in 1859.

Because of the availability of safe transportation by water, Hunnewell and Gore established in 1802 the Chelmsford Glass Company on the east bank of the canal in Middlesex Village. Glass workers from Germany produced window panes and ornamental glass. They were lodged in several small workers' cottages and in a long boarding house owned by the company and still standing today along the route of the canal. In 1827 or 1828 the glass works burned and Hunnewell and Gore failed. The concern was taken over by a local group who operated it until 1839, when the company moved to Suncook Village in Pembroke, New Hampshire.

Also in Middlesex Village were the Bent and Bush hat factory and Clark's Ferry to the north bank of the Merrimack River. All this commerce resulted in an increase in population and a demand for a church more conveniently located than the West Dracut meeting house on the north side of the river near the falls. Consequently, the Second Congregational Church (of Chelmsford) was constructed in 1821 along the Middlesex Canal and equipped with a bell cast by Paul Revere.*

The second settlement on Chelmsford Neck developed near the Pawtucket Falls. John Ford, who owned a sawmill purchased from Judge Jonathan Tyng, lived there. This mill located at the falls was one of the few enterprises to use the waterpower of the Merrimack River before the great mills seized it in 1822.

---

*When the meetinghouse was sold in 1859 the bell was removed to the Pawtucket Congregational Church where it is still in place.

Ford was a sergeant in the Chelmsford Minutemen and served at Concord Bridge on April 19, 1775. After raising a company of men, he was commissioned a captain and served with distinction and valor at Bunker Hill.

Also near the falls were the law office of Ashahel Stearns and the residence and store of Phineas Whiting, who owned also a small cotton spinning mill on the Concord River.

In 1792 the Proprietors of the Middlesex Merrimack River Bridge were incorporated; they built a toll bridge (known as the Pawtucket Bridge) from the Falls Village to West Dracut, connecting with Mammoth Road, also constructed in 1792 to be the main road to New Hampshire.

The building of the bridge and the opening of Mammoth Road helped develop West Dracut across the river. The West Congregational Church was built there in 1797 and was a convenient meeting house for the residents of Middlesex and Falls villages. In 1807, toll-free passage over the bridge was allowed to all persons attending meetings in the West Dracut church. All tolls were abolished in 1861 when the bridge was purchased for twelve thousand dollars by Middlesex County, Lowell, and Dracut.

The third settlement on the Neck was along the Concord River near the two sets of falls. In this area early settlers took advantage of the waterpower to set up an extensive and varied industry. Here also, as early as 1774, the first of Lowell's many bridges was built across the Concord River.

As early as 1737 a fulling mill for dressing cloth was built by Nicholas Sprake (or Sprague), Jr., at the Wamesit Falls on the east side of the Concord River near its confluence with the Merrimack. On the same side was a grist mill which later came into the ownership of Thomas Hurd. After it had been destroyed by fire, Hurd replaced it by moving to the site another mill he owned at the foot of the Pawtucket Falls. Hurd also owned a mill on the Concord's west bank. It had been built in 1813 by Phineas Whiting and Josiah Fletcher. Here he wove wool into satinets. This wooden mill burned in 1826; when the fire started the wooden waterwheel was put into motion so that its revolutions would immerse it and keep it safe. Although the mill was destroyed, the wheel was used in the replacement brick mill.

Hurd was a shrewd opportunist. While in Boston in 1821, he overheard a conversation dealing with land purchases in East

Chelmsford. Hurrying home, he bought the Bowers sawmill near the Pawtucket bridge along with considerable land on both sides of the falls. This put him in a position to strike a good bargain with the Merrimack Manufacturing Company. Not only did he make a profit on his land, but he also acquired the right to use water from the Pawtucket canal to help power his mills. The other old residents who had sold out cheaply must have envied Hurd's shrewdness. Hurd eventually failed and his property was taken over by the Lawrence brothers who built and incorporated the Middlesex Company there in 1830.

In the meantime, Hurd's mill on the east bank (in the Belvidere section of Tewksbury) was purchased by Winthrop Howe and later became the Belvidere Flannel mill.

Further up the Concord River was another industrial site. Here River Meadow Brook, after winding through the countryside from Carlisle, fell into the river. A short distance up the brook, Moses Hale in 1790 set up a mill for fulling, dyeing, and dressing cloth. By 1800, he had expanded the operation on a new site below the fulling mill, and added a sawmill and a grist mill. The new location permitted Hale to use the same waterpower twice. In 1801, Hale bought a picker and carding machine and started carding wool for the farmers of the area. Like Amos Lawrence some decades later, Hale publicized his product by giving samples of it to persons of influence. Once he had some of his carded wool spun and woven into cloth which he finished and had made into a suit for General Joseph B. Varnum of Dracut, who was then Speaker of the national House of Representatives.

In 1817, after building another dam further down the brook, Hale built a mill to manufacture gunpowder. The mill's opening was sufficiently important to bring Governor John Brooks to East Chelmsford for the event. The powdermill, the first in the area, was managed by Oliver M. Whipple who later married Hale's daughter and continued the business to as late as 1856. While the business thrived, it was dangerous. Consequently, Hale bought an island in Boston harbor to store the powder. To reduce the likelihood of accidents, the powder was transported to Boston in the dead of night in wagons pulled by horses whose hooves had been wrapped with cloth so that the iron shoes should not strike any sparks to ignite the powder and blow up the load, the cart, and the horse, as well as anyone else who happened to be venturing forth late at night.

Oliver M. Whipple was born in Weathersfield, Vermont, and came to East Chelmsford in 1818. He served on a committee to divide the town into school and highway districts, and was a member of the board of selectmen and an assessor of Chelmsford before the incorporation of Lowell. He was one of the first selectmen of Lowell, an alderman, and a representative in the legislature. In addition to being a trustee and vice president of the Institution for Savings, he was instrumental in founding the Lowell Cemetery: he sold the trustees the land on which the cemetery was built, and was its first president. He was responsible for the development of the area around the Concord River mills, where a street name today perpetuates his name.

Whipple put into effect one of his father-in-law's projects by digging a canal along the west bank of the Concord River in order to provide additional waterpower. Here on the Whipple Canal rose many small mills to which Whipple sold power. In 1865, the Wamesit Power Company purchased the water rights from which it continues to sell power to this day.

Another industry located on River Meadow Brook (now known as Hale's Brook in honor of its first developer) was started by Jonathan Knowles. After failing in the manufacture of cotton and woolen yarns in what later became Hurd's mill, Knowles devised a way of using the cotton waste from the mills—which previously had been dumped into the river—to manufacture cotton batting. To develop a market for his product, Knowles suggested sewing several layers of batting between sheets of cotton cloth to make comforters. Mrs. Knowles developed another source of business by using the batting to fill cushions for the pews in St. Paul's Methodist Church.

Finally, on the east side of the Concord River, on a promontory overlooking its confluence with the Merrimack, stood the estate of Judge Edward St. Loe Livermore. It was called Belvidere and eventually gave its name first to a real estate development by Thomas and John Nesmith, and then to an entire section of the city.

The son of the chief justice of New Hampshire, Livermore was born in Portsmouth in 1762, studied law in Newburyport, and practiced in Concord, New Hampshire. President Washington appointed him United States attorney for New Hampshire, a post he held until his appointment to the New Hampshire Supreme Court. After the death of his first wife, he moved to Newburyport, from which place he was elected to congress. Judge Livermore brought his family to East Chemsford in 1816. He bought the Gedney place, which he renamed "Belvidere" because of the spectacular view it commanded across and up the Merrimack River. Among his many daughters was Harriet Livermore, the world-famous "pilgrim preacher." She travelled in the Holy Land, did missionary work among the Indians, and preached in the Capitol in Washington. She was immortalized by Whittier in *Snow-Bound* as "a nature passionate and bold."

In 1811, no one living in the peaceful villages around the confluence of the Concord and Merrimack rivers knew that in Boston a gentleman merchant, in poor health, had decided to journey to England to improve his physical condition and—not incidentally—to have a look at how the British manufactured cloth. The consequences of that trip were to change the villagers' lives as surely as the arrival of the white men had affected the Indians' two centuries before.

Part Two

VI

Proprietors of Locks and Canals: The Founding of Lowell

By Harry C. Dinmore

On a clear day in November, 1821, a small group of Boston merchants made their first visit to the Pawtucket Falls. A light snow lay on the ground as they perambulated the area. With Nathan Appleton and Patrick Tracy Jackson of the Boston Associates were Kirk Boott, who had already been engaged to take over the management of their new enterprise, his brother, John W. Boott, Warren Dutton, soon to be the first president of the Merrimack Manufacturing Company, and Paul Moody, the master mechanic. It was Moody who had heard of the thirty-two foot fall of the Merrimack River while on a visit to his native Amesbury. All the investors shared Moody's enthusiasm, and it was decided to undertake the project. Before they left the spot, a remark was made that some of those present might live to see the place contain 20,000 inhabitants. In fact, when Nathan Appleton, the last survivor of the group, died in 1861, the population of Lowell was 36,827.

The Lowell Experiment, set in motion by this visit, was the result of the fortunate confluence of the capital accumulated by Newburyport ship-owners; the photographic mind of Francis Cabot Lowell; the initiative of his brother-in-law, Patrick Tracy Jackson; the inventive mind of Paul Moody; the engineering genius of George Washington Whistler and James Bicheno Francis; the untapped power of the Pawtucket Falls; the managerial

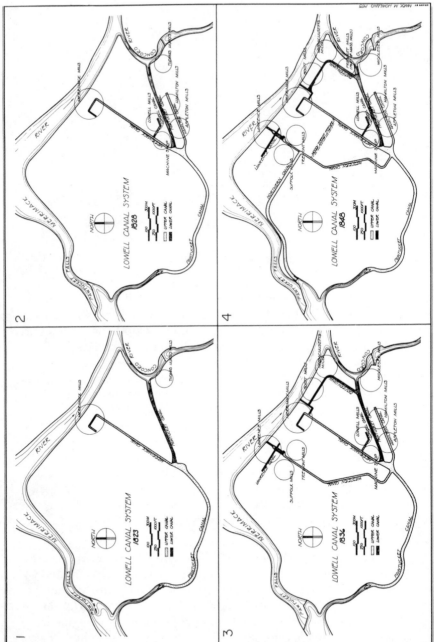

Lowell Canal System. Drawn by Mark M. Howland, 1975. Courtesy of Historic American Engineering Record, National Park Service.

talent of Kirk Boott; and finally a new domestic market hungry for cotton goods.

The earliest of these elements goes back to 1792 when a group of Newburyport merchants and ship-owners decided that the up-country of New England could be developed by better transportation down the Merrimack River through their seaport. The Merrimack, with its many rapids all the way back into the hills of New Hampshire, was a poor "trading" river. The worst spot for navigation was at East Chelmsford, where the river dropped thirty-two feet in a short distance. Log rafts had to be broken up and floated down, and other bulky goods, like limestone, had to be teamed around the rapids.

For thirteen hundred dollars, Dudley Atkins Tyng and his Newburyport associates bought the land for a canal to circumvent the rapids. On June 27, 1792, Governor John Hancock signed the charter of the Proprietors of the Locks & Canals on Merrimack River,* granting the new corporation water rights. The 1½ mile, four-lock Pawtucket Canal around the rapids was completed in 1796 at a cost of fifty thousand dollars.

Before the canal was even dug, Governor Hancock, on June 22, 1793, signed a charter incorporating a rival canal company. By 1803, the Proprietors of the Middlesex Canal had linked the Merrimack River at Chelmsford with Boston. The success of the Middlesex soon destroyed the dreams of a transportation empire through the Pawtucket Canal to Newburyport, and put an end forever to that town's prospects of prominence in New England trade. So it turned out that the original canal and transportation company was a failure; thirty years later, when the next generation used the neglected waterway to furnish the power to drive cotton mills, the little canal company became the basis of the Industrial Revolution in America.

The original Newburyport investors in the Locks & Canals Company—the Cabots, Lowells, Tyngs, Wendells, Clarks, Jacksons, and Duttons—intermarried and dominated the textile and financial world of New England for generations. Within their close-knit group, they had not only the shares of Locks & Canals, but also the financial resources and managerial skill to undertake the Lowell Experiment.

The other necessary ingredient, engineering innovation, fell

---

*This charter, still in existence and use, makes the Locks & Canals one of the oldest extant corporations in the United States.

Francis Cabot Lowell, 1775-1817. From an original
photograph in the collection of Harriet Ropes Cabot.
Printed by permission.

into place with Francis Cabot Lowell's trip through the English
textile mills. Because of British laws forbidding export of textile
machinery, he memorized the designs of the machines he saw.
After his return, in a loft on Broad Street, Boston, Lowell, with
mechanic Paul Moody, built a power loom from memory. In 1814
the loom was finished, and Moody, with the help of Ezra Worth-
en's machine shop, set up in Waltham the first fully integrated
cotton mill in the United States using power looms: the Boston
Manufacturing Company. Starting production in 1815, this
Waltham Experiment was successful enough to warrant a search
for an expansion site because the waterpower of the Charles
River at Waltham was insufficient.

Francis Cabot Lowell died in 1817 at the age of forty-two. His
brother-in-law, Patrick Tracy Jackson, the largest stockholder in
the company, and Nathan Appleton, a Boston merchant, took
over Lowell's leadership role in the project. To them fell the
waterpower problem, which they solved after a long search by
following the suggestion of Worthen and Moody to use the Pawtucket Falls on the Merrimack River at East Chelmsford. Jackson
and the other sons of the wealthy Newburyport associates

gathered in the shares of stock which their fathers had issued in building the Pawtucket Canal thirty years earlier. They also engaged Kirk Boott and Thomas M. Clark to buy up the East Chelmsford farmlands which are now downtown Lowell. The Tyler, Fletcher, and Cheever farms cost them $18,339, and the Canal shares $30,217.

The first company formed by these entrepreneurs was the Merrimack Manufacturing Company. On December 1, 1821, Nathan Appleton and Patrick Tracy Jackson each subscribed for 180 shares; Kirk and John W. Boott bought 90 shares each, and Paul Moody 60 shares. Shortly afterwards, nine other investors were allowed to purchase shares: Dudley Atkins Tyng (one of the original proprietors of the Locks & Canals Company), Warren Dutton, Timothy Wiggin, William Appleton, Eben Appleton, Thomas M. Clark, Benjamin Gorham, Nathaniel Bowditch, and Daniel Webster.

After the Merrimack Company was operating (and it took only two years), the need for more mills, canals, and machinery was obvious, and a new corporate set-up was required. The charter of the Locks & Canals Company was amended by the legislature in 1825 to permit the corporation to acquire and hold real estate, water rights, and mill privileges. On January 2, 1826, the Merrimack Manufacturing Company conveyed to the proprietors of Locks & Canals all its real estate in East Chelmsford,* and simultaneously took back a deed of the area occupied by its mills. All the rest, including locks, canals, water rights, and land, belonged to the Locks & Canals Company which thereafter constructed new mills, dug new canals, and built new machinery as needed.

The mill owners used the reorganized Locks & Canals Company to keep the economy of Lowell growing with new mills and with new engineering ideas for water measurement, power transmission, and basic cotton manufacturing improvements for new and better fabrics. To do this, they hired some of the best engineers of the nineteenth century. It is important to remember that in 1823 in New England no other method of driving manufacturing machinery existed than waterpower; steam was not introduced until the 1850s, and electricity not until the twentieth century. Thus it was essential to develop the science of hydraulics.

*This deed, which is recorded in the Middlesex North District Registry of Deeds in Book 6, Page 211 of the South District copies, is referred to as the "Great Deed," and is the source of title of most of the Locks & Canals property.

These engineers succeeded in taking a small half-dismantled canal, widening and deepening it, installing the controls and devices to channel the waterpower into the mills, and then harnessing the power to make the individual machines run. At first the water had to fall through the old type of breast waterwheels; the power was transmitted through giant belts and drive shafts running the length of the buildings to carding machines, spindles and looms which made the cotton cloth.

In order to distribute the water to the various mill sites, it was first necessary to dig feeder canals from the rebuilt Pawtucket Canal. The first of these was the Merrimack Canal, carrying a full thirty-foot fall of water to the Merrimack mills. All the other mills were supplied with either a thirteen-foot fall of water (on the upper level) or a seventeen-foot fall (on the lower level). This permitted each cubic foot of water to be used twice, to power the machinery in a mill on each level of the canal system.

The distribution of the correct amount of water into each branch canal was controlled by a system of gates and flow-measuring devices located in the operating heart of the system, the Swamp Locks, which were built in an old swamp on Dutton Street.

This original system of water distribution was enlarged and refined by the great hydraulic engineering studies of James B. Francis, who came to the Locks & Canals in 1834 as a young assistant to Major George W. Whistler, and remained as chief engineer and agent until 1885. Francis' published *Lowell Hydraulic Experiments*, along with the work of his associates, Ithamar Beard and Uriah Boyden, greatly advanced, if it did not establish, the discipline of hydraulic engineering.

By 1843, it became apparent that water from the river needed to flow in greater volume and more equitably to the ten mill sites. To accomplish this, Francis engineered, and the Locks & Canals Company built, the Northern Canal. This followed the south shore of the river from the dam to the Tremont, Suffolk, and Lawrence Mills, with a special supplement to the Merrimack Company under Moody Street—the Moody Street Feeder. It fed into the Western Canal and reversed its flow back toward the Swamp Locks. After this modification, the canal system was complete and the mills were able to get their proper proportion of water, and even some excess when it was available.

James B. Francis, 1815-1892. (Lowell Historical Society)

The best operating level at the dam was eighty-six feet above sea level, with the water just breezing over the flash-boards. The canal system worked best when the Concord River was at the forty-two-foot level; this allowed for the best flow away from the wheels. High water in the Concord reduced power, because the water did not flow away from the wheels quickly enough.

The upper Pawtucket, Western, Merrimack, and Northern canals were (and still usually are) maintained at 82½ feet. The middle level of the canal is maintained below the Swamp Locks and below the Tremont & Suffolk Mills at 67 feet. The Tremont, Suffolk, Hamilton, Appleton, and Lowell Manufacturing Companies and the Lowell Machine Shop had a 13-foot drop, while the mills located between the middle level and the river (Middlesex, Boott, Lawrence, and Massachusetts) had a 17-foot drop into the river. There were various gates and by-passes which could change the volumes of water being delivered to different mills.

One of Francis' noteworthy accomplishments was the building of the Guard Locks on the Pawtucket Canal. These were essentially a boat lock with the addition of a flood control system (the Francis Gate) and a measuring gate. Francis' study of the water levels of the Merrimack River for the preceding century convinced him that there was danger that the canal system in time of flood would provide an easy avenue into downtown Lowell for the flood water. Therefore, in 1850 he built the Francis Gate to take a top level of 93 feet, thus keeping out of the canal (and downtown Lowell) excess water from any predictable flood. Although the Swamp Locks had flooded every spring, Francis' carefully thought-out engineering solution was promptly dubbed "Francis' Folly." It took only two years for the great flood of 1852 to prove the soundness of his theory. Subsequent floods were also contained by the gate, and the only one to exceed the planned height was the 1936 flood which crested at 102 feet, and which was contained by placing sandbags on top of the guard locks and dam.*

The total power available in the canal system was about ten

---

*On March 19, 1936, at 4:30 a.m., when Locks & Canals officials and employees climbed up into the superstructure of the Francis Gate to lower it, they found the hammer and chisel which had been placed there almost a century before. Using these tools to cut the link holding up the gate, they were pleasantly surprised to see the gate slide down smoothly into place, so meticulously had it been engineered.

STATEMENT

OF THE

MILL POWERS AND SHARES IN THE PROPRIETORS OF LOCKS AND CANALS,

TO WHICH THE SEVERAL MANUFACTURING COMPANIES AT LOWELL ARE ENTITLED.

NAME OF THE COMPANY.	Number of Mill Powers.	Quantity of Water in Cubic Feet per Second.	Fall in Feet.	Number of Shares in Proprietors of Locks and Canals.
MERRIMACK MANUFACTURING COMPANY,	$24\frac{20}{30}$	616.667	30	740
HAMILTON MANUFACTURING COMPANY, .	16	968.000	13	480
APPLETON COMPANY, ...	$8\frac{16}{30}$	516.267	13	256
LOWELL MANUFACTURING COMPANY, .	$8\frac{12}{30}$	508.200	13	252
LOWELL MACHINE SHOP, ...	$3\frac{9}{30}$	199.650	13	99
Total on Upper Level of Pawtucket Canal,		2192.117		
MIDDLESEX COMPANY, ...	$5\frac{23}{30}$	262.383	17	173
BOOTT COTTON MILLS, ...	$17\frac{26}{30}$	812.933	17	536
MASSACHUSETTS COTTON MILLS, . . .	$24\frac{16}{30}$	1116.267	17	736
Total on Lower Level of Pawtucket Canal,		2191.583		
SUFFOLK MANUFACTURING COMPANY, .	$6\frac{15}{30}$	393.250	13	195
TREMONT MILLS, ...	$6\frac{15}{30}$	393.250	13	195
Total on Upper Level of Western Canal, .		786.500		
LAWRENCE MANUFACTURING COMPANY,	$17\frac{9}{30}$	787.150	17	519
Totals, ...	$139\frac{11}{30}$			4181

JAMES B. FRANCIS, *Agent Props. of Locks and Canals.*

LOWELL, DECEMBER 17th, 1853.

Statement of mill powers and water rights, 1853. (Lowell Historical Society) thousand to thirteen thousand horsepower. But in Lowell the power was calculated rather by mill-powers. A mill-power was defined, on the basis of the Waltham experience, as that power necessary to spin No. 14 yarn on 3584 spindles with all the other machinery necessary to convert cotton into cloth. Alternately a mill-power was defined as the right to draw twenty-five cubic feet of water per second on a fall of thirty feet (or about sixty horsepower). Each mill was allotted its mill-powers when it bought its land. The right to so much water power came with the land. The original price paid by each mill was $4 per spindle or $14,336 per mill-power, plus a yearly rent of $300 per mill-power. Each company owned its own power generating machinery—Locks & Canals only delivered the water to the mill.

The Locks & Canals Company originally had acquired the right to flood the land adjoining the river all the way up to Lake Winnipesaukee, so that it could control water levels, within limits, at any time.* At the present time, water levels are controlled by the U.S. Army Corps of Engineers with their flood control projects upriver.

Besides distributing water for power, Locks & Canals also engaged in other varied activities. It originally built all the mill buildings, dug the canals, installed the penstocks and water-wheels. It set up the Lowell Machine Shop which built all the machinery for textile manufacturing and processing, and which spun off as a separate enterprise in 1845. Later the Machine Shop combined with other machinery-building companies and is known today as the Saco-Lowell Company.

As early as 1830, because of the difficulties of winter transportation on the Middlesex Canal, Patrick Tracy Jackson, treasurer of the Appleton Company (and later president of the Boston & Lowell Railroad) conceived the idea of building a railroad. After Jackson had obtained the best reports from England, the engineers of Locks & Canals designed and supervised the building of the Boston & Lowell Railroad, which went into operation in 1835. It was one of the early roads in the country. An engine was bought in England, shipped to Boston and thence to Lowell by

*The right to control the flow of water also produced interesting results down river. It is said that the starting time of the Lawrence mills was later than Lowell's, because it took some time for the water, which had been held back at the Pawtucket dam, to flow through the Lowell canal system and then down the Merrimack to the down-river city.

way of the Middlesex Canal.* The machine shop draftsmen copied its design which was used to build many of the engines for America's early railroads. The Boston & Lowell, financed by the mill owners, quickly took over the cotton mill business from the Middlesex Canal, and by 1845 was solidly established. Eight years later the canal went out of business.

Today, the Lowell canal system is still in use. Its water flow is still used to generate a limited amount of electric power. But instead of the old waterwheels, turbines—developed by Uriah Boyden at the Hamilton Manufacturing Company—are used. Instead of being turned by the force of water falling on the waterwheel's exterior surfaces, the turbine is moved by the force of water rushing against fins on its interior. This change resulted in a power generating system many times more efficient than the old waterwheel. An agreement with the Massachusetts Electric Company calls for sending any excess power to that company when available, and for pulling in power when needed. The city also relies heavily on the canals for water for fire protection in the downtown area: a special distribution system of water for firefighting is maintained at a sufficient pressure by a reservoir atop Belvidere Hill.

The five-mile network of power canals constructed in nineteenth century Lowell was a uniquely successful solution to the problem of how to harness natural power to drive the machines of the new industrial age. The energy supplied by its carefully controlled waterpower gave birth and enduring life to the Industrial Revolution in America. The canals were a wonder then; they remain intact today, a silent testament to an age when energy was neither expensive nor dangerous, but readily available to anyone who had the vision and the know-how to capture it.

---

*In a marvelous example of self-destruction, the canal not only transported the engine parts to Lowell, but also deposited the granite ties at the desired spots along the route of the railroad.

VII

The Golden Age

By Joseph W. Lipchitz

In the fall of 1814, Francis Cabot Lowell completed his difficult task of re-inventing the power loom, whose design and operation he had carefully watched in the English and Scottish factories he had visited. On returning to this country, he had locked himself into a loft on Broad Street in Boston, and set himself the laborious task, with the help of a mechanic, of reconstructing a power loom. When it was finally done, he invited Nathan Appleton to inspect it. Appleton was duly impressed:

> I well recollect the state of admiration and satisfaction with which we sat by the hour watching the beautiful movement of this new and wonderful machine, destined, as it evidently was, to change the character of all textile industry.

The story of Lowell's beginnings and its rise as one of the foremost manufacturing cities in America is the story of the change of character of the textile industry. The Industrial Revolution resulted in mass production of goods by machines, use of energy sources (such as water power and, later, steam and electricity) to power the machines, and a concentration of labor within factories. With its coming the merchants of Boston were able to create an urban industrial complex.

In the early 1820s, the area which was to become Lowell was Chelmsford farmland bordering the Concord and Merrimack rivers; industrial Lowell awaited its creation by shrewd men able to use the opportunities which existed in the area, not only

by harnessing the waterpower, but also by combining and utilizing other components of the new industrial revolution. The
waterways, including the Middlesex and Pawtucket canals, had
been used for transporting produce and lumber to Boston and
Newburyport. More important, in its forty-eight mile course from
the New Hampshire boundary to the sea, the Merrimack River
drops ninety feet with more than one-third of the total fall occurring over a one-mile stretch at the Pawtucket Falls. This created
a tremendous source of energy which could be tapped. While the
Boston merchants were the first to capitalize on the waterpower,
they were not the first to use it. Some time prior to 1710, John
Varnum of Dracut had erected a grist mill on the north bank of
the Merrimack. In the first quarter of the eighteenth century,
Judge Tyng of Dunstable ran a saw mill on the Chelmsford side
of the Pawtucket Falls. (This was later acquired by Captain John
Ford and became known as Ford's Mill.) In 1737, Nicholas
Sprake (Sprague) built a fulling mill on the east side of the
Concord River; it was the first textile plant within the confines of
what is now Lowell. In 1790, Moses Hale built a fulling mill on
River Meadow Brook for fulling, dyeing, and dressing home-
woven cloth, and in 1801 he added the first picker and carding
machine in the area. Hale also operated a grist mill on the same
brook, which eventually became known as Hale's Brook.

In 1812, a factory built on the Concord River by Whiting and
Fletcher was rented by John Goulding to spin cotton. The factory
was bought by Thomas Hurd and converted to woolen manufacture in 1818 with sixteen hand looms to make satinets. By 1830
this mill was to become the Middlesex Company, the foundation
of the fabulous wealth of the Lawrence brothers. A glass factory
was begun at Middlesex Village by Hunnewell and Gore of
Boston; it operated from 1802 to 1839, and was the first industry
in the area to maintain a boarding house for its workers. The
Boston textile men who came here in the 1820s would raise the
boarding house to an indispensable position in their enterprise.

Another major early nineteenth century industry was the powder mill of Oliver Whipple, who had come from Vermont and
married Moses Hale's daughter. Started just after the War of
1812, the powder mill soon acquired an international reputation
and Whipple was shipping gunpowder all over the world.

By and large, these early mills were isolated attempts at manufacturing by individuals, as contrasted to the more heavily financed, thoroughly planned and integrated textile manufacturing
undertaken by corporations after 1822.

The man who had the greatest influence on the direction of growth of industrialized Lowell and for whom the city was named never saw Lowell and died before its foundations had been laid. Born in 1774, Francis Cabot Lowell, the son of Judge John Lowell, graduated from Harvard College in 1793. He established himself successfully in international trade and in 1811 he traveled to Scotland and England, both for his health (which was never strong) and for business. Because of the embargo which had been in effect since 1807, business in the United States was not good and Lowell was seeking lucrative investments for his capital. The textile industry he saw abroad so fascinated him that upon his return he convinced his brother-in-law, Patrick Tracy Jackson, as well as Nathan Appleton and his Cabot relatives to help finance his first experiment, the Boston Manufacturing Company, in Waltham in 1813. Appleton was somewhat skeptical of Lowell's scheme to implement the power loom and invested only $5000 instead of the $10,000 Lowell sought. As Appleton put it:

> I told them that, theoretically, I thought the business ought to succeed, but all which I had seen of its practical operation was unfavorable; I, however, was willing to take $5000 of the stock in order to see the experiment fairly tried . . . and I should make no complaint . . . if it proved a total loss.

But the experiment was a success, and before Lowell died in 1817 he not only had established the textile industry in New England, but also had set the pattern of industrialization for others in this country to follow. This pattern was that of the large plant, containing the total process of manufacturing from raw material to finished product, the combination of large capitalization and professional management, the use of labor in the factory itself for all the processes, the production of cheap goods in quantity, and the protection of infant industries by tariffs. The devices were not Lowell's invention, but his successful integration of them all reflected his genius.

The other "Boston Associates" were equally interesting, aggressive men of substance. Nathan Appleton, born in New Ipswich, New Hampshire, in 1779, was the seventh son in a family of twelve children. A good student, he had been accepted at Dartmouth College, but decided instead to go into trade where his Yankee ingenuity quickly made him rich and powerful. The history of Lowell and the New England textile industry would have been very different without him, and yet in his lifetime he was more respected for his knowledge and views on banking

Nathan Appleton, 1779-1861. Portrait by G.P.A. Healey. Courtesy of City of Lowell and Lowell City Library.

than on textile manufacturing. Appleton was one of those who
devised the Suffolk Bank system: any New England bank that
left $5000 on reserve deposit with the Suffolk was entitled to
have its paper currency redeemed at par. In an age when most
unfamiliar bank paper was looked upon with a jaundiced eye,
this was an important advance. The plan proved successful; in
time six other Boston banks joined, which forced the two
hundred or so banks in New England to redeem their notes in
specie. The sanction was the same as that used by the Bank of the
United States. Banks unwilling to provide a redemption fund
were presented with their notes in large quantities for immediate
redemption—an aggravating and embarrassing pressure that was
quite effective. As a result of this successful system, New England had an almost uniform currency from 1825 to 1860 and the
Suffolk Bank had about a million dollars of working capital on
which no interest had to be paid.

Appleton controlled much of Boston's finance capital which he
was able to invest in textile manufacturing; but he was not concerned with profits alone. In the textile industry he advocated
reducing costs of goods for consumers and pleasant working
conditions for employees—in lieu of higher wages and shorter
hours. In 1830, he was elected to Congress and did not seek
re-election, although he later served another term in the 1840s.
In his later years, Appleton affirmed that he would have been
satisfied financially with the first $200,000 he made in an early
trading company, as money making had not been his main purpose in life. As far as the textile industry was concerned, he had
gone into it by chance and he claimed that it was "accident and
not effort that made me a rich man." In fact, it was a series of
fortunate accidents, brought about by the careful and shrewd
planning of a resourceful man, which made him wealthy.

The most colorful individual in the city's early years was Kirk
Boott. An early investor and the first resident agent of the Merrimack Company (the first textile mill in Lowell operated by the
Boston Associates), Boott had more influence than any other
single person on the early planning and operation of the new
town. Born in Boston in 1791, he was educated at Rugby School
in England and at Harvard, where he displayed more inclination
for the social than the academic life and left without graduating.
Instead he purchased a commission in the British Army and
fought under the Duke of Wellington in his Peninsular Campaign against Napoleon's army. When his regiment was ordered

Kirk Boott, 1790-1837. Portrait by Chester Harding. Courtesy of City of Lowell and Lowell City Library.

to America during the War of 1812, Boott resigned his commission and returned to this country. After joining with his brother in an unsuccessful trading partnership, John W. Boott & Sons, he was unemployed when, in 1822, Patrick Tracy Jackson recommended him as agent for the Merrimack Company. As agent Boott became the town planner, architect, engineer, and production manager, as well as the leading citizen of the new community. Boott had many talents—energy, application, drive, and ambition—but he was not a popular figure. He was quick to use his riding crop on boys whom he deemed "impudent." An anglophile, he raised both the Union Jack and the American flag on the Fourth of July. He flew the Union Jack on top. This naturally infuriated the patriotic locals who gathered before Boott's house and demanded that the flags' positions be reversed. When Boott refused, they did it for him. Despite his lack of popularity, the members of the Merrimack Corporation were rightly satisfied with their appointment of Kirk Boott. It was he who drew up the plans of the company's land holdings, made the ground plans and elevation drawings of the buildings, wrote the deeds, and kept the records of the company's transactions. He also made two trips to England on company business, entertained visiting celebrities and directors, and several times served as representative in the state legislature. At noon on April 11, 1837, Kirk Boott toppled from his chaise in front of the Merrimack House, and died instantly of either apoplexy or a cerebral hemorrhage.

Patrick Tracy Jackson succeeded Boott as agent of the Locks & Canals Company, the holding company which, by its control of the land and waterpower, determined who could start a mill in Lowell, where, and at what price. As Francis Cabot Lowell's brother-in-law, Jackson had been an early investor in the Lowell textile mills. In addition to intuitive business sense, Jackson had a penchant for speculation that more than once cost him a fortune. But each time he managed to bounce back from such reverses, start again, and make another fortune. In addition to his textile interests, Jackson found other fields attractive. Railroads caught his attention, and he was the prime mover behind the development of the Boston & Lowell Railroad.

At this time, Jackson was treasurer of the Appleton Company. He persuaded the directors of the Locks & Canals to invest in planning a railroad. The charter request was bitterly opposed in the legislature by representatives of the Middlesex Canal, who

Patrick Tracy Jackson, 1780-1847. Portrait by G.P.A. Healey. Courtesy of City of Lowell and Lowell City Library.

claimed that there was no need for an alternative method of transportation, and that, in any event, no one would travel on such a fast, terrifying conveyance. Despite such arguments, the charter was granted on June 5, 1830. Work started immediately. James F. Baldwin, one of the sons of Colonel Loammi Baldwin, the builder and superintendent of the Middlesex Canal, was engaged to survey a route. Ironically, Baldwin found among his father's papers a map showing a discarded route for the canal. Using this same map, young Baldwin traced on it the route used for the construction of the railroad, which paralleled for some distance the old canal. This made it possible to deposit the heavy granite railroad ties along the route where needed, which was obligingly done by the Canal proprietors. The engine was imported from England. It was named the "Stephenson" after its maker, and was transported from Boston to Lowell, again by canal. In Lowell, it was dismantled in the Locks & Canals machine shop, under the superintendence of Major George W. Whistler, and the parts copied before it was reassembled. This provided the patterns for the subsequent locomotive building business of the machine shop.

Finally, on May 27, 1835, the "Stephenson" made the first trip to Boston carrying a load of distinguished passengers, including Jackson, Whistler, and Baldwin. All went well and the Boston & Lowell Railroad was launched, while the Locks & Canals machine shop went on to build two more locomotives for the Boston to Lowell run. The first home-made engine was to be named in honor of the treasurer of the Appleton Company who had masterminded the whole operation, but, at that time, "King" Andrew Jackson, the anathema of local Whigs, reigned in the White House, so the engine had to be named the "Patrick." It was followed by another called the "Lowell," a popular and noncontroversial name. The railroad was an immediate success and, within a very few years, drove out of business its accomodating rival, the Middlesex Canal. From the beginning the new line carried just under four thousand passengers a week.* The charter required a minimum legal fare of seventy-five cents one-way, and in order to live within the letter of the law, the railroad provided a special car with unpadded pine benches. In more conventional and comfortable coaches the fare was one dollar. In 1838 the Nashua & Lowell Railroad was created and in 1850 the

*In 1974 trains from Lowell to Boston averaged only 5430 passengers per week on a much larger population base.

Salem & Lowell Railroad opened service between the respective cities.

The Lawrence brothers, Amos, Abbott, Luther, William, and Samuel, all had varying degrees of financial interest in textile manufacturing in Lowell and elsewhere. Abbott and Amos Lawrence made an interesting contrast and an effective combination. Amos was the more measured and practical sort who early in life renounced such vices as smoking, drinking, and the theatre. Abbott was more libertarian and extroverted. Amos was not politically inclined while Abbott had political ambitions. He married the daughter of Timothy Bigelow, the speaker of the Massachusetts House of Representatives, member of the Hartford Convention, director of several Boston banks, and a relative of the Baring banking family of London.* Abbott was not only gaining a wife, but he was securing a niche in politics as well. He served in Congress, campaigned for General Harrison in 1840, and expected to be named secretary of the treasury in the new administration, but failed to be appointed. In 1848, he refused to support Daniel Webster's bid for the presidency because Webster opposed the extension of slavery. Instead, he backed Zachary Taylor with the expectation of being offered the vice-presidency. Again, Abbott Lawrence was disappointed; as a consolation, he was appointed minister to London. In addition to his political exercises, Abbott was one of the founders of Lawrence, Massachusetts. His nephew, Amos A. Lawrence was the eponym of Lawrence, Kansas, to whose settlers he had contributed generously during the fight for "Bleeding Kansas."

The Lawrence brothers might have had disparate interests beyond the business world, but they all had one trait in common—they were determined to be rich, and they succeeded. In 1825, William and Samuel Lawrence took over the selling agency for Thomas Hurd's small woolen mill. Hurd's business was not good; the brothers loaned him $45,000 in advance of sales, and on May 8, 1827, took a mortgage on the property for $55,000. By December, 1828, Hurd had failed owing $370,000, and the Lawrences took over the property by foreclosing the mortgage. They reorganized it in 1830 as the Middlesex Company, enlarged the plant, improved the machinery and increased production: soon the new corporation began returning profits.

Luther Lawrence was a lawyer, president of the Railroad Bank in Lowell, and the city's second mayor. His career came to an

*Luther Lawrence married Bigelow's sister.

untimely end soon after his re-election when in 1839 he had the misfortune of slipping from a platform into a wheel pit in one of the Middlesex mills and fracturing his skull in the seventeen-foot fall.

Such men seized the opportunity to build a new city economically based on the textile industry. Lowell was, in contrast to older cities, particularly European ones, a completely planned city. It was, as one French observer said, "a speculation of the merchants of Boston."

For such speculators the first order of business after organizing was to find a suitable site and to purchase the necessary land. In Amesbury, Ezra Worthen told his friend and former partner Paul Moody, the superintendent of the Boston Manufacturing Company, of the potential of the Pawtucket Falls on the Merrimack River at East Chelmsford. Moody inspected the site on his way back to Waltham and informed Appleton and Jackson. Having approved the site, the Boston Associates had Kirk Boott and Thomas M. Clark buy the land as quietly as possible to keep speculation at a minimum. They paid $18,339 for the farms of Nathan Tyler, Josiah Fletcher, Joseph Fletcher, and Moses Cheever. In addition, they bought the shares of the Locks & Canals Company which owned the Pawtucket Canal. The merchants now owned most of an island bounded on the north by the Merrimack River, on the east by the Concord River, and on the south and west by the Pawtucket Canal. With the construction of a low dam at the head of the Pawtucket Falls, the enlargement of the Canal, and the construction of branch canals, the necessary water power was available for a large complex of mills.

On the first of February, 1822, the Merrimack Manufacturing Company, by Kirk Boott, Agent, contracted with the Boston Manufacturing Company, P. T. Jackson, Agent, to build for it ninety-two spinning frames, with sixty-four spindles each, half for spinning warp and the other half for spinning fillings, as well as all the machinery needed to warp, dress, and weave the yarn into cloth. All the machinery was to be of the same quality and design as that used in Waltham, and was to be installed in East Chelmsford by the Boston Manufacturing Company. The Merrimack was to pay $28 per spindle, or a total of $164,764 for the equipping of its first mill.

The only remaining problem was labor. The Boston Associates had determined as a matter of policy to avoid creating another industrial slum like Manchester, England. There probably was some altruism in this decision, but, on a more practical level, the decisive factor was the shortage of potential industrial workers in this country. The Boston Associates hoped to attract the daughters of New England farmers to East Chelmsford to work in the new mills. In order to attract the women, and even more to allay the fears of their parents, the associates planned and built handsome, substantial, and clean brick boarding houses where the operatives could be housed in relative comfort and with moral safety. These boarding houses were to be the trademark of the Lowell Experiment and were copied by all the subsequent textile communities.

On September 1, 1823, the great wheel of the Merrimack mill first started to turn, and on January 3, 1824, Kirk Boott wrote in his diary: "10 bales of goods sent off to Boston—being the first lot sent off from the Merrimack." The Lowell Experiment had been successfully launched.

With the mills constructed, the mill girls settled in their boarding houses, and the machinery humming, the new town became a thriving community. Soon the population was sufficient for a separate town. Local pride of the inhabitants and the desire of the mill owners to control the town's expenditures, rather than be subject to taxation by the town government miles away in Chelmsford Center, combined to result in the incorporation of East Chelmsford as an independent town. Kirk Boott, who had done so much of the planning, hoped to name the town Derby after his family's native town in England, but Appleton's opinion that the town should be named for Francis Cabot Lowell prevailed. On March 1, 1826, Lowell was formally incorporated as a town with a population of twenty-five hundred.

In its first decades Lowell grew and developed so rapidly that much of the early careful planning was trampled underfoot by boom town economy and psychology. When the Merrimack Company proved to be enormously successful, other companies were quickly established. In 1825 the Hamilton Manufacturing Company purchased water power and land from the newly reorganized Locks & Canals Company in order to produce twilled and fancy goods. In 1828 the Appleton Company and the Lowell Manufacturing Company were formed, and even the financial panic of 1829 (when the Merrimack Company paid no dividend) was not enough to deter investment as Amos and Abbott Lawrence bought water power and land at reduced terms to establish the Suffolk, Tremont, and Lawrence companies the following

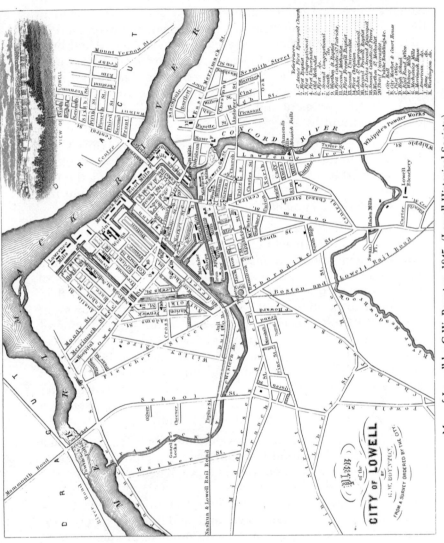

Map of Lowell by G.W. Boynton, 1845. (Lowell Historical Society)

year. Although most of these firms manufactured cotton goods, the Lowell Company early specialized in making carpets and the Middlesex Company made woolens.

The Merrimack Company that began it all was also the most profitable in the early years, returning an annual dividend as high as sixteen per cent per year. By 1845 it ran 5 cotton mills, 155 boarding houses for its workers, and a print works. In the first important years of operations, the print works depended on a skilled English print master, John D. Prince, who was brought to Lowell from Manchester. When Prince demanded five thousand dollars per year salary, Boott was taken aback. "Why, man, that is more than we pay the Governor of Massachusetts." Prince's retort was simple and direct: "Well, can the Governor of Massachusetts print?"

As in all the new industrial cities, the companies paid low wages. In relation to what a woman could earn in the early nineteenth century, for example as a country school teacher, the mill girls did fairly well, certainly better than their counterparts in the English textile factories. But on an absolute scale the wages were low. In the early years the companies paid unskilled labor between $1.50 and $2.00 a week above the fee (between $1.25 and $1.50) deducted for room and board. Hours were long, even for the young workers.

Despite the low wages the workers were frugal. The mill girls had entered the work force for specific reasons: to accumulate a dowry, to put a brother through school, to help pay off a family mortgage. In response to the workers' desire to save, as early as 1827 the Hamilton Company began holding their savings, issuing bank books, and paying interest. The company had no state charter for this activity which was of questionable legality. Lowell needed a proper bank and in 1829 the Lowell Institution for Savings accepted its first deposits. The bank's promoter was its first treasurer James G. Carney, a Lowell businessman. He had as associates some prominent Lowell men, including Reverend Theodore Edson, who served on the first board of directors and as the bank's second president, 1835–1883. It became a tradition that the rector of St. Anne's Episcopal Church should serve on the board of directors. The bank thus projected an aura of respectability, some admirers have said philanthropy. The companies and Lowell's leading citizens had responded to the mill girls' needs and had created one of the city's durable institutions.

The cotton industry's market declined in the 1840s and as profits shrank the companies' managers sought to avoid paying lower dividends on shares by a more rigorous exploitation of the labor force. Wages were cut about ten percent for the skilled weavers and up to twenty percent for the unskilled. The companies also tried to increase the profit margin by speeding up the machinery and by increasing the number of machines each worker tended. Perhaps the most demoralizing of the companies' innovations was the hated premium system which granted bonuses to overseers and second hands who succeeded in getting more work out of the operatives than was expected. Because it changed the whole relationship between the girls and the overseers from one of general informality and congeniality to one of rivalry and antagonism, this system probably contributed more than any other single factor to the demise of the mill girls as a labor force.

For years the existence of the famous mill girls had aided the manufacturers in selling their products, justifying their profits, and improving their own social image. As one author asked rhetorically, "If a Lucy Larcom read Milton and translated Schiller, after a long day in front of the machines, did it not follow that a Nathan Appleton was a sage, a man of honor, and a public benefactor?"* Under the premium system, overseers became tyrannical and hard driving and the girls resentful and suspicious. Such conditions, combined with a growing influx of Irish workers fleeing famine conditions in Ireland in the 1840s and 1850s and the failure of mill workers in Massachusetts to win passage of a ten-hour bill in the legislature, effectively closed one of the brighter chapters in the early industrial and cultural history of Lowell.

The strained relationship with the labor force might have been avoided had the mill owners been more farsighted. Smaller gross profits were caused largely by the early practice of paying too large a percentage of profits in the form of dividends which left little or no reserves for needed repairs, new equipment, or replacement of worn equipment. By the 1840s, when maintenance of plant and equipment required money, wages had to be lowered to maintain the dividends for stockholders.

Despite such problems the overall economy of the growing town was healthy enough to assure continuing expansion. In 1836, the town of Lowell, with its growing variety of businesses

*Hannah Josephson, *The Golden Threads*, p. 95.

and mills, became a city. By 1856 Lowell had 400,000 spindles and 12,000 looms which converted 36 million pounds of cotton and 5 million pounds of wool into more than 115 million yards of cotton cloth, calicoes, broadcloths, and cassimeres and into more than a million yards of carpet. In addition to the major textile firms there were wadding and batting mills, machine shops, dye houses, screw-bolt factories, card factories, bobbin and shuttle factories, bedstead factories, a wire fence factory, a bagging mill, a grist mill, a kyanizing plant, and a brewery. Even this list fails to include one of the greatest of the nineteenth-century businesses —patent medicines.

Between 1826 and 1836 Lowell's population jumped from twenty-five hundred to eighteen thousand. With this growth came attendant problems and demands for municipal services. Therefore, on April 1, 1836, Lowell received the third city charter granted by the Massachusetts legislature. The population continued to grow steadily until mid-century, when it declined briefly because of the discovery of gold in California.

The citizens' insistence on schools over the objections of Kirk Boott suggests that not all the city's wisdom resided in its wealthy. As early as the 1826 town meeting the citizens ordered a report on school districts so that proper planning could be started. Five such districts were outlined and formal elementary schooling was begun. By 1832, a more efficient organization of education and the proper housing for school programs were proposed and two modern, grade schools were built. The following year the South Grammar School opened on the South Common, and soon thereafter the North Grammar School was opened. A high school program began in December, 1831, in one room at the Middlesex Street schoolhouse, and for a time in 1835 the high school was a half-time operation because of a lack of funds. In 1840, however, a high school was constructed on the land between Kirk and Anne Streets, on the site of the present high school.*

Progress in education did not come easily since most of the property in town was still owned by the textile companies, and the owners, through their agent Kirk Boott, fought proposals for the higher property taxes necessary to finance schools. In 1832, Rev. Dr. Edson of St. Anne's Church spoke out in favor of the

---

*Among the members of the first class of Lowell High School were General Benjamin F. Butler and Gustavus V. Fox, Assistant Secretary of the Navy during the Civil War.

St. Anne's Church, 1825. Engraving from the *Lowell Offering*. (Lowell Historical Society)

proposal to build the two large grammar schools at a cost of twenty thousand dollars. Kirk Boott was adamantly opposed; when the motion passed the town meeting, he stopped attending the church.

After the parish's lease expired in 1842, William Appleton and the other directors of the Merrimack Company demanded that the parish purchase the church building, which had been so widely advertised as a free gift of the corporation. A price of twelve thousand dollars was agreed upon, but one of the conditions of the settlement was that the rectory be vacated. In 1856, on the advice of its attorneys, John P. Robinson and Benjamin F. Butler, the parish sued for return of the rectory and for recovery of the price paid for the church. The basic question was whether, by allowing the property to be dedicated to religious services, the company had surrendered its claims to the property. The company argued that it was still the owner, that it had never dedicated or deeded away control in perpetuity, and that the

Rev. Theodore Edson, 1793-1883. Engraving after the portrait by Thoman Bayley Lawson. Courtesy of Rector, Wardens, and Vestry of St. Anne's Church.

religious society of St. Anne's was not the only recognized religious organization which could claim sole usage of the property, since the property had been given over to religious uses, not to any particular religious organization. The decision in the Supreme Judicial Court was against the parish. It was not until 1866, when the Merrimack Company had finally agreed to sell the rectory, that the parish raised the funds to purchase it, and Dr. Edson moved back to the house he had been forced to leave twenty-four years before.*

The action of the directors might have been incompatible with Christian ethics but not with business instincts. St. Anne's had been established as an Episcopal Church by the Merrimack Company because Kirk Boott was an Episcopalian. Although the mill girls were Congregationalists, Baptists, or of some other denomination, they had to contribute 37½ cents every quarter to support St. Anne's and were obliged to attend services there until they formed their own congregations. Not all new congregations were welcomed by the company directors. When Jonathan Morrill began holding prayer meetings at his home for Baptists who resented being assessed for a "foreign church," Kirk Boott told Morrill that if he continued to hold such meetings, he must leave his company owned house. Fortunately, Morrill was soon appointed postmaster of Lowell and moved his family and his prayer meetings to an apartment over the post office. Less fortunate was T. J. Greenwood, an overseer at the Merrimack Company, who was discovered passing the hat in the mills to raise money to build a Universalist Church. The Universalists held the then unorthodox view that it was God's purpose to save every human being through divine grace—a kind of spiritual democracy in the next world. This notion alone was enough to offend Kirk Boott, but when Greenwood, unable to wait for the hereafter, proclaimed the principles of the Jacksonian Party and its egalitarian ideals, Boott dismissed him on the spot.

Boott, a staunch Episcopalian, preferred hierarchical and authoritarian religious organizations to the more democratic ones, and went out of his way to help the Catholic Church establish a parish. Large numbers of Irish laborers had come to Lowell in the early years to construct the buildings, canals, and roads. But

---

*During Edson's exile the rectory was occupied by the agent of the Merrimack Company. It was during this period that the parish installed a chime of bells in the church and refused an offer of two thousand dollars from the distraught Merrimack agent to silence the bells.

since the corporations had made no provisions for them in contrast to the provisions made for the factory workers, the Irish laborers were crowded together in a squalid settlement known variously as "Paddy's Camp Lands," "New Dublin," and "The Acre." Acts of vandalism were attributed to the Irish and there were frequent fights between the Irish and the Protestants. Boott hoped that the discipline and authority of the Church would help resolve the problems, and he invited Bishop Benedict Fenwick to dine, offered him the old Merrimack Company schoolhouse building as a temporary chapel, and soon gave him a lot on which to build a church.

As the city grew, the remaining water power sites were filled with the construction of the Boott and Massachusetts Cotton Mills. Since Kirk Boott's house stood on the proposed site of the Boott Mills, it was moved about a mile to the head of Merrimack Street on the heights overlooking the Merrimack River. In 1839, after Boott's death, the textile companies bought his mansion for a corporation hospital for sick operatives. The Lowell Corporation Hospital became St. Joseph's Hospital which has continued to grow and remains on the same spot to this day.

Twenty years after its founding, Lowell had begun to change, and the changes affected more than management and labor relationships. Some areas were already congested and slums were spreading within the city. Company managements began to be challenged on the one hand by dissident stockholders complaining of mismanagement and lower dividends, and on the other by less submissive workers, who had begun to rise against constantly increasing pressures to increase production combined with lower wage scales. Even the rooms in the corporation boarding houses became more crowded in the 1840s than they had been in the 1820s and 1830s. It was small compensation that the women spent less time in these rooms because they worked longer hours in the factories. By 1841, the workday was fifteen minutes longer than it had been in 1829. Lowell, which had been a model of working conditions for other parts of the world, now suffered in comparison.

As the town's planner, architect, and chief engineer, Kirk Boott had been primarily concerned wih the proper planning of mill sites and housing for the workers and supervisors; in this work, he was most painstaking. In planning for the rest of the city, Boott was almost neglectful. In the plans for the city, the area along the river and the power canals was given over to industry.

Behind the factories, neat, clean, attractive housing for the workers was laid out. Beyond this, Merrimack Street formed the commercial area with shops for such necessities and luxuries as clothing, shoes, dry goods, groceries, hardware, linen, china, drugs, and books. Beyond that, however, there was not such careful planning, and the area just grew. Boott's lack of interest in commercial development can be attributed to the fact that, unlike firms in most mill towns, Lowell's corporations did not have company stores; instead, they paid their employees in cash and thus attracted scores of independent merchants and shopkeepers.

In other parts of town inadequate planning for the tremendous growth of the young city led to improper utilization of land, with houses crowded together in some sections and large vacant areas in others. It was not until 1845 that the Locks & Canals Company auctioned off many parcels of land. Unfortunately this came too late to alter the congested pattern of the city. The glamorous view of Lowell presented by owners and visitors of the early years was fading into a dim past, and a grimmer reality was taking its place. In 1837, Mayor Dr. Elisha Bartlett reminded his fellow townspeople:

> The graves of our fathers are not here. The haunts of our childhood are not here. . . . . The large and gradually accumulated fortunes of nearly all our older towns are not to be found here. The great mass of wealth which is centered here, and which has made our city what it is, is owned abroad. Its proprietors do not reside among us. Its profits are not expended among us.

Lacking a heritage of wealth or tradition and depending on the success of the mills for its very existence, Lowell could not admit to failures, setbacks, or faults. In many respects the successes were real and worthy of acclaim. Economically the mills were a success. Any city would have been proud of Francis Cabot Lowell, who first realized the possibilities of the modern corporation for large-scale manufacture. Any city would have been equally proud of Nathan Appleton, who had modernized the concept of the corporation, utilizing finance capital in banks and insurance companies, and selling stock to the public while management retained the control. The early Lowell entrepreneurs were truly men of ingenuity and ability. They deserved much credit; they were not reluctant to take it. In a letter dated December 30, 1846, to the Middlesex Mechanics Association, Nathan Appleton wrote:

> I certainly look back with satisfaction upon the part which I

have had in leading to this result [the successful establishment of Lowell]. I do not say this with any reference to pecuniary interest. I could not say it, did I not conscientiously believe that the introduction of the cotton manufacture has added greatly to the mass of human happiness in those immediately concerned in it, as well as to the aggregate wealth and prosperity of the whole country. I could not say it, did I perceive in the system any tendency toward a relaxation of the moral purity which has ever been a characteristic of our beloved New England. My mind was early turned to a consideration of this question. I could never perceive any just ground for the opinion which formerly prevailed extensively, that occupation in manufactories was less favorable to morals than other manual labor. This opinion has, I believe, universally given way before the light of our experience. It is the elevation of all labor above the right to a mere subsistence, which gives it character and standing in society, and constitutes the elementary difference between American and European labor. That this elevated position may be strengthened and perpetuated by our institutions, is my ardent wish.*

In the early period of Lowell many citizens, made optimistic by the city's successes, viewed any deficiencies or faults as minor shortcomings that would be remedied with time. Certainly this was a realistic interpretation of the overall picture, although some people got carried away by the heady success. When Lowell's population neared the 18,000 mark in 1836, it was predicted with far greater enthusiasm than accuracy that in ten more years Lowell would have a population of 32,000 and in twenty years of 256,000. The early prediction was close to the mark as the population reached 32,000 in 1845, but the wilder forecast of 256,000 was never realized; Lowell's population peaked at 112,759 in 1920. An optimistic frame of mind prevailed throughout the golden age of Lowell. It is true that dissident stockholders found fault with high salaries paid to company officials, with nepotism, and with extravagant purchases of raw materials to help close associates. In exasperation James C. Ayer referred to those in control of the companies as exhibiting "pompous imbecility" while glutting themselves "with fabulous remuneration."

Conditions in the nineteenth century industrial cities were unhealthy, although Lowell may have been better than most. People died, most while still fairly young—as people had done down through the centuries—of the epidemic diseases which were often the product of ignorance or of indifference to the relationship between sewerage, bad drinking water, and disease.

*Ironically, at the time this letter was written, wages were being reduced and the work day lengthened.

Even if there was a warning against it, people would drink water from the canals. So the city bill of mortality would list deaths from cholera, typhoid, and typhus. The mills then put in a vaccination program, yet mortality figures remained high. Hygiene made its slow progress. Though vaccination was available, smallpox killed forty-one people in 1849. Tuberculosis, infant deaths, and childhood diseases dogged the factory population well into the twentieth century.

The mill city had critics even in its golden age. As early as July 13, 1839, a famous controversy, the Battle of the Books, began. On that day, after an uninterrupted series of favorable and flattering reports from visitors, politicians, and millowners, there appeared in the Boston *Daily Times* the first published article critical of the establishment. There were two objects of the attack: on the one hand, the unhealthy and inhuman conditions to which the mill girls were subjected; on the other, the decline in morals among this sad manufacturing population. The same charges were made by Orestes Brownson, the unpredictable and passionate religious philosopher in a scholarly article about the "Laboring Classes" in the July, 1840, issue of his *Boston Quarterly Review*.

The criticism called forth a spirited defense by the local establishment, including the mill girls' voice—the *Lowell Offering* in which Harriet Farley wrote a strong attack on Brownson. The *Lowell Courier* published a series of articles by former mayor Dr. Elisha Bartlett, which later appeared as a pamphlet entitled *A Vindication of the Character and Condition of the Females Employed in the Lowell Mills against the Charges Contained in the Boston* Times *and* Boston Quarterly Review. Bartlett made exaggerated claims that work in the factories was actually beneficial to the operatives' health. This claim, based upon dubiously interpreted statistics, was easily rebutted in a reply entitled *Corporations and Operatives: Being an exposition of the conditions of factory operatives and a review of the "Vindication" by Elisha Bartlett, M.D.*, written by "A Citizen of Lowell." The "Citizen" attacked especially the long hours of labor in the mills (made longer by alleged tampering with the clocks) and likened the slaves of the loom to those of the cotton fields.

Although the system continued to have many defenders— notably the *Offering*—still the unthinkable had occurred: the Lowell System had been publicly and skillfully attacked. A few years later, a labor newspaper, the *Voice of Industry*, began publication in Lowell under the editorship of a former mill girl, Sarah G. Bagley. The weekly complaints against injustices mounted and eventually merged into the controversy over the ten-hour day and deteriorating labor relations. But even these troubles became insignificant with the onset of the Civil War which triggered the long, slow decline of the textile industry.

75 Young Women

From 15 to 35 Years of Age,

WANTED TO WORK IN THE

COTTON MILLS!

IN LOWELL AND CHICOPEE, MASS.

I am authorized by the Agents of said Mills to make the following proposition to persons suitable for their work, viz:—They will be paid $1.00 per week, and board, for the first month. It is presumed they will then be able to go to work at job prices. They will be considered as engaged for one year, cases of sickness excepted. I will pay the expenses of those who have not the means to pay for themselves, and the girls will pay it to the Company by their first labor. All that remain in the employ of the Company eighteen months will have the amount of their expenses to the Mills refunded to them. They will be properly cared for in sickness. It is hoped that none will go except those whose circumstances will admit of their staying at least one year. None but active and healthy girls will be engaged for this work, as it would not be advisable for either the girls or the Company.

I shall be at the Howard Hotel, Burlington, on Monday, July 25th; at Farnham's, St Albans, Tuesday forenoon, 26th, at Keyse's, Swanton, in the afternoon; at the Massachusetts' House, Rouses Point, on Wednesday, the 27th, to engage girls,---such as would like a place in the Mills would do well to improve the present opportunity, as new hands will not be wanted late in the season. I shall start with my Company, for the Mills, on Friday morning, the 29th inst., from Rouses Point, at 6 o'clock. Such as do not have an opportunity to see me at the above places, can take the cars and go with me the same as though I had engaged them.

I will be responsible for the safety of all baggage that is marked in care of I. M. BOYNTON, and delivered to my charge.

I. M. BOYNTON,

Agent for Procuring Help for the Mills.

(1870)

Recruiting poster, circa 1870. Courtesy of Baker Library, Harvard Business School.

VIII

Daughters of Freemen: The Female Operatives and the Beginning of the Labor Movement

By Nancy Zaroulis

On October 8, 1823, Deborah Skinner stood at her loom. She checked to see that the warp yarn was properly sized, brushed, and dried with the ends drawn in through the harness and reed. Then, as waterpower from the Merrimack Canal turned the great wheel in the basement, she began to weave the first piece of cotton sheeting produced by the new Merrimack Manufacturing Company at Lowell.

Skinner formerly had been employed at the Boston Manufacturing Company at Waltham. Paul Moody brought her to Lowell in his private carriage—a privilege granted because of her importance to the managers of the new factory. Because she was a skilled weaver, she had been chosen to teach a group of newly hired female operatives how to work the looms. She alone was on the payroll from October 8 to 19; almost certainly she was not alone in the mill, but the new girls whom she instructed were not given any salary until they had learned the process of weaving.

These first female employees at Lowell—not more than one hundred and fifty—were soon joined by thousands more. The corporations hired women rather than men because labor—

manpower—was scarce in New England at that time. But if there were not many men available for hire, there were many "solitary" women, never married, or deserted by their husbands, or widowed, whose presence was tolerated in the home of some relative in return for endless and unpaid domestic service. Harriet Hanson Robinson, who worked in the mills in the 1830s and 1840s, recorded the change in women's status brought about by the opportunity to earn wages, however small, in the textile mills. There, she said, a woman could become a "money earning" rather than a "money saving" member of the community. With all professions closed to her except miserably paid teaching (when she could find a job), domestic service in a stranger's home, or sewing, the factories in Lowell offered a woman a chance to live independent of some relative's grudging charity.

The English writer Harriet Martineau, in what now seems an overly optimistic assessment of the benefits of the American factory system which she fleetingly observed in the 1830s, said of these women:

> The institution of factory labor has brought ease of heart to many; and to many occasion for noble and generous deeds. The ease of heart is given to those who were before suffering in silent poverty, from the deficiency of profitable employment for women, which is even greater in America than with us. It used to be understood that all women were maintained by the men of their families; but the young men of New England are apt to troop off into the West . . . .

From the manufacturers' point of view, women were the preferred workers not only because there were so many of them so poorly employed, but also because hiring women would help to keep down the cost of production. In a letter to a prospective investor, Nathan Appleton, discussing the prospects of cotton manufacture in the United States, stated, "the material is cheaper and the wages of labour, considering the larger proportion of female labour, scarcely if anything higher."

In the 1824 wage table for the Merrimack Company, women's pay ranged from $2.25 to $4.00 per week. Men were paid from $4.50 to $12.00 per week. Thus, the lowest-paid man earned more than the highest-paid woman.*

Still, factory work paid better than any of the other possible occupations for women, and so, at least for the first two decades of manufacturing at Lowell, enough women went "on the Corpo-

---

*The women's net pay was from $1.00 to $2.75 per week after the compulsory deduction for board. In the late 1840s, men paid $1.75 per week for board; the price for women rose to $1.37½.

ration" to provide the factories with a seemingly endless supply of operatives.

But they would not have come—or at least not in such numbers—had the corporations not provided for their living conditions, health, and moral welfare during their employment. The Boston Associates did not want Lowell to become another Manchester, England—that symbol of all the horrors of the Industrial Revolution. Therefore, even though the women were to be occupied in the mills from twelve to fourteen hours a day, the remainder of their time also had to be supervised.

The corporation boarding houses thus became an important part of the Lowell Experiment. They had been successful on a small scale at Waltham, where they housed the operatives of the Boston Manufacturing Company. Now, at Lowell, they went up by the hundreds, each with its matron responsible for the behavior of the women in her charge. She was responsible, too, for providing good meals and clean rooms. Very often she was a widow with small children to support, and, at least in the early days, she was able to survive and to fulfill her duties adequately with the money given to her for each operative's board. The position of boarding-house keeper may have been awarded often to friends or impoverished relatives of the corporation managers. These women, responsible for the conduct of their boarders, were themselves expected to be above reproach; corporate connections or no, they were as subject to dismissal for "bad conduct" as were the operatives. Harriet Robinson's mother was dismissed from her post as keeper of a Tremont Company boarding house when Harriet, age eleven, led the spinners out of the mill in the unsuccessful turnout of 1836.

The boarding houses, at first semi-detached and made of wood, later built in brick rows, stood close to the mills. The first floor contained a room for the landlady, a dining room (converted to a parlor after supper), a kitchen, and washing and storage rooms in the rear. Each of the upper floors usually contained four bedrooms; as many as four, six, and sometimes eight women slept in a room. From twenty to forty operatives and occasionally more lived in a house, depending on its size.

The boarding-house keepers tried to feed their charges as well as they could. Competition was close; the operatives were free to live at any corporation house which had a vacancy, and a landlady without tenants was a landlady out of a job. As reported by an operative in 1850 (to prove that she was indeed better off than

a Southern slave), a typical day's menu would include: for break-
fast, biscuit or toast and pie, bread and butter, coffee and tea; for
dinner, meat and potatoes, vegetables, tomatoes, pickles, pud-
ding or pie, bread and butter, coffee and tea; for supper, bread or
biscuit with "sauce," cake, pie, and tea.

When times became hard, however, and the price of food rose,
the boarding-house keepers presented a pathetic picture of
hard-pressed businesswomen struggling to maintain their standards. Many went bankrupt. Lucy Larcom, who became a fairly
well known writer, was compelled to go to work on the Lawrence
Corporation at the age of eleven because her mother could not
adequately feed her boarders with the money alloted to her. The
child's dollar-a-week salary and the dollar and a quarter allowed
for her board saved Mrs. Larcom from financial disaster.

Other problems plagued both landladies and tenants. "Filthy
vermin" often inhabited the bedrooms. Privacy—let alone peace
and quiet—was impossible. The air was almost as bad as that in
the mills, and it became worse as the area was increasingly built
up. Eventually, after the Civil War, the corporations sold their
boarding houses to private owners, and conditions degenerated
even more.

The corporations published extensive regulations to ensure
that their operatives behaved themselves. These rules of conduct
demanded compulsory church attendance, boarding in a company house, working for a full year after employment, giving two
weeks' notice upon leaving, and prohibited stealing anything
belonging to the corporations.

Boarding-house keepers had to obey rules, too. They were not
allowed to board persons not employed by the corporation which
owned their house, nor persons guilty of "disorderly or improper
conduct;" they had to enforce a 10 P.M. curfew; they were required to give information about their boarders' conduct and
church attendance; they had to keep their houses "in good order;" they were not allowed to keep swine.

Additionally, there were many unwritten rules. The Reverend
Henry A. Miles, in 1845, recognized that mill productivity depended on an "industrious, sober, orderly and moral class of
operatives." He commented favorably on the "moral police"
system, whereby the operative even suspected of "immoralities"
or "improprieties" was shunned and silenced by the others. If
the matron did not dismiss the offender, her fellow boarders
would leave the boarding house. Miles attributed the adoption of

REGULATIONS

FOR THE

BOARDING HOUSES

OF THE

MIDDLESEX COMPANY.

THE tenants of the Boarding Houses are not to board, or permit any part of their houses to be occupied by any person except those in the employ of the Company.

They will be considered answerable for any improper conduct in their houses, and are not to permit their boarders to have company at unseasonable hours.

The doors must be closed at ten o'clock in the evening, and no one admitted after that time without some reasonable excuse.

The keepers of the Boarding Houses must give an account of the number, names, and employment of their boarders, when required; and report the names of such as are guilty of any improper conduct, or are not in the regular habit of attending public worship.

The buildings and yards about them must be kept clean and in good order, and if they are injured otherwise than from ordinary use, all necessary repairs will be made, and charged to the occupant.

It is indispensable that all persons in the employ of the Middlesex Company should be vaccinated who have not been, as also the families with whom they board; which will be done at the expense of the Company.

SAMUEL LAWRENCE, Agent.

JOEL TAYLOR, PRINTER, Daily Courier Office.

Regulations for the boarding houses of the Middlesex Company, 1846. (Lowell Historical Society) this system to "the sagacity of self-interest" of those who had invested large amounts of capital in Lowell. Yet the female operatives who informed on each other had invested no money in the corporations.

It is here that we can see the internalization by women of the laws of conduct promulgated by men—entirely to the profit of men. Just as the writers of the *Lowell Offering*, the mill girls' magazine, became the unwitting tools of their employers (some would have said of their oppressors), so the females of Lowell, in strictly policing themselves, did the corporations' work. By jealously guarding their good names, they made it possible for the corporations to recruit and hire more decent, thrifty, hardworking, Yankee farm girls like themselves. The female operatives, ill-paid and overworked as they were, did not want to lose even this slim chance at independence. They did not want factory work to become a degraded occupation as it was in England and thereby become unsuitable work for decent Yankee women. The corporations used the women's need to earn money to ensure a continuing supply of new workers for the mills.

"*She has worked in a factory,* is sufficient to damn to infamy the most worthy and virtuous girl," wrote Orestes Brownson, a social critic, in 1840.

"I affirm that it is *not*," replied Harriet Farley in the *Offering*. "The state of morals and intelligence is not low."

In other words, the operatives accepted without question the paternal, corporate dictate (which, it should be noted, pervaded the entire society) that Woman—no matter what her station— must remain a Lady. Harriot F. Curtis, writing in the *Offering*, said that a woman who spoke up for equal pay (hardly a demonstration of immorality, although perhaps of impropriety) was accused of "indelicacy," "boldness," "presumption," and of having "unsexed herself."

This universally held belief in the proper conduct for women was to have tragic consequences for the operatives in later years, when their determined gentility led them to quit the mills, rather than organize effectively to oppose the increasingly harsh working conditions and declining pay.

Meanwhile, as the factories were being built and the boarding houses filled with tenants, the women who flocked to Lowell from the farms and mountain villages had their jobs to learn. Weaving, which Deborah Skinner had demonstrated, was only one of the positions available. Weavers were the most highly skilled and highly paid female operatives. An inexperienced woman might start out in the carding room, working at the drawing frame. Here the cotton, having been picked clean, passed through the lapper, carded onto wooden cylinders, and "finished" (all rough, and therefore men's work), was twisted into a coarse roving in which all the fibers were laid in one direction and stretched out into a thick strand. An operative in the spinning room spun the roving into warp and filling for the looms. Then the warp yarn (or thread) was taken to the dressing room, where a warper wound it onto a section beam. A dresser sized, brushed, and dried the yarn; then a drawer-in transferred the prepared yarn from eight section beams to one loom beam and drew in the ends through the harness and reed (the only hand process in the entire manufacture). The weavers then made the cloth. In 1845 each cotton mill had two weaving rooms employing about one hundred and forty weavers in each room. The completed fabric was taken to the cloth room, where operatives trimmed, measured, folded, and recorded it. The cloth was then either baled and sent to the selling agent, or delivered to the print works.

Both the Merrimack and the Hamilton mills had calico printing establishments. The first step in the process was the singeing of the fabric on hot copper cylinders to remove the nap. The male operatives bleached the cloth by an extremely complicated process (without a good white, no true or brilliant color could be obtained). Then a copper roller imprinted a pattern of paste containing the mordant on the fabric; when fabric so treated was immersed in large vats containing one or another dye-wood, it emerged the desired color. After another series of hot soap and chemical baths, the cloth was finished and dried.

The mill buildings were, in the beginning, attractive and impressive examples of utilitarian architecture. They did not at first cut off the view of the river entirely. Double-pitched slate roofs crowned the five-story red-brick buildings; a white cupola topped the central one. The mills were grouped much like college dormitories around a quadrangle of trees and flowers. Ample windows gave good light (but not air, since they were nailed shut to maintain humidity). Smaller, fireproof outbuildings were used to store the raw cotton from the South and to house the initial picking operation. The counting room and agent's office were next to the entrance gate, which was always locked except to allow the operatives to pass in and out.

Merrimack mills and boarding houses. Engraving by O. Pelton. (Lowell Historical Society)

Boarding houses of Lawrence Manufacturing Company. (Lowell Historical Society)

The corporation agents were the resident managers of the mills; they took overall direction from the hierarchy in Boston, but it was they who were responsible for the day-to-day operations of the factories. They were the only members of the corporation management who lived in Lowell; as such, they were at the top of the city's rigid caste system. Below them were the first and second overseers and skilled (male) workers. Then came the operatives, mostly female; then the domestics and day laborers, the Irish. Somewhat apart, both physically and psychologically, were the townspeople—lawyers, doctors, ministers, shopkeepers.

After spending twelve to fourteen hours a day in the mills, an operative might have been expected to collapse in her crowded dormitory until the rising bell awakened her at or before dawn the next day. In the early years, however, many of the women were determined to make the most of their stay in the new city. For a fee of twenty-five cents a month an operative could borrow books from the circulating library; for fifty or seventy-five cents she could subscribe to a series of lectures given at the Lowell Lyceum. Here she could hear learned gentlemen, many of them professors at Harvard or other universities, discourse on such topics as history, biography, astronomy, literature, or phrenology. Professor A. P. Peabody of Harvard recalled that he had never seen such attentive note-taking as in the audience of young women whom he addressed at Lowell. Lucy Larcom studied German; other operatives got up classes in everything from English grammar to botany. Church attendance was obligatory in the early years, when the mill owners were attempting to establish the moral purity of the participants in their Experiment; in the 1840s, however, some of the women could not afford pew rent, much less the required "Sunday best" costume, and so that regulation, at least, was quietly overlooked. Many of the women taught Sunday school.

It was, in fact, through the churches that some of the operatives were at last able to find an outlet for their hard-won self-education. Harriet Robinson speaks with some bitterness about the numbers of men whose college educations were paid for by the wages of their women-folk in the mills; women, of course, could not have been admitted to any college even if they had kept their savings for themselves.* But in 1839 the Reverend Abel Thomas

*In 1837, fourteen years after the opening of the Lowell cotton factories, Mary Lyon established the Mount Holyoke (Massachusetts) Female Seminary. In the late 1830s, three women were admitted to Oberlin College in Ohio, but they were not accorded the same rights and privileges as the male students.

of the Second Universalist Church organized an "Improvement Circle" (one of several in the city) for his parishioners, both male and female. He encouraged them to speak on various topics, but the women declined: the prevailing mores, to which they strictly adhered, prohibited females from speaking in public. The Reverend Thomas therefore designated a collection box where his "pupils" could deposit anonymously written articles, stories, poems, etc. When he saw the excellent quality of some of these attempts, he proposed that they be published.

And so the *Lowell Offering* was born. Ironically, it made the mill girls famous, but it might never have appeared had the women not been brought up to believe that to speak in public was a thing that a decent woman did not do.

The first issue, appearing in October, 1840, contained twenty-four pages consisting of one story, fourteen essays, three poems, an editorial, and two letters. At first glance it was perhaps not very different from the numerous literary publications of the time, many of which were directed to a female audience; but when the public realized that it had been written entirely by female factory operatives it became a sensation. Even in America—supposedly the home of the un-oppressed worker—people were surprised at its existence and the quality of its contents. Foreign visitors to Lowell found it miraculous—proof of the virtues of the American factory system.

The *Lowell Offering* appeared more or less regularly through 1845. But it failed to find a permanent audience — probably, at least in part, because its female editors refused to do battle with the corporations over the increasingly deleterious working conditions in the mills. By 1845 the battle for the ten-hour day had begun in earnest. Articles such as "The Pleasures of Factory Life" must have seemed increasingly irrelevant to the hard-pressed operatives. Harriet Farley, one of the editors of the *Offering*, attempted to revive it as the *New England Offering* in 1848–49, but that effort, too, failed. At no time was either publication directly subsidized by the corporations, although at one point an agent did buy up one thousand back issues—an indirect subsidy. The mill managers endorsed the *Lowell Offering*, however, and saw that it was widely distributed: what better advertisement to attract new workers to the proliferating mills?

Some of the *Offering*'s contributors had success as professional (as opposed to avocational) writers, most notably Lucy Larcom. Others, like Harriet H. Robinson, worked for women's suffrage. Lydia S. Hall became a missionary to the Choctaw Indians; later she ran a temperance "Wayside Inn" in Kansas, where she owned considerable real estate. At one time, after the Civil War, she served as acting Treasurer of the United States.

Not all the lives of the *Offering*'s writers ended happily, however. Harriott Curtis provides an especially touching example of the way in which women were expected to devote their lives to others—their proper "sphere." After a promising career both as a writer and editor (Robinson credits her with the idea for the *Offering*), she was obliged to give up her life in Lowell and return home to care for invalid relatives. This she continued to do, "despondent and despairing," until her death in 1889. "I have grown rusty," she wrote to Robinson from Vermont in 1860. "I could not earn a dollar *here* to save my life."

Some of the nonliterary operatives had interesting lives after they left Lowell. Clementine Averill, who in 1850 defended Northern mill operatives against charges that they were no better off than Southern slaves, herself went south to Florida to found a cooperative industrial home for unemployed workers. Margaret Foley achieved some success as a cameo cutter in Boston after she left the Merrimack Company; later she went to Italy where she became a sculptor. She exhibited some of her work in the Centennial Exposition at Philadelphia.

Fewer than a dozen success stories out of the lives of many thousands is hardly exceptional. More typically, many women achieved the more modest goals of a small amount of money earned, a glimpse of city life, an acquaintance with a more varied population than that offered in a country village, and, perhaps most important, the achievement, however temporary, of an independent life.

Work in the mills drove some operatives, however, "on through pain, disease and privation, down to a premature grave." In a time when life expectancy was much shorter than it is now, and when most diseases were incurable by the primitive medical knowledge of the day, working in the mills for a year or more could seriously weaken an individual's health. Critics of the factory system cited two major dangers to the operatives: the long hours and the badly ventilated, overheated, lint-filled rooms. These conditions not only fostered lung diseases, but also weakened formerly healthy constitutions so that the operatives were more likely to contract diseases such as typhus and cholera. Dr. Josiah

Mill girls with shuttles. Courtesy of Merrimack Valley Textile Museum.

Curtis, investigating the effect of factory labor upon the operatives in 1849, was especially critical of the foul air which they
were forced to breathe. In a typical room containing fifty-five
operatives, he estimated that each person needed 10 cubic feet of
air per minute for healthy breathing: 450,000 cubic feet per day.
In fact, the room with windows nailed shut, fifty solar (or whale
oil) lamps burning, lint flying, contained only about 65,000 cubic
feet of air. Moreover, the buildings, which should have been
aired hourly, were never ventilated from month to month. After
twelve to fourteen hours per day in this polluted atmosphere the
operatives hurried to their boarding house dormitories where, as
they slept six, eight, and more to a room, their lungs found little
relief.

John Allen, who for a time edited the *Voice of Industry* (a
Lowell-based labor newspaper), charged in an open letter to
Abbott Lawrence that the factory system in Lowell was worse
than that in England. Allen stated that the operatives here
worked two or three hours more a day; he condemned the evil of
forcing the operatives to stand so long at the machinery that
"varicose veins, dropsical swelling of the feet and limbs, and
prolapsus uter, diseases that end only with life, are not rare but
common occurrences." These and other criticisms of the Lowell
mills are startlingly similar to those made of the mills in Manchester, England, by Frederick Engels in *The Condition of the
Working Class in England* (1845).

The Kirk Boott house had been bought by the corporations in
1839 for use as a hospital. Male patients paid four dollars a week,
female, three. If they were unable to pay, the fee was charged to
their future earnings. But apparently many workers were reluctant to use its facilities. Dr. Curtis reported that boarding-house
keepers were threatened with discharge by the corporations if
they did not persuade sick operatives to go to the hospital. The
editors of the *Offering* proposed a "Plan for Mutual Relief,"
whereby every worker would contribute 10 or 12½ cents monthly to a fund which would provide three dollars a week to females,
four to males, who were certified as genuinely too ill to work. But
this early version of paid sick-leave (paid entirely by the workers,
with no contribution from the corporations save bookkeeping)
was never adopted, and so, then as now, a protracted illness
meant financial disaster. Many operatives went home to die: it
was cheaper.

It was universally agreed that the long hours of labor required of the operatives were detrimental to their health. Even the corporations admitted it, but excused themselves on the grounds that the operatives frequently returned to their country homes for (unpaid) vacations. In the early days, in the 1820s and early 1830s, a seventy-two-hour week tending one or two machines was undoubtedly tiring as well as boring, but it was not unbearable. In the late 1830s and early 1840s, however, came the speedup and the premium system. Weavers were required to tend three or four looms each; spinners, carders, and other workers were pressed accordingly. The long day which had been tolerable in the early years rapidly became intolerable. In addition, overseers, who received a bonus for extra cloth produced, drove their employees increasingly hard. Agitation began in earnest for the ten-hour day.

Before the 1840s the few impromptu "turnouts" in the Lowell mills had occurred because wages were cut. In 1834 the corporations lowered wages by twelve to twenty-five per cent. Nearly eight hundred women turned out in protest, but the corporations held fast and most operatives returned to their jobs in a few days. Those who refused to work at the lower wages went back to their homes in the country. In 1836 the corporations increased the amount withheld from the operatives' pay for room and board by 12½ cents (for a total of $1.37½ per week) to save many boarding-house keepers from financial ruin; for the same reason they also reduced the rent paid by the landladies for their houses by the same amount (12½ cents per week). For several days from twelve to fifteen hundred women stayed off the job; they formed a short-lived Factory Girls' Association of more than two thousand members. But again they lost. They had no income during the turnout, and at that time the corporations could easily find new hands to take their places. The Factory Girls' Association failed. Most of the women returned to work at the new wage. In 1842 there was a brief turnout after the announcement of a reduction of piece rates at the Middlesex Mills. Again the protesters were swiftly replaced by new workers.

By the 1840s, with conditions worsening, the operatives focused their demands on shortening the long working day to ten hours. Petitions were got up and surreptitiously passed around (an operative caught circulating one was instantly dismissed and blacklisted). The workers began to organize. Mechanics' and Laborers' Associations sprang up in most of the factory towns. In October, 1844, they came together in Boston as the New England

Workingmen's Convention (or Association). In December, 1844, Sarah G. Bagley, with half a dozen other women, formed the Lowell Female Labor Reform Association (LFLRA). This group, through its ownership of the *Voice of Industry*, was to have a great, although ultimately unsuccessful, impact on the labor struggles of the mid-1840s.

In fact, had there been no Sarah Bagley, there may well never have been a women's association at all. She seems to have been an extraordinary person, although we know very little about her. Naturally, since she was poor and a member of what had already become the "working class," she never had a portrait or daguerreotype made. She was described as a "common-schooled New England factory operative." In 1836 she came to Lowell to work in the mills. In the *Lowell Offering* of June, 1841, she contributed a "Tale of Factory Life" describing the course by which the heroine, "Sarah T.," became a factory girl. The impoverished and widowed mother, the cruel necessity of sending the daughter to work as a servant, the privations and humiliations of that life, the escape—barefoot—to Lowell were all familiar incidents of both life and fiction in the nineteenth century; it is probable that the story was largely autobiographical. Bagley also wrote an article on "The Pleasures of Factory Life" in the *Lowell Offering* for December, 1840. She enumerated these "pleasures:" the opportunity for contemplation while tending the machinery; the enjoyment of cultivating flowers and plants in the workrooms; the chance to earn money; wide acquaintanceship; the moral guardianship of the corporations; opportunities for education through public lecures; and, finally, the abundant religious instruction available at Lowell's many churches. In view of Bagley's violent denunciations of the factories just four years later, it is tempting to read this article as satire. The editors of the *Offering* refused to print her later vehement criticism of the Lowell Experiment.

For a few years in the middle of the decade Sarah Bagley devoted herself to the cause of labor reform. She organized, travelled, testified, wrote the *Factory Tracts*, wrote for and briefly edited the *Voice of Industry*, and made many powerful and effective speeches at labor conventions. During this time she struggled to make a living. Having left the mills, she worked in 1845 at dressmaking and straw weaving. In 1846 the magnetic telegraph was completed from Lowell to Boston. Bagley became the first woman telegrapher in the United States. Later she travelled as a correspondent for the *Voice* through northern New England. It is not known where or when she died.

In February, 1845, the legislature, having been presented with ten-hour petitions from the workers for three successive years, finally agreed to have a committee investigate the hours of labor in the state's corporations. William Schouler, the representative from Lowell, publisher of the *Lowell Courier*, and former publisher (1840–42) of the *Lowell Offering*, was unexpectedly elevated to chairman.

The committee sent notice to Bagley that she must appear to testify; despite the prevailing sentiment against females who spoke in public, she and several other operatives, men and women, traveled to Boston to appear before the legislators. Bagley gave her evidence; she also insisted, over the vehement objections of Schouler, upon interrogating a fellow witness, a male operative, who said, in response to her questions, that he had been cautioned by his superintendent to say as little as possible.

The committee was unable to reach a conclusion, and so it travelled to Lowell to inspect the mills at first hand. It found nothing amiss; the corporations even had grass and trees around the factory buildings. Everything seemed in good order.

The members recommended against the legislation. Although the corporations had been created by the legislature, the committee hesitated to regulate them. Further, it did not want to abridge labor's "freedom of contract." Nor did it want to penalize corporate manufacturers by enacting a ten-hour day which applied only to corporation employees and not to employees of unincorporated manufacturers. Relying on the legislature's constitutional right to regulate corporations, the proponents of the legislation had limited their request to corporate employees.

"Labor must look out for its own interests," reported Schouler for the committee. "The remedy is not with us."

The operatives, outraged but not discouraged by this setback, concentrated on further organizing, on communicating with operatives' associations in other New England towns, and on publicizing their grievances. An effective strike seemed beyond their capabilities. In fact, the most important point about Lowell's pre-Civil War labor organizations is that they never achieved a major or an effective strike to win their demands. The

LFLRA in its constitution specifically declared that the operatives were opposed to strikes, turnouts or other "hostile measures."

No one lacked for words. The columns of the *Voice of Industry* were filled with speeches, articles, and letters stating in sometimes violent terms the operatives' demands. In addition Sarah Bagley wrote a series of *Factory Tracts*, brief, inflammatory pamphlets intended to further the propaganda war against the "drivelling cotton lords," the "so-called Christians" who supported missions to the heathen but "care nothing for the bodies and intellects" of their employees.

After a promising beginning—with the convention of the New England Workingmen's Association (NEWA) at Boston in October, 1844, and again at Lowell in March, 1845—the labor organizations foundered and ultimately died. They could not agree on what they should call themselves; they could not agree on their objectives. The NEWA became the Labor Reform League of New England (1846); the LFLRA became the Lowell Female Industrial Reform and Mutual Aid Society (1847). In an effort to attract new members, the women's group refined its initial, somewhat vague, objectives and offered "something more definite:" a mutual aid society and a sick-fund to be administered by the Sisters of Charity. Meetings continued, although attendance declined so sharply that they became a "matter of ridicule and contempt on the part of their oppressors." The last convention was held in Lowell in March, 1848; nothing was done except to appoint delegates to the Industrial Congress in Philadelphia.

Several factors worked against successful labor organizing at this time. The corporations held powerful weapons: workers who protested bad conditions (or anything else) were not only fired but blacklisted from employment at textile factories in other New England towns. Since the "old man" (the overseer) was quick to dismiss with a bad conduct slip any malcontent who spoke up, it is easy to understand why Bagley and other organizers found it difficult to recruit members. The corporations were also in firm control of the legislature and of most of the press.

In addition, not all the operatives wanted shorter hours (the major demand of the petitions to the legislature), because shorter hours meant less pay. To women who could scarcely survive on the two or three dollars which they received for a seventy-two to seventy-eight-hour week, long hours were preferable to a wage cut. (These women, of course, did not plan to stay long at Lowell;

in 1845 the average length of time for an operative at the mills was four and a half years. By 1850, after repeated speed-ups, the influx of Irish mill workers, and the failure of the Ten-Hour movement, it was nine months).

Also the nascent labor organizations allowed themselves to be seized upon by proselytizers for the several Utopian philosophies springing up at the time, partly in reaction to the Industrial Revolution and its effect on American society. As a result, meetings called ostensibly to consider the workers' plight ended in calls for land reform, cooperative societies, Associationism (a kind of planned, quasi-industrial community), and other social experiments. Anti-slavery and temperance resolutions were passed. These may have been worthy causes, but they were not particularly relevant to the ten-hour day and the blacklist. The first issue of the *Voice of Industry*, in May, 1845, contained on page one a serialized Utopian fiction: "Meadow Farm; or a tale of Association." In 1847, at a meeting of the Labor Reform League of New England, a resolution was passed declaring that "American slavery must be uprooted before the elevation sought by the laboring classes can be effected." The Utopians did not want to reform society; they wanted to abandon it and start over. They attempted to gain a popular base for their proposals by joining and assuming control of the new labor organizations. When this tactic failed, they withdrew, leaving the workers to reassemble and attempt to carry on their struggle alone.

Perhaps most important of all, women—the majority of the operatives—were not psychologically ready for the disobedience to paternal authority implied in joining a labor organization, much less for the overt rebellion of an organized strike. Although Bagley thundered against the corporation "drones" (the capitalists), she must have understood that a strike was out of the question until women found a greater strength in sisterhood than they had been able to achieve until that time. The constitution of the LFLRA eschewed direct action. No female operative, even an angry one, wanted to be called "disorderly." Sarah Bagley, the most determined and radical of women, felt compelled to reassure the men of the NEWA that the women who had organized "claim no exalted place in your deliberations." She and other "daughters of freemen" asked only to "be permitted to furnish the soldiers with a blanket or replenish their knapsacks." She then presented to their convention (in May, 1845) a typically feminine offering: a banner which she and other women in the

LFLRA had embroidered. Its motto was "Union for Power."
And, indeed, the women were only too well aware that they
needed the men's support. "What shall we expect at your
hands?" asked Bagley.

Very little, apparently. In 1846 the LFLRA bought the type
and presses of the *Voice of Industry*. The paper printed increasingly feminist articles — attacks on the institution of marriage, on
the denial of education and equal pay to women, pleas for the
vote, exhortations to sisterhood.* Although many men supported
the women's cause, neither men nor women subscribed in sufficient numbers to the *Voice* or to its editorializing; neither men
nor women, in the face of the worsening economy, cared to lose
the jobs which provided at least some sustenance. The *Voice*
ceased publication in 1848.

The economic recession of that year threw thousands of hands
out of work. The legislature continued to uphold the corporations' position. The labor organizations languished and died. In
1847 the corporations granted from fifteen to thirty minutes extra
time for meals. Although "slavers" continued to scour the up-
country farms for new workers, the defeated Yankee women
began to desert the mills. Their places were taken by the
thousands of immigrant men and women, who, fleeing the potato
famine in Ireland, had no choice but to work under conditions
which the native-born women would not tolerate.

The fight for the ten-hour day was revived in the next decade
by politicians who included it in their platforms. There had
been, through the 1840s, a continuing debate at the labor conventions about whether to take political action to gain the workers' demands—that is, whether to organize support against the
corporations' candidates. In 1845 William Schouler was defeated, but he won back his seat in the legislature the following
year. The Utopians, who had for a time dominated the workers'
associations, wanted to politicize the issue, thus effectively removing the majority—women—from having any voice in the
controversy. The activist women, on the contrary, wanted to help
themselves as much as they could, even though they realized
that ultimately they were dependent on men to ameliorate their
condition. The women wanted to organize themselves and to
appeal to public opinion (an indirect resort to politics, since

*These writings were published before the Seneca Falls Declaration of 1848,
which is generally regarded as the beginning of the feminist movement in the
United States.

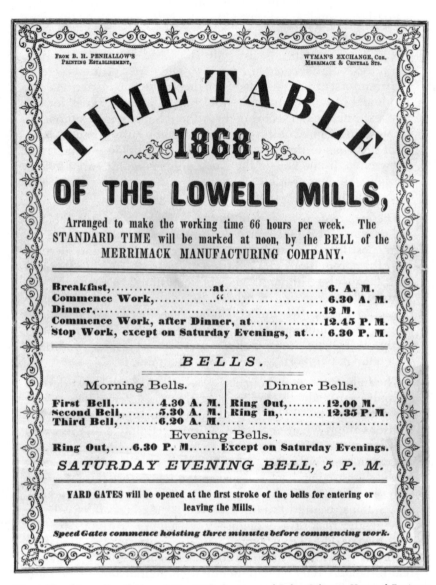

Timetable of Lowell mills; broadside, 1868. Courtesy of Baker Library, Harvard Business School.

presumably "public opinion" would force the legislature to enact a ten-hour day). They also had a short-lived hope that the corporations would be moved by the workers' pleas.

The difficulty of the women's position was nowhere more clearly shown than in *Corporations and Operatives* (1843), the angry reply by a "Citizen of Lowell" to Dr. Elisha Bartlett's whitewash of the Lowell manufacturers. For seventy pages the anonymous "Citizen" spoke both to and about the female operatives. Although he believed that a woman's place was in the home, these oppressed operatives, now that they were in Lowell, had all his sympathy. Falling wages, long hours, foul air, insufficient food, lack of privacy—all demanded reform. The "Citizen" had the answer: the operatives themselves needed to "watch their own interests, and guard their own rights, *at the ballot box*" (italics added), where they should elect legislators who would see that *"the rights of man* [sic!]" were protected. Since the workers to whom the "Citizen" addressed himself had no access to the ballot box (women did not achieve suffrage until almost a century later), this remedy could hardly have given them much comfort. Of course, at that time, men, too, needed encouragement to vote against corporate interests, since the secret ballot had yet to be introduced. To vote against the Whig candidate was a risky thing to do in Lowell. Thus the defeat of Schouler, even for one term, was a triumph for the operatives, both male and female.

Benjamin F. Butler, beginning his long political career by running for the state legislature, capitalized on this corporate dictation in the election of 1852. Faced with possible defeat for their candidates, the corporations, just before the election, reduced the working day to eleven hours for men. In 1853 the corporations—not the legislature—set the hours for all workers at eleven. In 1855 a legislative committee reported out favorably a compulsory ten-hour law. But the corporations prevailed: their lobbyists killed the bill by buying up its supporters. It was not until nineteen years later, in 1874, thirty years after Sarah Bagley organized the Lowell Female Labor Reform Association, that the Massachusetts legislature passed a ten-hour law for women and children.

The history of the pre-Civil War operatives at Lowell is an important chapter in the history of American women. It is also an unusual and significant glimpse into the lives of ordinary

people—working people—who have seldom left any written records down through the centuries. By and large, history as we
know it has been history by and about a tiny fraction of the
population: educated men. Women, workers, peasants, slaves,
children—very few of these, who are the majority, wrote about
themselves until comparatively recent years. The Lowell mill
girls were not literate because they worked in the factories; but
because they were literate, in the New England tradition, they
were able to give to us a sense of what they were, what they
thought, what they wanted.

Almost half a century later, revisiting the city where she had
spent her girlhood, Harriet Robinson, after meeting the factory
girls of that later day, pleaded with the manufacturers to "mix a
little conscience with their capital" to "try to bring back the 'lost
Eden'" which she remembered. Lowell was never an "Eden,"
but as the place where American women first had a chance to
earn an independent living, and where the American Industrial
Revolution began, the Lowell Experiment marked the beginning
of a long road.

IX

The Civil War:
Patriotism vs. King Cotton

By Arthur L. Eno, Jr.

During the decades preceding the Civil War, King Cotton dominated the thinking, as well as the economy, of the city of Lowell. The Boston Associates and their successors, the manufacturers of Lowell, had many personal contacts with the South: business dealings, cotton-buying trips, and visits by Southerners to Boston and by Bostonians to the South. One such trip was the lengthy good-will tour by Amos A. Lawrence (the son of Amos Lawrence) in 1836 and 1837. The relationship was profitable and both the Yankee "Lords of the Loom" and the slave-holding "Lords of the Lash" hoped to continue it.

The same attitude prevailed among the lesser figures in the cotton textile industry in Lowell. It was felt by overseer and loom-fixer alike that the city's continued prosperity, as well as their own, depended on the continuance of the friendly and cooperative relationship with the southern cotton growers. If for any reason the flow of raw cotton into Lowell stopped, the mills would be forced to close, and all would be out of work.

This attitude was startlingly demonstrated in the fall of 1834. There came to Lowell on a speaking tour the English social reformer who had been responsible for Britain's abolition of slavery in the British West Indies. George Thompson was scheduled to deliver three anti-slavery lectures on consecutive

evenings in the town hall. A large audience was on hand for his
first lecture on "Slavery and the Bible." A rock was thrown from
the street below, but was deflected by the window frame and did
no damage. On the second evening his lecture on the "History of
San Domingo" precipitated some hissing and stamping of feet.
Three missiles were hurled at the building, including one
brickbat which crashed through a window and narrowly missed
the speaker. On Tuesday morning, the southern sympathizers
became more active: Thompson received an anonymous letter
advising him to leave town, and placards appeared throughout
the town:

> Citizens of Lowell, arise! Look well to your interests! Will you
> suffer a question to be discussed in Lowell which will endanger
> the safety of the Union?—a question which we have not, by our
> constitution, any right to meddle with. Fellow-citizens, shall
> Lowell be the first place to suffer an Englishman to disturb the
> peace and harmony of our country? . . . If you are freeborn sons of
> America, meet, one and all, at the Town Hall, THIS EVENING, at
> half-past seven o'clock, and convince your Southern brethren that
> we will not interfere with their rights.

That evening the freeborn sons of America turned out in force.
A noisy, threatening crowd gathered around the town hall and
threw stones at the upstairs auditorium windows. The ministers
who had invited Thompson to speak tried to convince him to
leave the hall and to stay off the streets. His supporters and the
selectmen agreed to postpone the meeting until the next afternoon when most of the mob would be at work in the factories.
Before a far smaller audience Thompson delivered his final lecture on the "History and Results of West India Emancipation".

It is perhaps startling that the workingmen of Lowell should
have concurred so completely with their employers, and that
they should have given such violent expression to their feelings.
In addition to what we may be sure were subtle hints from the
management about the precarious future of the textile industry,
the workers were also influenced by the local newspapers which
reiterated the views of the manufacturers.

It must not be supposed, however, that there was no opposing
point of view in Lowell. There had always been a small nucleus
of anti-slavery sentiment originating in Dracut and reaching
across the river into Lowell. The Varnums had been of this nucleus. Their efforts do not seem to have made much headway
against the pro-South flood emanating from the mills. In 1844,
one of the country's leading abolitionists, John Greenleaf Whittier, came to Lowell to edit an abolitionist newspaper, the
Middlesex Standard. The next two years probably represent the

high-water mark of abolitionist activity in Lowell. In 1845, Whittier left the city and the *Standard* soon moved to Worcester. During the same time, anti-slavery articles appeared in the *Voice of Industry*, a labor newspaper which led the fight, not only for the ten-hour day, but also for other "good causes" such as abolition and women's rights.

But Lowell, like all of Massachusetts, was dominated during this period by the Whig party. The convolutions of the Whigs are fairly representative of the attitudes and reactions of the majority in Lowell during the pre-Civil War decades. When Maine and Missouri were admitted to the Union in 1820 as part of the Missouri Compromise, northerners and southerners alike rejoiced that the troublesome question of the "peculiar institution" of slavery had been resolved once for all, and that the status quo had been preserved by balancing a new free state with a new slave state.

Despite their pro-southern bias, the Massachusetts Whigs had deep reservations about slavery as an institution. They finally adopted the legalistic position that the constitution protected slavery where it existed at the time of its adoption, but did not prevent Congress from legislating against it in the territories which sought admission to the Union. Since this was essentially the position of the northern Democrats, it represented the view of a vast majority of Lowell residents.

This consensus, however, was buffeted by several events on the national scene. The Mexican War, uniformly rejected by the Massachusetts Whigs as a Democratic pretext for the extension of slavery, aroused the consciences as well as the passions of some of the younger Whigs. The Compromise of 1850, designed to save the Union by having each section give up something, included a stringent Fugitive Slave Law. This fired the imagination of the younger Whigs, who revolted from the leadership of the old "Cotton" Whigs, and called themselves "Conscience" Whigs. Their consciences were further disturbed when the fight over the admission of Kansas broke out. From the Massachusetts Whigs—and primarily from Amos A. Lawrence—moral and financial support poured out to the free settlers of Kansas, who fought bloody battles to make Kansas a free state, despite the incursions of slave-holding Missourians and the connivance of President Franklin Pierce's Democratic administration in Washington.

Even the Cotton Whigs were shaken by the Kansas fight. They

felt that the great compromises of the past, which they had
supported in the face of strong attacks from the young Turks, had
been destroyed by the insistence of the southerners that the
slave empire be extended. For years, the Whigs had preached
protection for slavery in the original states, and had equally
loudly proclaimed their intention not to let it spread into the
western territories. In order to maintain this position, they had
even agreed to the infamous Fugitive Slave Law, which
abolitionist orators, novelists and even Boston mobs joined in
condemning.

As the presidential election of 1856 approached, all the various
anti-slavery groups, including some northern Democrats, formed
the new Republican party. Their first campaign was unsuccessful, in part because the die-hard Whigs refused to join the coalition and instead took over the American ("Know-Nothing") Party. This alliance widened the breach between the two wings of
the now defunct Whig party. The final straw came on October 19,
1859, when John Brown made his famous raid on Harper's Ferry
and tried to launch a slave rebellion. This terrified the South and
frightened the Cotton Whigs of the North, who were now desperate to find any means to save the Union.

Lincoln's election was the signal for the secession of South
Carolina; other southern states joined her in passing resolutions
of secession, but nothing decisive happened. Several northern
groups—pre-eminent among which were Amos A. Lawrence
and his associates—were trying still to reconcile irreconcilable
views.

In the election of 1860, because the opposition was splintered,
the Republicans swept not only the presidency, but also all the
state offices. John A. Andrew, a Free-soiler and abolitionist, was
elected governor, defeating both Amos A. Lawrence, the old-line
Whig candidate, and Benjamin F. Butler, the Democrat. Republican John A. Goodwin of Lowell was elected speaker of the
house, and former Lowell editor William Schouler was
adjutant-general of Massachusetts. Andrew was elected annually, and served as governor throughout the war. One of his first
acts after his inauguration was to order a hundred-gun salute
fired in Boston (and other salutes at the same time in several
cities including Lowell) to commemorate the victory of Andrew
Jackson in New Orleans (on January 8), and also to honor the
gallant resistance of Major Anderson at Fort Sumter in the harbor
of Charleston, South Carolina. The purpose of the salute was

General Benjamin F. Butler, 1818-1893. Lithograph by Dominique C. Fabronius published by L. Prang & Company (Private Collection)

patently to revive old patriotic memories. Massachusetts was leaning more and more toward Union and abolition, and away from cotton and slavery.

Finally, in April, 1861, the shooting began with the firing on Fort Sumter. Almost immediately, the Democratic *Advertiser* joined the Republican *Courier* in calling for an end to secession, and demanding punishment and military defeat for the South.

Despite the precarious position of Fort Sumter and the threat by the Confederates that they would consider any attempt to relieve the fort an act of aggression, Lincoln decided to try to send supplies to the besieged fort. He was persuaded to do this by Gustavus Vasa Fox, a native of Lowell and a member of the first class at the Lowell High School. Fox had graduated from the Naval Academy, but had later resigned his commission to become the agent of the Bay State Mills in Lawrence. He worked out a plan to relieve Fort Sumter by sea and proposed it to Lincoln. The president not only accepted the plan, but commissioned Fox to take command of the expedition. Despite elaborate preparations, everything went wrong. Some of the ships never reached the rendezvous, and a violent storm blew up and prevented the flotilla from reaching Sumter. Fox and his ships had to sail away, Major Anderson surrendered the garrison, and the Civil War had begun. Fox stayed on to work at the Navy department and a few months later the post of assistant secretary of the Navy was created for him.

When Lincoln called for troops, Massachusetts was ready. Also ready was a citizen of Lowell (and high school classmate of Gustavus Fox), who was destined to dominate the headlines during the Civil War and the decades that followed. Benjamin Franklin Butler's career as a Democrat had collapsed with the Democratic National Convention at Charleston, South Carolina, in April, 1860. Despite the preference of most of his constituents for Stephen A. Douglas, Butler voted fifty-seven times for Jefferson Davis, and ended up supporting the pro-slavery extremist, John C. Breckenridge. Although he defended his actions on the basis of his desire to preserve the Union and defeat secession, local Democtats ostracized Butler and shouted him down when he tried to explain his stand at a public meeting. When the Breckenridge Democrats ran Butler for governor that fall, he managed to get only 6000 out of 169,534 votes, far fewer than he had received in his previous campaign.

When Butler returned from Charleston convinced that war was inevitable he started preparing for action the Massachusetts Sixth Regiment, in which he was a brigadier-general. This regiment was largely composed of Lowell companies which, as early as January 21, 1861, at Butler's urging, voted to tender their services to the governor in the event the president called for troops. Governor Andrew was persuaded to secure funds for the proper arming of the Sixth Regiment, and a contract for cloth for new overcoats for the regiment was awarded to the Middlesex Company—which happened to be largely owned by Butler.

When the call to arms finally came,* the legislature had adjourned without appropriating any funds for transporting the troops. Butler rode to Boston on the train with James G. Carney, president of the Bank for Mutual Redemption, and asked him to loan the funds to the Commonwealth, and also to recommend Butler as commander of the brigade. The stratagem worked and Butler, although a political opponent of Governor Andrew, was appointed . This coalition of abolitionist governor and one of the most *ultra* of Breckenridge's supporters (and the bitterest of anti-Republicans) helped to demonstrate to the South that the free states were forgetting party differences and were unified in defense of the Union.

The first elements of Butler's brigade, consisting of the Sixth Regiment including four companies from Lowell, left Boston for Washington on April 17, 1861, after an enthusiastic ceremony on Boston Common with Governor Andrew personally bidding the regiment farewell. The regiment's progress through New York City and Philadelphia brought forth similar enthusiasm.

On April 19, the anniversary of the Concord and Lexington battles (an analogy which was often pointed out by orators describing the event), the regiment reached Baltimore. There the railroad cars had to be pulled by horses to the Washington depot on the other side of the city. Seven companies had already reached the Washington depot when the last four companies started out. By this time, a secessionist mob of ten thousand began hurling bricks, rocks, and oyster shells at the railroad cars, and pulled up the tracks to prevent the cars from proceeding further. The men had to disembark and continue on foot, all the while being assaulted by threats and missiles. Although the Mayor of Baltimore marched at the head of the column, someone

*The orders were delivered to Butler in open court as he was trying a case in Boston. He left immediately and, according to his autobiography, the case was never finished.

from the mob fired into the troops and one man fell dead. The soldiers were ordered to return fire and did so, but by the time the smoke cleared, a large number of the Massachusetts men were wounded, and four of them lay dead: Luther C. Ladd and Addison O. Whitney of Lowell, Sumner H. Needham of Lawrence, and Charles A. Taylor, residence unknown.

The bodies of Ladd, Whitney, and Needham were returned to Massachusetts for burial. After lying in the vault of King's Chapel in Boston, the remains of Ladd and Whitney were transferred to Lowell for formal funeral services. They were interred in the Lowell Cemetery with all the honors due the first casualties of the Civil War.

Butler, following with the rest of his brigade, heard of the Baltimore riot and proceeded toward Washington by way of Annapolis, where he occupied the Naval Academy and seized the USS Constitution ("Old Ironsides")—both threatened by the secessionists. While the Sixth Regiment continued to Washington, Butler's troops captured Baltimore, thus preventing Maryland from seceding and breaking the supply lines from the North. The Sixth was the first of the volunteer militia regiments to reach Washington; it was quartered in the Senate chamber of the Capitol. On the night of their arrival, the men of the Sixth were visited by President Lincoln who personally thanked them for saving the Union. Ninety days after they were mustered, the enlistments of the Massachusetts brigade expired and the regiments returned home to a heroes' welcome.

Lincoln commissioned Butler to return to New England to recruit and and train a volunteer force of not more than six regiments. He recruited throughout New England, not without sharp clashes with Governor Andrew who was simultaneously recruiting state volunteer militia.

The attack on the Sixth Regiment in Baltimore and the shedding of local blood aroused the people of Lowell and spurred the recruiting of new companies of militia, which were equipped with the help of a municipal appropriation. Thereafter, there were frequent appropriations both for the relief of the volunteers and their families, and to pay bounties for enlistments.

This patriotic enthusiasm continued throughout the war, although it declined slightly with the bad news from the front and with each new call for troops. Nevertheless, the city was able to send 5266 men into the Union forces; except for one draft, all were volunteers. The effort was helped by the patriotic speeches of the mayor and other politicians, by the newspaper appeals to the youth to enlist, and by fairly generous bounties for enlistments.

The women, too, shared in the war effort. Throughout the country, women participated in the work of the Sanitary Commission, organized to take care of the men at the front, especially the wounded. Through such local activities as "Sanitary Fairs," money was raised to further the work of the commission.

The shift in thinking about slavery in Lowell was exemplified by the changes in General Butler's thinking. After voting for the pro-slavery wing of the Democratic party at the Charleston convention, he was the first to volunteer for active military duty once war became inevitable. While occupying Baltimore, he offered assistance to put down by force a threatened Negro insurrection, much to the disgust of Governor Andrew and the Massachusetts "Conscience" Republicans. Then, in May, 1861, while he was commanding Fortress Monroe in Virginia, he anticipated the Emancipation Proclamation by holding slaves belonging to rebels as "contraband of war." His legal argument was that any property belonging to rebels, especially that which could be used against the United States, was subject to seizure as contraband. Passing the question whether human beings could be considered property, Butler argued that the southern rebels, having made the ownership of slaves as property a constitutional right, could not deny the government's right to seize that property in wartime.

After his recruiting duty in New England, Butler was sent to participate in the capture of New Orleans. He arrived after Admiral Farragut had captured the city, but he set up its military administration. He cleaned it, reduced disease, and kept the citizens from starving. This was accomplished at the expense of the unreconstructed rebels who missed no occasion to try to humiliate the Union troops. Butler's response was stern. A rebel who cut down the Union flag was shot. Any southern woman who insulted Union troops in the street was to be regarded and treated, according to the famous General Order No. 28, "as a woman of the town plying her avocation." These actions aroused the entire South against Butler, resulting in his being proclaimed a felon and an outlaw by Jefferson Davis. A reward of $10,000 was offered for his capture and delivery to the Confederates, and his reputation as the "Beast of New Orleans" persists to this day in the South.

When he tangled with the European consular corps, Butler was removed as commander of the New Orleans Department and replaced by General Nathaniel P. Banks, the former "bobbin boy" who had worked in the Lowell mills and served as governor of Massachusetts. *Harper's* magazine, which was to publish many vitriolic editorials and cartoons of Butler after the war, criticized Lincoln for removing Butler. And even the Republican legislature of Massachusetts adopted a formal resolve tendering its thanks to Major-General Benjamin F. Butler "for the energy, ability and success characterizing his late administration and command of the department of the Gulf."

In his farewell address to the citizens of New Orleans, Butler completed the long journey from Breckenridge Democrat to Abolitionist and spoke of ". . . the institution, cursed of God, which has taken its last refuge here, [and which] in His providence will be rooted out as the tares from the wheat, although the wheat be torn up with it."

On April 2, 1863, Butler was the guest of honor at a reception at the Academy of Music in New York, attended by a tumultuous crowd. He was then detailed to represent the United States in talks concerning the exchange of prisoners. Butler enjoyed the idea that the Confederates would be forced to treat with one whom they had outlawed and pronounced a felon.

When the November, 1864, elections approached there were rumors of a possible riot at the polls in New York City, managed by southern sympathizers, and looking to the election of General McClellan. Butler was dispatched to New York to keep the peace. Because the troops had already voted in the field by absentee ballot, and the law provided that their votes could not be counted if they were in New York on election day, Butler's legal mind worked out a plan to deploy his troops on ferryboats, anchored in New Jersey waters, so that they could be ferried to any part of Manhattan Island in which they were needed. By a combination of tact and bluster, Butler succeeded in keeping New York calm, and returned to his post in Virginia, in command of the Department of the James [River]. There followed several weeks of attempts to cut off Richmond, disagreements with General Grant and long justifications of himself, placing the blame for failure to take the city on others (usually West Pointers).One of the most humiliating defeats he had to explain was being "bottled up" in Bermuda Hundred by an inferior Confederate force. Finally on January 7, 1865, Butler's military career came to

Don Quixote (Lincoln) and Sancho Panza (Butler). Cartoon by Adalbert J. Volck. Courtesy of The Maryland Historical Society, Baltimore.

an end when General Order No. 1 of the War Department relieved him of command and ordered him ιo "repair to Lowell,
Mass. , and report *by letter* to the adjutant general of the army."
In his last farewell to his troops, he singled out the Negro troops
of the Army of the James, and boasted of their bravery and of the
fact that he himself had been the first to enlist blacks as soldiers
instead of as laborers. Butler's conversion to the abolitionist
cause was now complete.

Even among the Republicans a similar transformation took
time. In 1861 the Republican state convention refused to adopt
Charles Sumner's abolitionist plank for the party's platform. In
1862 the convention readily adopted the same declaration that
had been turned down the previous year.

On March 15, 1865, as the war was coming to a close, George
Thompson, the abolitionist who had been mobbed in 1834, again
visited Lowell. He came with William Lloyd Garrison to speak
on behalf of the Lowell Freedmen's Aid Society. His speech was
delivered in Huntington Hall, practically across the street from
the town hall where three decades before he had been the target
of hisses and brickbats. This time, instead, he was greeted with
applause and honor.

In April, Lee surrendered at Appomatox Court House. On
April 19, 1865, dedication exercises had been scheduled in Lowell for the monument erected in memory of Ladd and Whitney,
the Lowell martyrs and first victims of the Civil War. This
monument had been proposed within weeks of their death, and
was jointly paid for by the state and the city. Five days before the
date set for the dedication, President Lincoln succumbed to an
assassin's bullet. The ceremony was postponed until June 17,
1865. Governor Andrew gave the principal address from a bal-
cony of the Merrimack House overlooking the monument, in the
presence of the executive council, most of the members of the
legislature, and the soldiers of the Sixth.

The Civil War years were a dividing point in Lowell's history.
The successes of the prewar decades could not be matched in the
new era after the north's victory, and while enormous profits
would continue to be made from the textile mills, they would be
made increasingly at the expense of the mills' operatives.
Perhaps, given the fossilized corporate structure of the Lowell
factories and the increasing demands for profits on the part of
stockholders, no other outcome could have occurred. But when
the mills were again operating at full employment after 1865, a

"First Blood." The Sixth Massachusetts Regiment fighting its way through Baltimore, April 19, 1861. *Harper's Weekly*, May 4, 1861.(Lowell Historical Society)

Dedication of the Ladd & Whitney Monument, June 17, 1865. *Harper's Weekly*, July 8, 1865. (Lowell Historical Society)

new, grim epoch was at hand; already, at this time, the famous
Yankee mill girls and their "philanthropic" employers were historical figures, surviving copies of the *Lowell Offering* were
brittle with age, and no one seemed ever to have heard of a
labor newspaper called the *Voice of Industry*.

X

Decline and Fall:
The End of the Dream

By Fidelia O. Brown

On April 27, 1861, four men held a directors' meeting of the Merrimack Manufacturing Company at the treasurer's office in Boston, and voted to appoint the acting treasurer and the selling agents as a committee to reduce production by stopping a portion of the machinery and the works. The committee later reported to the directors that production was suspended as of August 24, 1861. The inventory of raw cotton was then sold at great profit to other New England mills, instead of being manufactured into cloth.

The other companies (governed by interlocking directorates) naturally followed the lead of the giant Merrimack. The result was dramatic and tragic; it also marked the beginning of the long decline of Lowell's textile industry.

Historian Charles Cowley described both the action and its consequences:

> The impartial historian cannot ignore the fact, painful as it is, that nine of the great corporations of Lowell, under a mistaken belief that they could not run their mills to a profit during the war, unanimously, in cold blood, dismissed ten thousand operatives, penniless into the streets!

> This crime, this worse than crime, this *blunder*, entailed its own punishment,—as all crimes do by the immutable law of God.

When these companies resumed operations, their former skilled
operatives were dispersed, and could no more be recalled than the
Ten Lost Tribes of Israel. Their places were filled by the less
skilled operatives whom the companies now had to employ. So
serious was this blunder, that the smallest of the companies would
have done wisely, had they sacrificed a hundred thousand dollars,
rather than thus lose their accustomed help.

The closing drove the remaining native born mill girls back
home to their family farms in New Hampshire and Vermont.
When the mills reopened after the war, the mill girls did not
return and their places were taken by the new immigrants who
had joined relatives and friends already employed by the mills.
This was probably the greatest change in the industry since
Francis Cabot Lowell re-invented the power loom. After the
Yankee women had left, there was no longer any need for the
careful precautions to attract and pacify this homogeneous labor
force. The women were replaced by cheap, immigrant labor
which the management could press and oppress without qualms.
Symptomatic also was the sale of the boarding houses. When the
women left, the boarding houses became miniature Leagues of
Nations; the mill management had little patience with the dis-
putes and problems that arose, and no desire to act as interna-
tionality arbitrators. With the sale of the boarding houses disappeared the last of the major original elements of the Lowell
Experiment. As John Coolidge has phrased it, "Nothing of Francis Cabot Lowell's Utopia has stood the test of time"

The vote of April 27, 1861, was not, of course, the sole cause of
Lowell's decline. There are many theories as to the effective
cause, and the truth undoubtedly is a combination of many
theories.

As early as 1848, Charles Sumner had given currency to a new
term to express his conviction that there was no longer
utopianism among the manufacturers of Lowell. When he spoke
of "Lords of the Loom," the natural comparison he intended was
with the southern "Lords of the Lash." The increasing profits of
the owners kept pace with the increasing speed of the machines
and easily outdistanced the wages of the operatives.

Then came the attack from within—by the corporations' own
stockholders and officials. The battle started in 1858 with the
newspaper publication of a letter from "Historicus" (Charles
Cowley) attacking the nepotism into which the Lowell Experiment had degenerated:

Let no man fatten on corporation pay without a full equivalent in

labor. . . . Banish those decayed families and coteries that have sat
down in corporation offices as upon life estates. Banish the
clanism and nepotism which fill important posts with brainless
cousins and nephews, and allow no field for plebian energy and
skill. Disband that oligarchy of office-holding which now rules
supreme; which makes one man director of thirty companies and
president of nineteen.

Cowley's letter was occasioned by the publication of a pamphlet by Erastus B. Bigelow, former agent of the Lowell Manufacturing Company, entitled *Remarks on the Depressed Condition of Manufactures in Massachusetts with Suggestions as to its
Cause and its Remedy* (1858). Bigelow's thesis was that the
corporate form was unsuited to manufacturing operations and
carried within itself the seeds of its own destruction. According
to Bigelow, a "private" (as contrasted with corporate) enterprise
can react promptly to economic conditions and renew its plant or
build extensions during slow periods, in order to take advantage
of lower costs and to keep its personnel. A corporate treasurer, on
the other hand, cannot obtain from his stockholders funds for
expansion during bad times. Only when times are good (and
costs of building correspondingly high) can the money be spent.
In order to be successful, an enterprise should grow slowly and
naturally, and not by sudden and sporadic infusions of cash.
Bigelow pointed out that all the great British manufacturing
organizations of the time were "private enterprises" which had
grown from small, if not tiny, beginnings. Their prosperity contrasted vividly with the present lethargic state of the manufacturing corporations in Massachusetts where a new textile company
had not been incorporated for years.

The greatest and most active critic of the mills was himself a
manufacturer and capitalist owning large blocks of stock in
many of the textile mills. James C. Ayer, M.D., a patent medicine
manufacturer, became a corporation reformer when, in 1857, two
mills in which he was a substantial investor—the Middlesex
Company in Lowell and the Bay State Mills in Lawrence—
collapsed. He joined Ben Butler on an investigating committee
of the stockholders of the Middlesex, which published a report of
its findings. Almost every subsequent stockholders' committee to
investigate the operation of a company had Ayer as a member:
the Lowell Manufacturing Company, the Hamilton, and the Merrimack, among those in Lowell.

In 1863 he published his pamphlet *Some of the Usages and
Abuses in the Management of our Manufacturing Corporations*

in which he reported the scandals these investigations had
uncovered. With vitriolic pen, Ayer attacked the corrupt and
fraudulent practices he blamed for the low state of the industry:
holding stockholders' meetings in a small (seventeen by thirty-
two feet) treasurer's office in Boston, which accommodated only
a small fraction of the stockholders; calling meetings on short
notice, or at the same time as other corporations' meetings, or at
an early hour before the train from Lowell arrived in Boston;
taking proxies from stockholders by falsely representing the
proxy to be only a receipt for a dividend; keeping the stockholders' list (after stockholders had finally won the legal right to
inspect it) without including addresses. Using these practices,
management kept itself in office, by discouraging or making
impossible stockholder attendance at meetings, by securing
enough proxies to outvote any stalwart stockholders who managed to attend the meetings, and by preventing the stockholders
from communicating with each other and organizing.

Corruption not only existed, it was openly tolerated. An
$89,000 payment was described at a Middlesex Company annual
meeting only as a "bribe for Congress," without condemnation or
question.

Ayer also denounced nepotism, and cited a case where the
Hamilton treasurer's youthful, inexperienced son lost $50,000 of
the company's money on a cotton-buying trip. He railed against
the favoritism which awarded a year's salary to the retiring treasurer of the Lowell Company (a man Ayer thought hardly deserved his regular salary), and which cut off workers' wages
during periods of closing, while officers' high salaries continued
to be paid. F. T. Crowinshield, the Merrimack treasurer, was
paid a full salary for a supposedly full-time job, while he was
drawing salaries from three other mill corporations and also from
a railroad corporation, for which he was a bond trustee.

But the basic fault, said Ayer, was the system itself. When the
Lowell Experiment started, one of the few stockholders might
own $25,000 to $100,000 of stock in a company. Naturally, each
investor had strong incentive to follow the activities of the company management. Now, however, stock ownership was spread
more widely among many more individuals who owned an average of only $3,000 in stock apiece, and therefore could not be
expected to take the same interest in the corporation as a Nathan
Appleton or a Patrick Tracy Jackson. To make matters worse,
each individual probably owned a few shares in several corpora-

tions, making it impossible for him to follow them all, even if he
had the desire to do so.

Also wrong, according to Ayer, was the system of selling
agents—commission houses like A. & A. Lawrence & Company,
Lawrence, Stone & Company and J. W. Paige & Company—
which were responsible for all sales and so had considerable
influence in dictating the production of certain goods. These
commission houses were partnerships controlled by the inner
circle of the mill owners, and so offered a way of withdrawing
profits without sharing them with the small stockholders. Ayer
criticized the exorbitant charges of the selling agents (there were
special charges for auctions and other special services necessi-
tated by lack of sales, in addition to the standard sales commis-
sions and reimbursement for expenses), their lack of compe-
tence, and their conflict of interest in representing competing
companies. There was a further conflict of interest because, although they owned few shares, representatives of the selling
agents were usually elected directors, and so voted on their own
compensation.

Ayer did not stop at criticizing. After the Civil War, he gained
control of the financially ailing Suffolk and Tremont Companies.
Consolidating them into the Tremont and Suffolk Mills, Ayer
took personal charge of the corporation and made it a profitable
enterprise.

Benjamin F. Butler, for decades Lowell's most illustrious resident, attributed the decline of the city to the exodus of some
fifteen hundred of the city's most energetic and enterprising
young men who left for California during the 1849 gold rush.
Butler estimated that the capital thus lost to the city amounted,
through the years, to $1,250,000.

Speaking at the city's semi-centennial celebration in 1876,
Butler said: "Our city has been a hive of industry, and, as a rule,
the honey has been gathered by others." Butler pointed out that,
besides the initial investment in the mills, investors contributed
very little. Mill extensions were financed by reserves initially set
aside to cover depreciation. He pointed out also that the mill
owners did not live or spend or invest their money in the city;
and, he might have added, they made no enduring civic gifts.

When in the 1850s steam power became feasible because of
the reduction in the cost of obtaining and transporting fuel,
competing factories sprang up in such places as Fall River and

New Bedford, which were conveniently located for water transportation of coal, raw cotton, and finished products. By the turn of the century, both Fall River and New Bedford had surpassed Lowell in production and in number of employees. Even before the age of steam, the giant Amoskeag mill had been built on the falls of the Merrimack River in Manchester, New Hampshire, and had soon surpassed Lowell in importance.

After the first World War the textile industry looked to the South and found the grass greener and the cotton fields nearer. Living costs were lower and so were labor costs because of the lack of unionization. Although the workers were unskilled, being English-speaking they were, some overseers felt, easier to train than New England's polyglot immigrant population. The Southerners also courted the cotton mills, while New Englanders, by now disillusioned with the collapsing structure of a one-industry economy, tended to blame all their urban woes on the mills.

Labor troubles also contributed to the dispersal and decline. After almost a hundred years of operation, the New England textile industry was fairly well organized. As working conditions became worse and jobs more precarious, the unions pressed for new concessions to protect their members. The rigid managerial mind resisted the spread of unions and preferred to move the entire plant to more favorable climes. One by one, the mills packed up and moved South, leaving behind their empty buildings and their unemployed hands.

Even though Lowell suffered less bitter and violent strikes than those in other textile centers, notably Lawrence, the city's workers "went out" several times before the turn of the century.

In the years before the Civil War corporation operatives had failed to restore wage cuts or shorten their working day by "turnouts," or strikes. They were hardly more successful in the latter part of the nineteenth century: the moment a strike was called by one of the craft unions which had begun to organize, the corporations locked out the offending employees (and sometimes the entire work force as well). Often they hired new workers to take the strikers' places. Then, when the strikers could hold out no longer, the companies would offer to hire back the striking workers (except the organizers), but would not dismiss any new employee to make a place for one who had struck.

In 1867 the mule-spinners at the Hamilton, Boott, and Lawrence companies struck for a reduction of the work day from

Appleton Company plant and boarding houses, circa 1880. (Lowell Historical Society)

eleven hours to ten; the mills continued to operate and the
spinners returned after three weeks—to eleven hour days. In
1875 the Mule-Spinners' Association of the United States ordered a test strike at selected Lowell mills; all mule-spinners in
all mills were discharged and locked out, and the mills continued
operations with new employees using ring-spinning (a less complicated process). After six weeks the strike was broken, and the
operatives signed an agreement not to join the union. In 1878,
female operatives at the Lowell Manufacturing Company were
fired when they struck against a wage cut. In 1884 the same
company lowered wages again; weavers and creeler-boys struck
unsuccessfully. The depression of 1893 cut back work to half-
time at all the mills for several years; many operatives who
formerly would have protested now felt fortunate to have even
starvation-level pay. With the upturn in business at the end of the
decade, however, operatives again attempted to protect themselves against wage cuts.

In 1898 a strike by hand-shearers of the White Brothers Company, protesting a reduction of their wages, was resolved by the
State Board of Arbitration: the company's plan to use machines to
shear hides had proved unsuccessful, and the strikers were taken
back at the old rate. In 1898 and 1899 there was widespread
discontent among the operatives throughout the city: limited
strikes occurred at several of the major corporations. Some companies took note. In December 1899, and January, 1900, ten
percent wage increases went into effect at the Appleton, Boott
Hamilton, Tremont & Suffolk, and Middlesex mills, as well as at
the United States Bunting Company, and the Kitson Machine
Company. An operator who formerly earned $6.00 a week was
raised to $6.60.

The first major city-wide strike of textile operatives began in
March, 1903. It was called by the Lowell Textile Council, made
up of representatives from skilled workers' unions: weavers,
carders, beamers, mule spinners, loom fixers, knappers, and knit-
ters. These operatives comprised perhaps ten percent of all the
mill operatives, who numbered between 18,000 and 20,000 at the
six major corporations. The council had for the previous year
demanded a ten percent wage increase, which had been refused
by the corporations.* After conferences between the mill agents
and representatives of the Textile Council, a strike was an-

*In 1900 the average hourly wage in the mills was ten cents an hour for a
sixty-two hour week. But workers were not guaranteed fifty-two weeks a year of

nounced by the union leaders. Ring-spinners, who had been used to break previous strikes, were hastily signed into a union by visiting members of the nationwide United Textile Workers of America. This organization, along with the American Federation of Labor (AFL) led by Samuel Gompers, had promised aid to Lowell's strikers. On the day of the strike, all the mills except the Lawrence Company announced an indefinite closing. The State Board of Arbitration came to Lowell to hold hearings on the issue. After examining the corporations' books, it made a report which was largely favorable to the mills, saying that with the exception of the Lawrence mill the corporations could not afford to raise wages.

The effects of the strike began to be felt. Rents and grocery bills went unpaid and tenements were vacated. Many small stores in the city's ethnic districts were forced to close. The city's church leaders aligned themselves: the Protestant ministers condemned the strike, the Irish Catholic clergy supported it, and the French Catholic clergy, like their parishioners, tended to remain neutral. Many French-Canadians left Lowell. The Greeks were less able to leave; they supported the strike, although many of them were unskilled workers and had little knowledge of the union leaders' plans. The Greeks announced through their community leaders that they wanted no strike benefits from the Textile Council—they would, they said, provide support for their own people. The Poles and the Portugese also supported the strike and helped in organizing the unskilled workers.

After the strike had lasted for two months, Samuel Gompers came to Lowell to speak. His support for the Textile Council was lukewarm; the AFL offered only voluntary, not assessed, aid. Gompers did not seem to believe that the Lowell strike was vital to the national labor struggle—possibly because he saw it as an inevitable defeat for the workers.

Although many unskilled workers had supported the strike, they wanted and needed to return to their jobs. When Gompers' lack of enthusiasm was reported, the mill agents saw their chance for victory. Sure of a work-force, they announced that the mills would reopen at the old wages. The strong union supporters— skilled workers—remained out, confident that the mills could

pay, even at that rate, because the corporations frequently closed down when there was a poor market for their product or when a large inventory had been built up. Many operatives worked only nine months a year—and of course could expect no unemployment benefits for the remaining three.

not run without them. They were mistaken. The agents promptly moved up into skilled positions the Portugese, Poles, and Greeks. The Textile Council held out for three weeks more and then finally called off the strike, but it was too late; craft union strength had been broken. From that time, only industry-wide organization would give workers the strength needed to prevail against the corporations.

In June of that year, William Southworth, the agent of the Massachusetts Cotton Mills and spokesman for all the corporations, said that the mills would have closed in any case, strike or no strike, because of the high price of raw cotton. The corporations sold what cotton they had to mills in other New England cities; by doing so they made a higher profit than if they had stayed open and manufactured and sold cloth.

The most serious challenge to the Lowell textile corporations' hegemony occurred during the strike of 1912 led by the socialist-oriented Industrial Workers of the World. As opposed to previous attempts to organize skilled workers into craft unions, the IWW focused on industry-wide organization of all operatives as the key to successful strikes for higher pay and better working conditions. As early as the 1830s, when the cry of "outside agitators" had been raised against striking operatives, the mill management had feared industry-wide solidarity among all categories of their employees, unskilled as well as skilled, immigrant as well as native-born. Now, they watched with growing apprehension the turmoil occurring ten miles down-river in Lawrence where an IWW-led strike was already in progress. They realized that they were faced with an unprecedented situation. As the Lawrence strike continued, the IWW stepped up its recruiting in Lowell. "Big Bill" Haywood and Elizabeth Gurley Flynn descended on Lowell to exhort the workers to join them.

In March, 1912, the Lowell corporations announced a six to eight percent wage increase—part of the industry-wide response to the threat of the IWW. This raise was less than that granted in other textile centers; consequently it triggered the strike. The issues went deeper than wages, however. Operatives wanted better working and living conditions.

The Appleton Corporation was struck first. As had been its practice in the past, the management closed the factory and locked out the workers. The strikers proceeded to recruit operatives in other factories, making the strike—and thus the lockout—city-wide. The IWW promptly sent in its leaders, organized a strike committee, and established picket lines. The workers demanded four concessions: a fifteen percent wage increase for all employees, the weavers' right to weigh their own cloth, double pay for overtime, and re-hiring of all workers without discrimination. The IWW claimed that the operatives' committees presenting these demands were independent of the union, but the mill management saw them as socialist agitators influenced by outside radicals. They refused to bargain with the strikers.

Now the AFL-affiliated United Textile Workers, which for twenty-five years had represented the skilled operatives, entered the dispute, denouncing the IWW and its leaders. Its demands, however, were very similar, and were also refused by the corporations' officials. Internecine arguments erupted between the IWW and the UTW but the disagreement did not deter the IWW from carrying on a spirited campaign to sign up new members and keep its demands before the public. Organized picket lines were on duty every day at the silent, empty cotton mills; noisy parades made their way through the central business and mill district; daily meetings were held.

The success of the strike, as in previous years, depended on the solidarity of the unskilled workers. If they passed the picket lines and returned to work, the strikers once again would be defeated. The Greeks were the pivotal group. They supported the IWW, but they did not formally affiliate with it. They elected Dr. George Demopoulos as their leader; he dealt with the IWW and gave instructions to the Greek community. He wanted no bad publicity for his people who were working so hard to find a place in American society.

The IWW appealed for strike funds for Lowell from member unions throughout New England and as far away as Baltimore and Detroit. As before, the Greeks provided their own aid to needy fellow operatives. The UTW received limited aid from its affiliates. Typically, the poorest workers suffered most. Many, notably French Canadians, left the city in search of work elsewhere.

Four weeks after the strike began, the corporations received a blow to their pride as well as their morale: they were censured by the New England Association of Textile Manufacturers for not raising their wages a full ten percent. Faced with opposition from all sides, they agreed to the increase, thus bringing the Lowell mills in line with others throughout New England.

The offer was accepted by the UTW and by the Greeks. The IWW agreed—contingent upon the settlement of the workers' other grievances. The mill management acquiesced: one-and-a-quarter time pay was granted for overtime, weavers were allowed to weigh their own cloth, and striking operatives were to be rehired without discrimination. Perhaps the greatest victory for both sides was that, unlike Lawrence, Lowell saw very little violence during the strike.

The IWW-led strike of 1912 proved that the key to successful opposition to corporate practices lay in industry-wide organization, not "elitist" guilds of skilled workers. Although the IWW subsequently failed, its presence in Lowell, however brief, helped the operatives to achieve gains which they probably would not have made without it.

While workers wrested their gains from the corporations, the long decline of the Lowell textile industry continued.

Because Lowell was primarily dependent upon only one industry—textiles—and because that industry was highly susceptible to the seemingly inevitable cycle of economic depressions, or panics, the city's population suffered enormously during times that were harder than usual. Always, of course, reduced demand for cloth meant layoffs and cutbacks in wages and hours. In the panics of 1837, 1857, and 1873 there was little organized private charity outside of religious groups, and virtually no help from the city government. The City Poor Farm, which was the subject of several municipal investigations, represented the last miserable refuge of the destitute; many would rather have died than go there, and probably many did.

In the severe depression of the 1890s there was evidence of the financial squeeze on all economic classes: attendance at theaters and "socials" declined, and, as reported in the press, at-home games of whist became popular. In 1893 the Lowell Church League set up charity bread depots and tried to find other ways to help the needy. The mayor of Lowell, John J. Pickman, told the league that he felt the reports of poverty were exaggerated; city council members and other city officials were equally reluctant to accept the reality of large numbers of citizens totally without resources. Some money was appropriated, however, for public works to employ the needy.

The Lowell Church League began a fund-raising campaign. By

Christmas, 1893, the Catholic churches had begun to distribute food and clothing to those of their parishioners who were in need. Daily articles began to appear in the press about destitute families and individuals. Reports were published also of unusually large numbers of tramps begging from door to door. In May, 1894, unemployed workers demonstrated for public works jobs; the city council, however, could not bring itself to appropriate any more money, and even refused an offer from the church league to provide private funds for workers' pay if the jobs could be provided.

After the brief revival of the economy during World War I, the textile mills began to move away from Lowell. Therefore the city's working population was not unfamiliar with the troubles which beset the entire nation after the stock market crash of 1929. Hard times simply became harder; once again, in a kind of nightmarish repeat of past performances, the press kept the news from the front pages, reporting the activities of the stock market only on the financial pages until frantic stockholders at Lowell brokerage offices made it imperative to print the disastrous news on page one. And again, the city government talked and talked (as did every other city government in the nation) but no money could be found for public works to hire the increasing numbers of unemployed. Once again private and church charities dispensed the necessities of life—food, clothing, and fuel—to the hundreds and thousands who could not find work. Like the rest of the country, the citizens of Lowell somehow survived the Great Depression of the 1930s and were employed again in the general mobilization of World War II.

The city's past economic history is once again being re-enacted in the recession of the mid-1970s, although in this latest economic crisis the single remaining newspaper, the *Lowell Sun,* is less wedded to the tradition of ignoring the obvious. From 11 to 15 percent of the city's population was unemployed in January, 1976 (as opposed to a nationwide figure of 8½ percent). Now, however, in contrast to the laissez faire policy of the late nineteenth and early twentieth centuries, the federal and state governments provide some financial support to the unemployed; that fact does not solve the problem of a sick economy, but it does enable people to survive without begging in the streets or having to prove themselves worthy of aid from private groups.

Whether the reasons were nepotism, emigration, mismanage-

C.I. Hood advertising puzzle. (Lowell Historical Society)

ment, depression, labor troubles or strikes, Lowell's decline continued.

The cotton hegemony started breaking up at the end of the nineteenth century. The Lowell Manufacturing Company early turned from weaving cotton cloth to producing carpets, and in 1899 merged with the Bigelow Carpet Company. In 1896, the Lawrence Company converted to knitting. In 1912, the Lowell Machine Shop merged into the Saco-Lowell Company. Between 1912 and 1918, the Middlesex Company ceased production, and the Bigelow Carpet Company left the city. In 1926, due to vast management and financial problems, the Hamilton Company went into receivership.

The next five years were critical. The Suffolk mill was sold to the Nashua Manufacturing Company and then closed in 1936. The Tremont mills were bought by the Merrimack and torn down. The huge Massachusetts Company plant was sold to Pepperell Manufacturing Company, which shortly afterwards discontinued production. The Appleton Company moved to Anderson, South Carolina, and the Ipswich Mills (which had taken over the Middlesex Company plant) sold out. The Saco-Lowell shops moved to Maine and the plant was razed. The Lowell Bleachery closed in 1930. Even the smaller companies followed the pattern. The Faulkner mills closed in 1927, the Belvidere Woolen Company in 1929, and the Stirling mills in 1940.

By 1940, only three of the original Big Eleven textile mills were still in operation: the Merrimack (reorganized in 1952; closed and razed a few years later); the Boott (closed in 1956 but still standing as mill space for several smaller companies); and the Lawrence (taken over by Ames Textile Company and still operating on a reduced basis.)

As the textile industry began its decline, there appeared on the scene another industry which, for a time, again sent Lowell's name and products around the world. The patent medicine industry, although it employed far fewer workers, rivalled the textile industry in activity and profits and surpassed it in volume of advertising. The two giants locally were J. C. Ayer & Company and C. I. Hood & Company.

James C. Ayer was born in Ledyard, Connecticut in 1818. Having lost his father at an early age, he was sent by his mother in 1835 to live with her brother, James Cook, agent of the Middlesex Company and later mayor of Lowell. After working in

Jacob Robbins' apothecary, young Ayer bought it in 1841. This drugstore was the seed from which J. C. Ayer & Company grew. The firm established a huge complex of buildings for its laboratory, pill-making, and printing operations. Ayer personally invented most of the machinery for the company, including such diverse items as pill-making and paper-folding machines.

In 1852, Ayer started publishing annually Ayer's *American Almanac*, a series which continued until after the first World War. In time it was published in ten languages and thirty national editions; some fifteen million copies were printed each year in the company's own print shop. Besides the standard almanac fare of calendars, dates of noteworthy past events, and phases of the moon, Ayer's almanacs contained an equal amount of advertising and testimonials for Cherry Pectoral and other Ayer nostrums. One Henry A. Alford, of Weratah, Tasmania, wrote: "Six bottles of Ayer's Sarsaparilla cured me of a very badly ulcerated leg." The same issue gave the same preparation credit for curing a bad case of syphilis.

Ayer's flamboyance contrasted strongly with the conservative, inbred management of the textile mills, in which Ayer was a substantial stockholder. After the collapse, in 1857, of the Middlesex Company and the Bay State Mills, Ayer took up the crusade against corrupt management of the mills which, he said, was stealing from both the stockholders and the workers. Besides exposing the fraudulent practices in his monograph *Usages and Abuses*, he lobbied for the passage of laws to permit stockholders to examine lists of the holders of their corporation's stock; to restrict the giving of proxies; and to permit the formation of corporations without the necessity of going to the legislature.

Refusing to pay the freight bills demanded by the monopolistic Boston & Lowell Railroad, Ayer formed a competing road, the Lowell & Andover, which connected with the Boston & Maine Railroad and provided an alternative route to Boston.

In 1874, Ayer was an unsuccessful Republican candidate for Congress, having been nominated while on a lengthy European tour. As a result of his gifts of ornate boxes of Cherry Pectoral sent to foreign sovereigns, his fame was such that he was invited by the Czar of Russia to a naval review and to the wedding of one of the imperial princes. Besides this invitation, Ayer's public relations gesture earned him unsolicited endorsements from

Neschid El Hassan, Pasha of Trebizond* and the Emperor of the Ming Dynasty in China.

An amateur poet, classical scholar, and linguist, Ayer also displayed wit in his practical jokes. When he donated a bell for the new carillon of St. Anne's Church, he at first suggested that it be cast with the inscribed words: "Cherry Pectoral and Cathartic Pills."

His philanthropic donations to the city of the statue of Victory in front of the City Hall, and to many charitable institutions are outstanding. His home, the former Stone Tavern, became the Ayer Home for Children, which he endowed. His generosity to the town of Ayer resulted in—or from—the naming of the town in his honor. He died in 1878, widely known and mourned.†

In the depths of the depression, in 1931, *Harper's Monthly Magazine* published an article by Louis Adamic on the "Tragic Towns of New England," describing Lowell, among several towns in Massachusetts, as a depressed industrial desert populated by a beaten, discouraged, and hungry people. Although the article was sympathetic and did not attempt to place blame for conditions, it was bitterly attacked in the press by the Chamber of Commerce, which maintained that conditions were not as desperate as Adamic had depicted them.

One looks in vain in the inaugural addresses of the mayors in the late 1920s for any recognition of the problem of the vanishing textile industry, let alone recommendations for improving the situation. Finally, in 1949, a special legislative commission was set up to study the textile industry and make recommendations to prevent its removal from the Commonwealth. In 1950, the commission made its report. It found that the differential between North and South in wages and worker productivity was the chief cause of industry moving south; that manufacturers (unjustly, in its opinion) considered taxes in Massachusetts excessive, and that the social legislation in this Commonwealth had indeed placed Massachusetts manufacturers at a competitive disadvantage. The only recommended legislation, however, was a bill to

*"As the life of my people is dearer than camels and gold, we shall pray for you in our heart when they are raised up from the tent of sorrow by this product of your deep learning and beautiful wisdom. . . . "

†But not by all. William S. Robinson ("Warrington") had written of him during his congressional campaign: "He probably slew more rebels, real or incipient . . . than General Grant in all of his [campaigns] . . . I suppose the real trouble has been the indiscriminate character of his slaughterings. For every Southern stomach disarranged, a Northern kidney has been 'devilled.'"

permit the employment of women and children for eight continuous hours.

The situation in Lowell was not unique. It was striking, however, because of the former predominence of the textile industry, and because there was no secondary industry to rely on. Gradually, especially during the second World War, electronics firms began to develop locally and came to be the area's prime industry. At present, only three major plants in the city are still engaged in the weaving of cloth—the Ames Textile Corporation, (parent of the Lawrence Manufacturing Company), the Wannalancit Textile Company (in the old Suffolk mill), and Joan Fabrics Corporation (which occupies the former Massachusetts Mohair Plush Company plant). The textile industry in Lowell indeed has changed in one hundred and fifty years.

Part Three

XI

The Mills and The Multitudes: A Political History

By Mary H. Blewett

The founders of Lowell organized and built the mill system with little initial attention to politics or town government. Indeed the village of East Chelmsford where the mills were built was governed and taxed by the town of Chelmsford for four years before Lowell became a separate town in 1826. Once involved in political matters, however, the Lowell mill interests exercised a profound influence on town and city politics.

In November, 1824, the Merrimack Manufacturing Company organized a committee to prepare a petition to the state legislature for the incorporation of the area as a town. East Chelmsford had grown in population from two hundred in 1820 to twenty-five hundred in 1826, and the mill management wished to exert more control over local taxation and school policy. It was unacceptable to them to have the property which they managed subject to taxation by a rural town government miles away which did not represent their interests.

The only disagreement concerning the proposed new town was what to call it. The area was at one time known as Wamesit Neck, a name apparently favored by the old residents of the East Chelmsford farms from which Lowell was being formed. Kirk Boott, the imperious agent of the Merrimack Company and the Locks & Canals, had attempted to organize the town to resemble

in many ways the English country life he idealized. He wanted
the name of Derby. According to Nathan Appleton's account,
Derby was an English country town with which the Boott family
had fond associations. Boott, who was in charge of the petition to
the legislature, dismissed Wamesit and narrowed the choice to
Derby or Lowell. The name Lowell commemorated Francis
Cabot Lowell, the founder of the textile mill system developed
in Waltham and then under construction in East Chelmsford.
Meeting Appleton by chance in the State House in early 1826,
Boott bowed to the influence of the Boston capitalists and accepted Appleton's suggestion of "then Lowell by all means."
The legislature granted a town charter with provisions to settle
debts and taxes owed to Chelmsford. The warrant to call town
elections was issued to Kirk Boott as the leader of the town
charter movement by Joseph Locke, justice of the peace (appointed the first police court judge in 1833). Boott quickly called
the first town meeting five days later on March 6, 1826, at the
Stone House, a convenient tavern and meeting place near Pawtucket Falls. As moderator, Boott presided over the election of
three selectmen and one representative to the state legislature.
There was great interest in the choices and "quite a little
demonstration." Two of the men elected were old settlers,
lawyer Nathaniel Wright, who was also elected state representative, and Oliver Whipple whose business interests pre-dated the
mills. Only the third, Samuel Batchelder, directly represented
the mill interests, specifically the Hamilton Company. Both the
town clerk and the treasurer were tradesmen and old settlers. It
was clear immediately that the major issue of local politics in the
new town was to be a struggle between the old residents and the
new mill interests.

In 1826 the town also elected a five-man school committee
which presided over six school districts including three former
village schools and two which the corporations had provided for
the use of their workers. The school committee was led by Reverend Theodore Edson, the tough-minded Episcopal minister
whom Boott had personally imported from Boston to conduct
services for the Merrimack's employees. Ultimately, the Merrimack Company furnished Edson a stone church called St.
Anne's and a parsonage. Edson and the committee quickly alienated the old settlers' element by forcibly adopting modern school
textbooks. In order to gain more control over the decentralized
school system, Edson and the committee decided to consolidate
the schools by building two large schools and introducing grades

to the old ungraded system. This policy required twenty thousand dollars of new tax money and the chief representative of mill property in the town and Edson's benefactor, Mr. Boott, was adamantly opposed to the idea. No one on the school committee but Edson would face Boott's opposition in a town meeting. Edson was warned by Boott that if he continued to advocate the building policy he would lose Boott's patronage at St. Anne's—parsonage and all.

At the September 3, 1832, town meeting, the new school policy was debated and sustained by the assembled citizens. Edson's courage in publicly facing Boott's opposition won the committee a close twelve-vote majority. Boott then arranged to call another town meeting on September 19 to try to get a reversal. Two high-powered corporation lawyers, John P. Robinson and Luther Lawrence, argued Boott's position against Edson. The vote on the question gave Edson a thirty-eight vote majority in an obvious reaction against Boott's pressure tactics. Outraged, Boott withdrew from St. Anne's church, and subsequently the Merrimack Corporation evicted Edson from his parsonage, precipitating a law suit. The church membership eventually settled by purchasing both church and parsonage, but it was not until 1866 that Edson moved back to the parsonage. Edson's opposition to corporation influence in municipal affairs made him a hero to the old residents.

As the town's population continued to grow rapidly, corporation lawyers such as Robinson and Lawrence appeared frequently as selectmen and representatives to the legislature from Lowell alongside representatives of the old settlers and small businessmen. Boott himself served four terms as state representative, the number of which reached thirteen from the town in 1835. These lawyers represented the mills not only in the General Court but also in the law courts in such important cases as the Melvin ("Paddy Camp" lands) suits which threatened the Locks & Canals property holdings in the "Acre" section of the town center. The Locks & Canals had apparently neglected to buy out all of the heirs of the Fletchers—one of the old farming families of East Chelmsford. Multiple suits were brought by the heirs, the Melvins, to recover what was by then extremely valuable property. According to historian Charles Cowley, when the state Supreme Judicial Court sustained the Locks & Canals position, local opinion never ran more strongly against the corporations.

Similar conflicts also occurred over the annexation of Belvidere from Tewksbury to Lowell in 1834, a move which Boott
strongly opposed because of the allegedly lawless nature of the
residents of Belvidere. For six years the residents of Belvidere
had worked for annexation; they had close business and social
ties to Lowell but were taxed and represented by Tewksbury
Center, some miles distant. Tewksbury valued the area for its tax
yield and resisted the annexation plan. The Belvidere people,
including the Nesmiths, Rogers, Hedricks, and Wymans, chose
to make themselves such a nuisance at the Tewksbury town
meetings that the town would be glad to get rid of them. Gangs of
boisterous men from Belvidere would descend on Tewksbury at
town-meeting time, drink rum flips at Brown's Tavern, and pro-
ceed to disrupt the day-long meeting. On one occasion they
assembled enough votes to schedule the next town meeting in
Belvidere, and Tewksbury gave them up.

The corporation representatives also opposed the local expression of anti-slavery sentiments originating from the Varnum family of Dracut and encouraged in Lowell in 1834 by two Varnum
brothers who were church deacons. A group of lawyers including
John P. Robinson met to prevent the use of the town hall for
anti-slavery meetings. They had no interest in inflaming the
question which could jeopardize the mills' supply of raw cotton.
The meetings were held in friendly churches in Lowell, but they
faced organized and violent mob attacks.

By the mid 1830s the mill interests in Lowell found that the
town meeting system of government with its annual appropriations voted by a majority of those present was uncontrollable and
unresponsive to their needs. The town meeting also seemed too
cumbersome a way to handle the complex problems of the area,
the population of which continued to soar. In 1835 ten long
meetings, held at the town hall, were required to handle the
town's business. The same year, public discussion of a city charter began. At the February 17, 1836, town meeting a city charter
committee chaired by corporation lawyer Luther Lawrence reported after two weeks' deliberations that a city charter was
essential to order and progress. The report cited the principal
defects of the town system to be "the want of executive power,
and the loose and irresponsible manner in which money for
municipal purposes is granted and expended." These concerns,
of course, were primarily of interest to the mill owners.

A city charter was drafted by the same committee on which

Old City Hall building, 1830. From an advertising card. (Lowell Historical Society)

were represented corporation interests as well as old resident interests, Whigs as well as Democrats. Because of the fairly equal division of party strength locally between Democrats and Whigs and the strength of the old residents' vote, a consensus was necessary. On April 1, 1836, the legislature granted a city charter—the third in the Commonwealth*—and the voters assembled at the last town meeting on April 11 to vote three to one (961 to 328) to approve it.† The charter established an elected mayor, a Board of Aldermen of six members, and a Common Council of twenty-four members: four from each of the six wards. Decisions on city policies made by the mayor with the consent of the two legislative bodies were confirmed by the voters in annual elections of officials.

The election of the first mayor of the city in 1836 was a close and hotly contested race. Editor of the Jacksonian Democratic newspaper, *The Advertiser*, and postmaster of Lowell, Eliphalet Case ran not only his own campaign for mayor in the spring of 1836 but also headed the local Martin Van Buren campaign for president in the fall. The Whig candidate, Dr. Elisha Bartlett, was neither a partisan politician nor a robust campaigner as he suffered from consumption. Bartlett's sympathies were known to be with the corporations, but he was a respected local figure and was not directly their candidate. However, he had cooperated with their opposition to anti-slavery meetings, and in 1841 physician Bartlett would publish a strong defense of the treatment of the mill girls by the corporations, especially the influence of the work on their health. The city had not had time to divide into wards, and the 1836 city elections were held at the town hall in the form of a town meeting. Bartlett won a close victory over Case, 958 to 868, but in the November elections the new city voted for Democrat Marcus Morton for governor and for Democrat Van Buren against the redoubtable Daniel Webster. This series of elections in 1836 represented a high point of Democratic strength in local elections. No Democrat was elected mayor in the city until the exceedingly close race of 1848 and none after that until 1877. The Whig party controlled the mayor's chair until the disintegration of the party in the crisis that led to the Civil War.

The new city government gradually expanded its activities to

---

*Boston (1822) and Salem (March 23, 1836).

†The total vote cast was 1289, presumably the total number of those who attended the last town meeting. This represents about nine percent of the total population of sixteen thousand in 1836.

reflect the growing size and requirements of its population. In 1844, the city began to pave streets at public expense. Two commons, North and South, were purchased and laid out in 1845. To discourage the public use of contaminated water drawn from the canals and from wells close to unsanitary drains and sinks, the city, after a long discussion of alternatives, began in 1855 to distribute river water untreated through a water works system. It was widely believed that the river water, although contaminated by upstream cities, purified itself as it flowed downstream. Filtration was adopted in 1870, but recurrent outbreaks of typhoid remained a serious problem.

The growth in economic importance of the city was also reflected in the prominent position which Lowell attained in Middlesex County prior to the Civil War. A red-brick courthouse topped by a graceful cupola was built on Gorham Street in the Chapel Hill section, centralizing the legal affairs of northern Middlesex County in Lowell. A registry of deeds for the Northern District of Middlesex County opened in 1855. A quite remarkable and controversial county jail built of granite with startling twin towers and separate facilities for men and women prisoners, designed by James H. Rand, a Lowell architect, was constructed facing the South Common in 1858. Historian Charles Cowley stated the timeless objections of generations of taxpayers against generations of county commissioners when he wrote in 1868, "To squander money thus approaches very nearly a crime."

The conservative tone of Lowell politics on the national level was set prior to 1826 and endured. Chelmsford was a traditional Federalist stronghold, and by the 1820s the old residents who had developed small mills and canals on the Merrimack and Concord rivers supported the Whig Party and its policies to develop industry and transportation. The mill interests established after 1822 were strongly Whiggish, largely because of the Whig position on the protective tariff. Francis Cabot Lowell was personally responsible for the 6¼¢ minimum tariff on each square yard of imported cotton fabric written into the tariff act of 1816. Tariff protection was a cardinal principle of Whig Edward Everett of Cambridge, the congressman who represented the Lowell district in the 1820s and who carried all twenty-two votes in the town's first congressional election. This concern to protect cotton textile manufacturers from foreign competition plus the local animus against anti-slavery discussions subsequently branded the dominant political group in

Lowell as Cotton Whigs. The split in the Whig Party between Conscience or Anti-Slavery Whigs and Cotton Whigs wrecked the party in the 1850s and led to the development of Republican power in Lowell as well as throughout the state.

The voters of Lowell continued to support Whig congressmen after the census of 1830 determined that the Middlesex Congressional district had enough population to split it north and south. After the reorganization of the district in 1832, Democrat Gayton P. Osgood of Andover represented the district for one term, followed by a succession of Whigs. These congressmen, however, resided not in Lowell but in outlying towns in the district. The election of 1852 finally produced a Lowell Whig, Tappan Wentworth, who was replaced in the next election by Whig journalist and abolitionist Chauncey L. Knapp of Lowell who served until the Civil War.

Whig strength was also reflected in presidential elections. Until 1892 no Democratic presidential candidate carried Lowell except Martin Van Buren in 1836, and Van Buren won by only sixteen votes. The Whigs and later the Republicans carried the city with comfortable margins, and no third party effort won more than a few hundred votes, usually away from the Democrats.

The dominant position of the Whigs in local and national party politics seemed unshakeable in Lowell prior to the Civil War. However, the growing Irish Catholic population in the city offered the Democrats a new base of power. Irish workers had done the backbreaking work of digging canals and laying foundations in the 1820s, and they were followed in the 1840s by hundreds of desperate refugees from the potato famines in Ireland. Under the leadership of a shrewd politician and reformer, Benjamin F. Butler, the Lowell Democratic party organized the Irish into a strong block of support. Until the Northern Democrats were traumatized by the Confederate secession, the local Democrats under Butler made significant political gains. After spending the Civil War and Reconstruction as a Radical Republican, Butler continued to build and strengthen the Democratic party in Lowell and to promote the cause of reform in Massachusetts.

While the mill work force consisted largely of women drawn from New England farms, there was no chance of labor politics in Lowell. Not only were the women under the control of the corporations, they could not vote. Their only means of political expression was to petition the state legislature or strike. Neither of these tactics developed among the female operatives until the late 1840s; by that time the mills could look to the Irish as a more tractable group of workers. As a lawyer and politician, Butler associated himself closely with both groups of mill workers and voiced their demands for a ten-hour day, women's suffrage, and the right to organize unions.

Butler came from a family of Jeffersonian Democrats settled in the intensely Federalist town of Deerfield, New Hampshire. His father was a stubborn maverick and an adventurer, characteristics which helped form Butler's politics. When Benjamin was six months old, his father died while operating as a privateer in the Caribbean for Simón Bolívar, the revolutionary hero of South America. As a boy Butler was raised by his arrogant and robust grandmother, but his mother accepted a position as a housekeeper of a Middlesex Corporation boardinghouse in 1828 and her son followed her to Lowell. Upon graduation from Colby College and after some indecision, he chose to read law in a Lowell firm instead of studying for the ministry. All this time he was living with his mother in the boardinghouse and teaching school in Dracut. His earliest clients were mill workers with grievances against the corporations. Most lawyers in Lowell refused to take their cases. Butler also made himself an expert on a new state bankruptcy law passed after the 1837 depression. Bankruptcy cases brought him closely in touch with debtors in the city. He also specialized in police-court cases and came to dislike heartily the police court judge, Nathan Crosby, and his methods. A high percentage of favorable verdicts brought him public attention and financial security.

Butler also went into Democratic politics in the city, joining forces with Fisher Ames Hildreth of Dracut and later marrying into the family. In 1844 Butler was a delegate to the Democratic national convention and campaigned locally for James K. Polk. He pointedly associated the local Democratic party with the interests of the mill workers. Two of the reforms he fought for throughout his career spoke directly to these interests: the secret ballot to protect workers from manipulation at election time* and the ten-hour day. Workers in the textile factories in the 1840s worked a fourteen-hour day, six-day week, and the corporations were unwilling to make any reduction in hours or to accept any legislation on working hours. Butler's advocacy of the ten-hour

*The owners' influence was made clear by placards on the outside gates of the Hamilton Corporation reading, "Whoever employed by this corporation votes the Ben Butler ten-hour reform ticket on Monday next, will be discharged."

day earned him the detestation of the industrial interests of Massachusetts and their allies.*

Not only an advocate of reform, Butler knew the necessity of organizing political power to bring about change. He quickly understood that the Whig party could be split in Massachusetts on the Free Soil issue—opposition to the expansion of slavery into additional western states. In 1849, he helped create a winning state-wide coalition between Democrats and Free Soil Whigs. The coalition platform contained the ten-hour day, the secret ballot, popular election of judges, reform of the bankruptcy laws, and a reduction of the poll tax. The coalition elected the governor and in 1850 won control of the state legislature which elected Charles Sumner a United States senator.

As a Democratic state representative from Lowell in 1852, Butler lobbied for a ten-hour law and also caused much excitement when he unsuccessfully sought state funds to rebuild the Ursuline convent in Charlestown which had been burned to the ground by an anti-Catholic mob in 1833. He was the hero of Irish Catholics in Lowell. As a grudging tribute to his efforts on the ten-hour bill in the legislature, the mills in Lowell voluntarily reduced the work schedule from fourteen to eleven hours a day in September 1853 in an effort to kill the ten-hour movement and undercut Butler's political support. When, in 1858, Butler bought a controlling interest in the Middlesex Corporation, a woolen mill on the Concord River, he adopted the ten-hour day plus overtime to vindicate his position and irritate his opponents.†

Early in his legal career Butler had joined the Lowell City Guard, a company of the Massachusetts Volunteer Militia. Rank was conferred largely by popular election, and Butler was quickly promoted to colonel. When the Know-Nothing party was at the height of its political power in the mid-1850s, Butler tangled with the rabidly anti-Catholic, anti-foreign group over the issue of his own Lowell company of Irish militia known as the Jackson Musketeers.‡ In 1854, the Know-Nothing governor, Henry J. Gardner, disarmed and disbanded the militia group and discharged Butler. Quietly, using the election procedure of the state militia, Butler, to Gardner's great dismay, had himself promoted to brigadier-general. Lowell itself voted overwhelmingly

*It is astonishing how long the frenzied attacks of his opponents were believed and how long their version of his career besmirched his historical reputation.

†Legislation on the ten-hour day was enacted in 1874 after the organization of a state-wide Labor Reform party.

‡This militia company later served in the Civil War as the Hill Cadets.

for a Know-Nothing mayor, dentist Ambrose Lawrence, in 1854. Mayor Lawrence promoted a series of outrageous investigations of the Notre Dame convent school by groups of Protestant vigilantes.* This persecution of Catholics by Yankee Protestants in Lowell bound the Irish more closely to Butler's Democrats. The Civil War, however, extinguished the Democrats as an active political force and destroyed the local party newspaper, *The Advertiser*. Lowell was a one-party Republican city throughout the war years and even Butler served as a Republican congressman during Reconstruction.

In 1866 Butler was elected as a Republican congressman from the Essex district (where he had a summer home) on the issue of impeaching President Andrew Johnson. He played a leading role in the indictment proceedings in the House and was one of the managers of the impeachment in the Senate. When Thaddeus Stevens' illness prevented his active participation, Butler led the battle. After impeachment failed by one vote, Butler quickly turned to other issues that concerned the common people and reform. One of these issues, the greenback controversy, led to his nomination as President in 1884.† The greenback issue concerned the paper money (not backed by gold) issued by the Lincoln administration during the Civil War to finance government operations. To withdraw these greenbacks from circulation after the war, as banks and bondholders insisted, would restore the dollar to the gold standard. To do so would also enrich the holders of government bonds purchased with paper money and the creditors who had lent in paper money. To withdraw the greenbacks also was to risk a severe economic contraction, a scarcity of money, and high interest rates. Butler could see no good in it. Indeed the economy of the post-Civil War period required a different, expansionist policy. The economic issue symbolized by the paper greenback continued to convulse national politics until it was decisively defeated in the election of 1896.

---

*From the Massachusetts Legislature came one Joseph Hiss and his infamous "Smelling Committee." While in Lowell, Hiss made the acquaintance of a Mrs. Moody, alias "Mrs. Patterson," with whom he passed the night at the Washington House. The Smelling Committee was discredited and Hiss was subsequently expelled from the Legislature by his embarrassed colleagues.

†Butler received the nomination of the Greenback-Labor party and the Anti-Monopoly party in 1884, but he vigorously sought the Democratic nomination with the backing of Tammany Hall of New York City. The Democrats nominated Grover Cleveland, and Butler won only 843 votes in Lowell as a third-party candidate.

WARD ONE.

DEMOCRATIC

REGULAR TICKET.

FOR GOVERNOR,
BENJAMIN F. BUTLER, of Lowell

FOR LIEUTENANT-GOVERNOR,
JAMES S. GRINNELL, of Greenfield

FOR SECRETARY OF STATE,
CHARLES MARSH, of Springfield

FOR TREASURER AND RECEIVER-GENERAL,
CHARLES H. INGALLS, of North Adams

FOR AUDITOR,
JOHN HOPKINS, of Millbury

FOR ATTORNEY-GENERAL,
JOHN W. CUMMINGS, of Fall River

FOR COUNCILLOR, 6th DISTRICT,
CHARLES S. LILLEY, of Lowell

FOR DISTRICT-ATTORNEY,
SAMUEL K. HAMILTON, of Wakefield

FOR COUNTY COMMISSIONER,
LEWIS P. TRUE, of Everett

FOR SPECIAL COMMISSIONERS,
SAMUEL STAPLES, of Concord
SYLVANUS POND, of Holliston

FOR COMMISSIONERS OF INSOLVENCY,
EDWARD B. QUINN, of Lowell
JOHN H. PONCE, of Cambridge
CLEMENT MESERVE, of Hopkinton

FOR SHERIFF,
HENRY G. CUSHING, of Lowell

FOR REGISTER OF PROBATE AND INSOLVENCY,
JOSEPH H. TYLER, of Winchester

FOR SENATOR, 7th MIDDLESEX DISTRICT,
JOHN H. MORRISON, of Lowell

FOR REPRESENTATIVE, 20th DISTRICT,
DENNIS J. CROWLEY, of Lowell

Democratic ballot for the 1883 state election when Governor Butler was defeated for re-election. Courtesy of Allen Gerson.

"The Cradle of Liberty in Danger." Anti-Butler cartoon by Thomas Nast. *Harper's Weekly*, April 11, 1874. (Lowell Historical Society)

Butler was defeated in 1874 in the Essex district but a group of
Lowell Republicans offered him the nomination for Congress
from the Middlesex district in 1876. Butler's candidacy and election created much tension within the local Republican Party;
therefore he did not run for another term in 1878. Overall his
congressional record (1867-75 and 1877-79) is admirable in an
era known for corrupt politics and chicanery. He supported a
federal department of education to establish national standards,
civil rights legislation for Negroes, women's suffrage, and an
income tax on investments. His vigor in debate on the House
floor produced a durable rallying cry for Republicans—the
bloody shirt. He punctuated a speech on a civil rights bill by
waving a nightshirt which he said had been taken from the back
of a white schoolteacher in a Negro school who had been flogged
by the Ku Klux Klan. Waving the bloody shirt to summon Civil
War memories was a device to galvanize the Republican faithful
down to the 1890s.

In 1882, after six campaigns, first as a Republican and then as a
Democrat, Butler became governor of Massachusetts while shiv-
ers of fear ran through State Street, Harvard Yard, and Back Bay.
Conservative Republicans had prevented him from gaining the
nomination as one of them, so Butler rebuilt his organization in
the state Democratic party. The legislature elected in 1882, however, was strongly Republican and blocked Butler's reforms. The
major controversy during his one term as governor was the grisly
investigation of the Tewksbury almshouse which had a ninety
percent infant mortality rate and which did a brisk business in
the cadavers of paupers with the Harvard Medical School.*

In the 1882 elections in Lowell the Democratic party's re-
surgence under Butler produced the first Irish Catholic mayor,
John J. Donovan.† Donovan was a successful businessman and
banker who lived in the fashionable Highlands area. His administration added buildings to the City Poor Farm, built schools
and bridges, and made the public library free to all citizens. In
1886 when Donovan ran for Congress, he scared the Republicans
by cutting their usual majority in congressional elections from
three thousand to four hundred votes. In 1888 he was chairman
of the Democratic state convention. Donovan's backers were the
same coalition which Butler put together: Yankee reformers and

*Harvard overturned a long-standing tradition by denying Butler an honorary
degree as governor.

†In 1882 Butler carried Lowell by a 1500-vote majority; Donovan beat his
opponent by 450 votes.

Irish voters. Their success pointed toward the major shift in political allegiance in the city away from Republicans and corporation interests toward the Democrats and ethnic and labor politics.

The number of foreign-born people in the city's population increased swiftly in the late nineteenth century. After the Civil War, French-Canadians, largely from Quebec province, came to be mill workers. In the 1890s Greeks, Poles, and Portuguese appeared in increasing numbers and established colonies in the city. The federal census of 1900 counted only twenty percent of the 100,000 population as native-born of native parents. The other eighty percent were Irish, French-Canadians or people of southern and eastern European origin. At the turn of the century ethnic groups far outnumbered the natives, but relatively few had become citizens, and only the Irish were politically organized. In addition to the efforts of Mayor Donovan and others in building a Democratic organization, the Irish established in 1889 a local trade council which would speak for the interests of the American Federation of Labor unions of building trade workers, leather workers, bottlers, and spinners. The trade council quickly became a Democratic force in local politics.

Beginning in the 1890s the Democratic party began to win consistently in local elections. One reason was a serious disruption of the Republicans over the anti-Catholic, anti-immigrant activities of the Lowell chapter of the American Protective Association. The Republican involvement with the APA disturbed a political alliance between the Yankee Republicans and the French-Canadians. The French had developed a middle class group of spokesmen, a community newspaper, *L'Etoile*, and usually voted Republican because of Irish influence in the Democratic party. The French also deeply resented Irish control of local Catholic affairs and had established separate, French language, Catholic churches in the city. A conservative Democrat of native background, William F. Courtney, attracted French voters alienated over the APA issue in 1894 and held them through his skillful use of patronage and his marriage during his second term as mayor in 1896 to Alice Brouilette, the daughter of a prominent French family. Courtney served three terms as mayor. It was becoming clear that the French community held the balance of power in municipal elections.

The city's ward lines had been redrawn in 1894 to create an odd number of wards (nine instead of six) to prevent deadlocked

votes in the Common Council. Irish Democrats controlled three
wards, Republicans controlled four, and the French held two.
. This arrangement further increased the importance of the
French-Canadian vote which by 1897 the Republicans had successfully recaptured. This pattern of both parties wooing the
French vote continued until the city charter change of 1911.
Meanwhile there was increasing evidence of local interest to
reform the structure of city government—a change which would
abolish ward-based representation and concentrate power in the
hands of a small number of representatives elected at-large. Support for this municipal reform movement came from dissatisfied
middle class Republicans, Yankee and French. Regular Republicans opposed and feared the reform movement at first because
the reformers had their own candidates and seemed uncontrollable. The effect was to divide Republicans and help Democrats
in the 1900 and 1901 elections.

Republicans, however, had one sure-fire issue to use against
the Democrats—temperance. Liquor licenses were issued and
liquor laws enforced by the politically charged Board of Police
appointed by the mayor. The political connections between the
liquor retailers, the members of the Board of Police and the
Harvard Brewery of Lowell were well known and involved
favors and campaign funds. The issue of corruption in liquor law
enforcement was highlighted by a series of raids on violators of
the Sunday laws led personally by the Republican mayor, William Badger, in 1902, and later by the Law and Order League, a
group of temperance-minded Protestant clergy. The targets were
Irish-owned hotels which alone had the privilege of serving
liquor on Sundays, provided it was accompanied by food.* Republicans used the temperance issue with success in 1902 but
the Democrats won control of the Board of Aldermen, a source of
future political talent.

After 1902 a new group of Democratic leaders emerged to set a
new tone and a new political style for the party. The old Yankee
leaders like Courtney disappeared from party councils, and new
men, James B. Casey and John F. Meehan, took over. Casey and
Meehan were rank-and-file Irish politicians who depended on
heavy votes from the Democratic wards. Both men, however,
were able to attract sizeable votes in the French wards (Six and
Seven) to deprive the Republicans of their alliance. Not only did

---

*There is a local legend about one dried-out sandwich that travelled from table
to table in observance of the Sunday law.

Casey and Meehan take care of most of the patronage demands of the French, but they openly courted French votes. Casey became mayor in 1904 and 1905 but was defeated in 1906 and 1908 by a split in the party over his use of the police board to obtain campaign funds. This raised the temperance issue once more to the benefit of the Republicans.

Casey's successor as Democratic mayor, John Meehan, did not repeat his predecessor's mistakes. Meehan was the ablest politician in the Democratic party since Butler and Donovan. He quickly reunified the party and deftly avoided the liquor-law issue. In two years the Republicans believed their party was finished as a force in municipal politics. Meehan was aided in his organizational work by another upcoming young Democrat, James E. O'Donnell, Jr.

Born in Lowell in 1875, Meehan resided in Ward Two in the city center, and worked as an accountant for a construction company. He was principal of the Butler Night School where mill workers could learn to read and write. In 1906, he served the first of three terms as state representative. Meehan won a primary fight with O'Donnell for the mayoral nomination in 1909 with a strong vote from the workingclass French sixth ward. In the election campaign he worked hard to reunite the party, concentrating on the other French ward. So large was his vote for mayor in 1909 that the *Courier-Citizen,* the Republican daily, mourned that the city would never again see another Republican mayor. In 1910, Meehan repeated his success with a landslide victory, demonstrating the durability of the Democratic coalition with the French voters, especially those in Ward Six. The Democrats had reserved two places on their aldermantic ticket for French-Canadians, Joseph Jodoin, and Hercule Toupin, who carried most of the 1882 registered Republican votes in the French wards. The Board of Aldermen went nine to zero Democratic, Democrat Edward Foye became purchasing agent, and the Democrats on the Common Council in combination with the aldermen controlled all city appointments.

The crushing defeat in 1910 convinced the Republican leadership that their party was in shambles, and they moved to revive interest in municipal reform. The immediate motive was to prevent the Democrats from becoming the only viable political force in the city by changing the rules of the political game. Long term dissatisfaction with growing city indebtedness and rising taxes, the liquor scandals, and the takeover of city jobs by Democrats provided wide support for a municipal reform movement, organized and directed in 1911 by a group of lawyers in the Lowell Board of Trade.

The Board of Trade proposed a new city charter in 1911. A four-member commission and mayor elected at-large would conduct the affairs of the city much as a board of directors conducted the affairs of a corporation, an analogy which the reformers emphasized. Each commissioner would be responsible for the operations and finances of a separate city department. Wards would be abolished as representative units; political party designations would end. Elections would be non-partisan and city-wide. The School Committee was to be elected at-large, again eliminating a representative from each ward. Recall, referendum, and initiative procedures would replace annual elections but beginning the process required the signatures of twenty percent of the voters. The liquor licensing and enforcement functions of the police board would be separated.

The proposed charter struck deeply at the power of the Democrats in the city. The ward system was the foundation of Democratic representation on the Common Council, the School Committee, and in the state legislative districts. The dual functions of the police board provided campaign funds. Meehan and the Democrats saw the reform proposal as a direct assault on their strength and success as a party, and they struggled fiercely to defeat it. Hecklers at pro-charter rallies claimed the reform was anti-democratic elitism and a conspiracy of business interests against the working man. Meehan testified at the legislative hearings on the proposal in March, 1911, that the charter was backed by men who have "dinner" against men who have "supper." He described Lowell as a city which needed the ward system to represent its different neighborhoods and nationalities. Nonetheless, the Republican-controlled legislature voted approval, and the charter proposal came to a vote in Lowell in the November elections.

The strategy of the Democrats was to turn out a heavy vote against the charter based on the landslide vote of the preceding year. It became evident however that the French community would split on the charter issue; L'Etoile and middle class French lawyers, small businessmen, and doctors came out strongly for the charter change. Their spokesman, Dr. Joseph E. Lamoureux, argued in a column in L'Etoile called "Oui ou Non?" that the political influence of the French would increase with the new charter because the influence of the Irish, whose power lay in the wards, would decline. Meehan and the Democrats attempted to counter Lamoureux by taking political ads in French in *L'Etoile* to argue that the French risked the loss of all representation in the city government and on the school committee in non-partisan at-large elections.

The middle-class voter was the major target of the proponents of charter reform. The old system, they explained, was corrupt and expensive, directed by men who made politics a profession. The new city charter meant efficiency, reduced expenditures, lower taxes, and a more business-like conduct of city programs. Meehan and the Democrats worried about the impact of these arguments on middle class Irish voters. One major defection was James E. O'Donnell, Jr., who announced his neutrality on the charter question and his intention to run for mayor whichever system won in November.

O'Donnell was born in Lowell in 1875, the son of a well known undertaker in the Irish community. He attended Boston University Law School and was a typical middle class professional man, yet he had a political sense. O'Donnell saw that the middle class Irish vote would desert the party on charter reform in the election on November 7. The vote on the charter in the regular elections divided along class lines. The Yankee middle class wards voted heavily for the charter. The French wards split, as many had predicted, with the working class, "Little Canada" Ward Six voting against the charter, and the more affluent Ward Seven in Pawtucketville, across the river from the mills, voting for the charter. Traditionally Irish, Democratic, and working class wards Two, Four and Five voted heavily no; but wards Three and Eight in the Highlands, an area where middle class Irish families were moving away from the central city, and which voted Democratic on all other issues, provided the winning margin for the charter. The charter reform carried by a 1294-vote majority at the same time as Democratic Governor Eugene Foss carried the city by 2381 votes. The defection of middle class Irish votes was obvious; Meehan's work and hopes were smashed.

The primary to nominate candidates for mayor was a curious affair. Although formally non-partisan, everyone in the city knew that O'Donnell would be the Democratic candidate after he defeated primary opponents in the party too closely identified with Meehan and the old system. The Republicans, however, had a problem in the primary. None of the reformers were interested in interrupting their professional lives to take on the mayor's office. Dr. Lamoureux, for example, refused to disrupt his medical practice. The pro-charter groups decided to back Colonel Percy Parker, an ex-West Point officer and Indian fighter, who lived on his investments in banking, real estate, and trolley lines. His manner was stiff and condescending; his only political experience was on the Park Commission. Backed by the solid Republican vote, Parker won the nomination. Another major result of the primary vote was to eliminate all French-Canadian candidates for the commission or the School Committee; none would appear on the ballot.

O'Donnell concentrated on unifying the Democrats and winning the loyalty of Meehan's supporters. All of the old line Democrats knew that if they could elect three members of the commission, they would control the city government. O'Donnell's neutrality on the charter question enabled him to appeal to middle class Irish voters, and he relentlessly campaigned in the French wards, walking the streets and tracking down voters. In contrast, Parker merely allowed himself to be driven through the French neighborhoods in an expensive touring car, nodding occasionally to passersby.

On election day O'Donnell and the Democrats won control of the commission and the school committee, capturing the city government under the new charter. This decisive shift to Irish Democratic control reduced to insignificance all other political forces in the city. The Democratic wards delivered heavily for O'Donnell, who led the balloting, and for two other Irish Democrats, Lawrence Cummings and James E. Donnelly. Their three votes controlled the commission. All four Irish Democrats nominated in the primary were elected to the school committee with the only other place going to Yankee John Jacob Rogers. This was an historic and impressive reversal of control typifying the decline of Yankee power in municipal politics. One of the major factors in the school committee election was the massive registration of women voters under an 1870 state law which permitted women to vote in school elections. Organized mostly by Irish Democratic candidates for school committee, women registered by the hundreds. When each ward was guaranteed a representative on the school committee, their votes were not needed. In an at-large election they were vital. The day the books closed before the election, women voters had increased by 5435 or an increase of six hundred percent.

The Democrats in the city literally went wild over the election.

The vanguard of a cheering crowd of ten thousand led by a brass band unhitched the horses from O'Donnell's carriage and drew him through the streets of the business district. Red torches and roman candles lit up the scene until supplies in local shops were exhausted. The cheering became deafening in front of the *Lowell Sun* building in Merrimack Square. The *Sun*, owned by John H. Harrington, had endorsed Parker, and the crowd jeered. After many speeches and many ovations O'Donnell, bursting with satisfaction and joy at the returns, finished the celebration by singing several vaudeville tunes.

The Yankees were silent, the French deeply resentful. *L'Etoile* now saw that Mayor Meehan had been right:

> Now that the candidates are elected at-large how can the French or any minority group hope to hold the balance of power which was the only weapon we had. . . . We must say with bitterness that for the present the political influence of the French-Americans is finished under the new charter.

Charter reformers had organized in 1911 to prevent the Democrats under Meehan from enjoying a powerful coalition with the French. The result was to eliminate both Yankee and French influence in the city's political life and to deliver municipal politics into the hands of the Irish.

After 1911 the shift to Irish Democratic political strength in the city was capped by the adoption of a strong mayor, Plan B charter* in 1924 and by an astounding turnout in the 1928 elections. The key element was the presidential candidacy of Irish Catholic Al Smith of New York on the Democratic ticket against Republican Herbert Hoover. Local party workers, their relatives, and youngsters more than doubled the registration of Democratic voters in Lowell. This enormous new registration became the source of a new generation of Democratic leaders with a very large constituency in the city.

Smith and the Democrats, local and state, swept Lowell in the elections of 1928. Hoover carried only two of the city's wards, and Smith won the city by 10,000 votes. The election, in which an amazing 93.5 percent of the voters turned out, laid the basis for Franklin D. Roosevelt's victories in Lowell starting in 1932.

The city's Democratic party fared much less well during the years of the Depression and the New Deal. Many of the textile mills had departed en masse in the late twenties, and some of the mill owners decided to tear down the brick structures instead of paying property taxes on the buildings. The mills literally began

---

*Plan B is one of several standard charter forms provided by the General Laws of Massachusetts.

to disappear, while the value of the inner city property declined quickly. Falling tax revenues and general helplessness in the face of economic difficulties paralyzed the city government. Republican leadership, bent on economy, returned to city hall. Democrats on the council worked hard to get the unemployed on relief and on city work, partially financed by federal WPA money and partially by borrowing from the state. However in 1938 almost forty percent of the population of Lowell still received some kind of relief. The stagnant economy of the 1930s greatly increased the value of political jobs, which produced serious factionalism among the Irish Democrats. This factionalism reached a critical point during the early 1940s resulting in a change from the strong-mayor, Plan B government to the city manager-council government of Plan E.

In the 1939 elections former city laborer and state representative George T. Ashe got the backing of Democratic ex-mayor James J. Bruin to recover control of the mayor's office from the Republicans. Organization and money for rallies and radio speeches plus Ashe's image as a workingman's candidate helped him win easily against Republican warhorse Thomas H. Braden. The key issue of the campaign was Ashe's promise to cut both city spending and the tax rate, taking the economy issue from the Republicans. Cuts in city spending, however, struck at the political base of the local Democratic party which depended heavily on the bloc votes of city employees and on patronage for the unemployed. The new mayor quickly found himself in angry conflict with his own party's leaders. Furthermore, Ashe was unable to cut taxes sufficiently to please the Taxpayers' Association, and he therefore risked alienating the anti-tax forces which had backed him in 1939.

In an effort to regain the support of the Taxpayers' Association for another mayoral try in 1941, Ashe pushed a departmental merger plan to place all city employees under one head and thus eliminate all department heads. This, he argued, would increase efficiency and decrease expenditures. Enraged city employees hired Bruin as their attorney to fight the plan. The city council defeated the idea, but it was good politics for Ashe to advocate among economy minded voters.

Meanwhile the mayor moved to undercut Bruin's hold on city employees by supporting expansion in the Water Department and by using WPA funds to raise the salaries of city workers. Shut off from Bruin's sources of support in the local party, Ashe built his own campaign treasury and organization. In August, 1941, with employment rising from defense contracts in the area, the incumbent mayor could announce a $5.60 tax cut in time for the September Democratic primary against William C. Geary who was backed by Bruin. Ashe won narrowly and again faced Braden whom he defeated but by a much smaller margin than in 1939. The fight with the Bruin Democrats nearly cost Ashe the election.

The re-elected mayor faced immediate trouble. He had alienated the regular Democratic party which controlled local campaign financing. He needed to raise money for his own political organization. Then in February, 1942, a Middlesex County grand jury began to investigate scandals in the City Water Department and in city purchasing. In April Ashe was indicted on one count of conspiracy to defraud dealing with kick-backs on city purchases and on one count of bribery arising from school renovation contracts. While the trial proceeded, a movement organized in Lowell for a new city government to eliminate the strong mayor and replace him with a city manager who would use the mayor's powers efficiently and with no attention to politics. Mayor Ashe was convicted on both counts in November, 1942, and the strong-mayor system in Lowell was on its way out.

The movement for the adoption of Plan E was headed by Harvard educated Yankee lawyer, Woodbury F. Howard. City government under Plan E would consist of nine councilors elected at-large by proportional representation. The majority of the councilors would then select a city manager to administer the city. Howard deftly got backing for the new charter from those groups discouraged from political activity under the old charter. The committee for Plan E featured prominent Greek, French, and Yankee names plus several Irish ones along with a lone Polish name. The reform movement implicitly opposed ethnic divisions and explicitly condemned partisan politics.

A special election was held in November, 1942, to vote on the new charter. Despite the strong opposition of the city employees led by Hubert L. McLaughlin, former city solicitor under Ashe, and from the local Democratic leaders, Bruin and Geary, the new charter won by a small margin. The victory margin came from heavy voting in French Ward Six and in Republican Ward Eight with significant support from traditionally Democratic wards, indicating strong disenchantment with the Ashe conviction and the local party.

Woodbury Howard became mayor in 1943 because of his iden-
tification with Plan E and the election of four other reform councilors who voted for him. The key choice of city manager, however, went to ex-city treasurer, Democrat John J. Flannery, the
personal candidate of Councilor Joseph J. Sweeney who as acting mayor had replaced Ashe. On the vote to choose the manager,
reform sentiment vanished and the Democrats won on a straight
party vote, five to four. Woodbury Howard and the Republicans
on the council continued to advocate reform in city government
and oppose moves by Bruin and Geary to get rid of proportional
representation. Howard, however, lost his bid to be mayor again
in 1945 and ended his career on the council in 1950.

An integral feature of the new Plan E charter was proportional
representation, a weighted system of voting in elections which
favors minority group participation in city affairs.* The PR system increased the power of groups which had formerly played a
limited role in city politics. The most noticeable new groups
were the Greek-Americans and the Polish-Americans. By 1950,
most major ethnic groups in Lowell—Yankees, Irish, French,
Polish, and Greeks—were represented on the city council by
Hockmeyer, Callery, Ayotte, Janas, and Eliades, among others.
Until PR was dropped in 1958, the Irish held four seats, picking
up another when the Yankee representative failed to get elected,
the French held two seats, the Poles one (beginning in 1947) and
the Greeks one (beginning in 1949).

In response to persistent efforts by Democrats locally and
through the state legislature, a referendum on PR was placed on
the ballot in November, 1955 allegedly to end the complications
in the system's method of ballot counting. In a council vote
which precipitated a two-year court fight, and a new referendum
in 1957, five council members (the Irish and Polish councilors)
voted to waive a state requirement that all voters be mailed
notices of the referendum, a move which demonstrated hostility
to PR. Against the waiver and in support of PR were two French
votes, one Yankee, and one Greek vote. The electorate voted
strongly against PR in the disputed election, but Councilor
Samuel A. Sampson brought a suit in Superior Court which

---

*The proportional representation system permits a voter to cast a ballot for as
many candidates as he wishes from a long ballot, by numbering the choices. After
all ballots are counted, the candidate with the lowest number of first place votes
is eliminated and his ballots are distributed to the next choice on the ballot. The
process is repeated until the requisite number of candidates is elected. The
process is time-consuming and it often took several weeks to decide the
election—one of the arguments used to defeat the voting system.

"Council Meeting, Plan E Style." Cartoon by George Gagan. *Lowell Sunday Telegram*, November 21, 1943. Courtesy of Lowell Sun Publishing Company.

invalidated the election on the grounds of violation of state election laws by failing to notify the voters by mail.

The fight over PR began again in November, 1957. It involved a tussle between the League of Women Voters who supported PR and anti-PR Irish-American councilors who directed the city solicitor to stop the League from campaigning for PR from a booth owned by the city in Kearney Square. The booth was dismantled. In the referendum vote, PR was defeated again by a wide margin. Anti-PR forces carried a substantial vote in the Greek stronghold in Ward Two while the majority of Greeks, Yankees, and French voted to retain PR. In the next election Irish candidates took seven council seats, thereby dominating the city government. Minority group representation in city politics was by no means eliminated by the defeat of PR, but it was definitely limited, and the crucial votes to choose the city manager were held by the Irish councilors. This pattern of Irish strength in at-large elections and the choice of city manager remains the distinctive feature of local politics.

Prior to 1975, with the exception of the 1875–77 term, the congressional representatives from the Lowell district since the Civil War have been Republican.* Many of them were residents of the city: Benjamin F. Butler (1877–79); Frederic T. Greenhalge (1889–91) later governor of Massachusetts; Butler Ames (1903–1913) the grandson of Ben Butler; John Jacob Rogers (1913–25) whose widow Edith Nourse Rogers succeeded him in 1925 and held the seat until 1960, followed by F. Bradford Morse (1961–72) and Paul W. Cronin (1973–74). Paul E. Tsongas, the district's first Democratic representative since 1877, was elected in 1974. Success in the congressional elections was aided by persistent factionalism within the district's Democratic party, largely a tug-of-war between Lawrence and Lowell Democrats over the party's nomination. Most Republican representatives also paid close attention to the particular needs of the city through depression and war. The best example of this was the remarkable career of Edith Nourse Rogers who served the district ably and far longer than any other representative. Although labor and ethnic issues dominated municipal politics and the city voted solidly Democratic in presidential elections after 1924,

*In 1872 the congressional district had been redesigned to place both Lowell and Lawrence in the same district. The exception to Republican rule came two years later when Democrat John K. Tarbox defeated James C. Ayer of Lowell in a heavy Democratic vote. Only three Democrats have ever represented Lowell in Congress: Gayton Osgood (1833–35), Tarbox (1875–77), and Paul E. Tsongas (1975–   ).

Yankee Edith Rogers consistently convinced the voters of Lowell to split their tickets and give her an unparalleled personal following for over thirty years.

Edith Nourse was born in Saco, Maine, in 1881, the daughter of a Yankee mill company executive. The family came to Lowell when she was a young girl. She attended the Rogers Hall School and a finishing school in Paris where she was captivated by French culture. But Edith Nourse also acquired from her father a thorough knowledge of textile mills and their financial, labor, and trade problems. In 1907 she married the son of another Lowell textile executive, John Jacob Rogers. Her deep love of western European society and her interest in the problems of textile manufacturing in New England would be two formative experiences in her political life.

In 1917 Edith and John Rogers (he had been elected to Congress in 1912) involved themselves deeply in World War I. They both toured the French war zone and she worked for the YMCA and the Red Cross caring for the wounded. In 1918, they returned to Washington where Rogers enlisted. She continued her work at Walter Reed Army Hospital until 1922. Her work with World War I veterans made her and Rogers popular with veterans' organizations which became politically powerful after the war. In the 1920s she served without pay as an inspector of veterans' hospitals, and her work was recognized and supported by three Republican presidents. When her husband died in March, 1925, the state Republican party insisted she succeed him. She expected to serve only for a few years but found she greatly enjoyed the life and the work. She spoke her mind on the floor of Congress and dealt aggressively and perceptively with national issues. Her secure Yankee background, travel, and education as well as the unshakeable political base in her district made her a formidable representative.

Congresswoman Rogers was a liberal and an internationalist, typical of successful Republicans of the northeast. She voted for most of the key New Deal programs of the thirties—the Wagner Act which protected union organization, the Social Security Act of 1935, and the minimum wage law of 1938—in line with the needs of her Lowell constituents, if not with the Republican leadership. However, she strongly opposed the Roosevelt administration's program of flexible and negotiable tariff rates. In 1938, fearful of competition in shoes, she attacked a trade treaty with Czechoslovakia and insisted on high tariffs on all textiles coming from Japan. Her attachment to her happy days in Paris and her work in World War I made her an early opponent of Hitler. In 1937 she voted to amend the neutrality legislation which prevented Roosevelt from demonstrating opposition to German and Japanese expansion and later she became an active supporter of the United Nations.

During World War II Edith Rogers served on both the Veterans' Affairs Committee and the Armed Services Committee;* she sponsored major legislation including bills for a Women's Army Corps in 1942 and for a G. I. Bill of Rights which granted housing, education, and medical benefits to veterans. Her busy staff spent hours each day on constituents' problems, particularly the needs of armed-service widows. She subsequently introduced legislation to grant pensions to war widows. Defense contracts awarded to Lowell businesses greatly improved the local economy. All of her activities were well publicized in the district; she was a good politician and unbeatable at election time. Representative Rogers died of a heart attack at the age of seventy nine in the midst of her re-election campaign of 1960.

The voters of Lowell were devoted to Republican congressional representatives, but less so to Republican candidates for president especially since the 1920s. The magnetic spell of Civil War Republicanism lasted until 1892 when Lowell voted for ex-President Grover Cleveland. The 1896 election, however, shattered the Democrats over the issue of the gold standard for the dollar, and William McKinley swept the city. The city continued to vote Republican for president until the 1912 elections, when the Republicans split and ran two candidates, both former presidents. While William Howard Taft and Theodore Roosevelt both did well, they divided the Republican vote locally as they did nationally, and Democrat Woodrow Wilson carried Lowell in 1912 and 1916. This forecast a strong trend away from the Republicans in the mid 1920s.

After the turmoil of American involvement in World War I the conservative candidates of the Republican Party seemed attractive to Lowell voters, but in 1924 the electorate showed a strong

*She also served on the House Foreign Affairs Committee and on the Civil Service Committee, two very important assignments. Democratic strength in Congress in the 1930s greatly reduced the number of Republicans in the House and good committee assignments were available. When the Republicans won the Ninetieth Congress in 1946 during the Truman administration, Rogers had to choose between chairing the Veterans' Committee or continuing on Foreign Affairs. She chose the veterans and remained the ranking Republican member until her death.

interest in the reform-minded Progressive party candidate, Robert LaFollette of Wisconsin, although voting was light. After the 1924 campaign there was an unprecedented increase in the numbers of voters in the city (38.4 percent) and the beginning of a massive voter realignment. The 1928 campaign of Irish Catholic Al Smith of New York began the pattern of landslide Democratic victories in Lowell which lasted through 1972. In national party politics, even in the controversial 1948 and 1972 elections and during the Eisenhower years Lowell was a solid Democratic city.

The two major influences that explain why Lowell was a Whig-Republican city in the nineteenth century and a Democratic city in the twentieth were, first, the economic power of the textile mills and, later, the impact on politics of the multitude of ethnic groups that came to work in the mills. While the power of the textile interests was balanced in part by the old settlers and the Irish Democratic organization faced anti-tax and anti-corruption "reform" groups, the prevailing pattern in the city mirrored its textile industry—the mills—and its immigrant people—the multitudes.

XII

The New People: An Introduction to the Ethnic History of Lowell

By Peter F. Blewett

The new people, the immigrants, have always been a part of Lowell. On April 6, 1822, a labor contractor named Hugh Cummiskey led thirty Irish laborers to the vicinity of Pawtucket Falls. They had walked up from Charlestown along the Middlesex Canal to begin the work of deepening the existing Pawtucket Canal and digging others which were to channel the water to power cotton mills. They were met by the lordly Kirk Boott, who gave them tools and bestowed on them a little money for their "refreshment." This was about as much provisioning as they would get from their employers, the mill owners, who set up no living quarters for them, and had no intention of making this foreign born group a part of the mill town's work force. Their plan called for the employment of young, native born women in the cotton mills. The Irish were initially necessary but extraneous and perhaps unwelcome in the long run.

In the 1820s and 1830s Lowell was a boom town. New factories, a railroad, boarding houses, even a stately home for Kirk Boott were built, and the Irish stayed on to provide the labor. They lived, segregated, in a shantytown, variously called "Paddy Camp Lands," "New Dublin," or "The Acre," on property over which the companies chose not to exercise control. And so, before it was even finished the planned city of Lowell had its first slum. As early as August, 1822, long before the mill girls began to arrive, the Irish had established families living in the new town. They increased in numbers, attracted by the opportunities for work, and became an important element in the population. The mill agents were forced to deal with them; hence in the name of good discipline Boott provided the land for a Roman Catholic Church whose priest would, he hoped, keep the Irish in order.

The possibilities for work drew most of the new people to Lowell. From England and Scotland came experienced textile hands and masons. From Quebec province in 1841 a blacksmith arrived, followed four years later by the first French-Canadian carpenter, and then, over the next fifteen years, by the first wave of their countrymen drawn away from the poverty of the farms. In the late 1840s more Irishmen, potato famine refugees, arrived, just as the mill girls began to fail as a docile work force. They were hired by the companies as operatives at lower wages, and a pattern became set. Each new ethnic group entering Lowell rehearsed this experience with the mills, as its appearance in the city allowed the managers to undercut the existing wage structure.

Once the mill managers recognized the profit potential of low-paid immigrant labor for whom they did not have to provide subsidized housing, they began to recruit intensively. The same method which drew rural, Yankee women applied to Quebec farmers. French-speaking recruiters toured eastern Canada, especially after 1865, and convinced the inhabitants that Lowell offered high wages and good jobs. As a consequence, thousands of French-Canadians came to Lowell, leaving behind the deadend of small farms, harsh climate, overpopulation, and land hunger. By 1900 they composed about a fifth of the city's population.

In the nineteenth century the population of Europe rapidly expanded especially in the agrarian countries. There came to be more people than the land could support. Vast patterns of migration developed, at first from the farms into the cities, but inevitably out of the homeland and into the undeveloped parts of the world. Lowell, like the rest of the United States, was the destination of large numbers of migrants driven from Europe by a great depression during the last third of the nineteenth century. They could generally be classified as peasants, either farmers or herders; most were young; few had saleable skills. In short, they

"Bell Time." Workers leaving the mills. By Winslow Homer. *Harper's Weekly*, July 25, 1868. (Lowell Historical Society)

were ideal for the work force in the mills. Whether it was Poland, Portugal, Greece, or Russia that they left, the prime motive was economic. Some, like many of the Poles and Greeks, intended to work, to save, and to return home, perhaps to buy land. A few did, but most, like the Irish, came and settled almost inadvertently. Sometimes political oppression, religious persecution, or the need to evade conscription into a foreign overlord's army, set people on the road which led to Lowell. Once a few people of a nationality became established, they acted as magnets drawing in relatives, friends, and fellow villagers. An eastern industrial city like Lowell with its demand for low-wage, initially unskilled, labor was a natural place for the impoverished immigrant to stop. Even after the cotton mills died, the pattern remained and was replicated—so strong was the web of ethnic connection back to the homeland.

The actual journey to Lowell was slow and hard. Irishmen often tried their luck first in the industrial cities of England, then pushed on to America, pausing in port cities like New York, Boston, Quebec, or Montreal before reaching Lowell. While most French-Canadians came by train, some walked from Quebec. The late nineteenth century immigrants from Europe travelled a longer distance. Because most of the immigrants were young, the trip was a wrenching initiation into the world. It was an experience perhaps more fearsome than exciting or promising. They came from rural home villages, which few of them had previously left, even for short trips. Sometimes this meant a more difficult break even than leaving relatives and friends. For one teenaged Polish widow it meant leaving behind a young son, who sentiment insisted would join her in time, but whom reality told her she would never see again. Once aboard the train the immigrants were on a journey into an alien world. After contending with the bewildering "foreign-ness" of the port city of Bremen, Hamburg, or Liverpool, they faced the singular experience of the long sea voyage. Travelling by Belgian or English ships could be quite comfortable, but the usual experience on ships of other flags was dismal. Few had cabins and people were crowded into unpartitioned below-deck quarters, where all their human activities were carried out for as long as a month. The food was usually poor, and except in mid-summer, the weather on the ocean was bad. One Polish girl, travelling alone, experienced days of terror on a ship hove-to at sea waiting out a storm. Sixty years later she could remember still the experience of lying among hundreds of strangers in the claustrophobic below-decks as the ship, its bow facing into the wind, rose and dipped with every huge swell.

The European imagination perceived the United States as an economic Land of Oz. This image was shaped by agents for steamship lines, travel writers, labor recruiters, journalists, and, perhaps most important of all, by immigrants writing home. The newcomer came with exaggerated hopes. Sometimes experience confirmed promise. As one Greek remembered: "When I come to Staten Island [sic], when I come out, I found a dime on the street. Jesus, I said, Christ's sake, I just come here, I begin to get rich now!" For most of the immigrants, though, disillusionment began at Ellis Island. There were long lines, cursory but arbitrary medical checks, and sometimes rancorous dealings with officials. The place acquired a bad reputation. Here people lost ancient family names because officials could not spell or understand them. Poles were infuriated by this; Jews often did not mind: many would change their names when they became citizens. Here a little girl, who had red-rimmed eyes from crying all night, could be diagnosed as tubercular and prevented from landing. She would be detained until her mother could travel from Lowell to rescue her from the bureaucracy. Here the immigrant's dream could crash as the sick person was forced to return to Europe.

Many of the immigrants of the 1890s and early 1900s came through to Lowell consigned to relatives, wearing tags sometimes inscribed with simply the city's name as a guide for ticket sellers and train conductors. The Jewish community in Lowell maintained someone at the Middlesex Street depot to meet all trains. He greeted the newcomer in Yiddish, elicited the name of the person's relatives in Lowell, and directed him to them. Within days a relative, or *landtzman*, a person from the same area of the old country as the newcomer, helped him to find a job. All the ethnic groups beginning with the Irish provided lodging and help for the newcomers: no matter that a French-Canadian family of twelve was crowded into a four-room tenement in "Little Canada;" it somehow accommodated the new arrivals. This sense of community obligation was perhaps the most powerful social accomplishment of the immigration period, and represented the maintenance of an old agrarian social attitude in the new environment of a foreign industrial city. To many immigrants this aid meant survival—emotional as well as physical or material. Each ethnic group created its island of separate culture, language, and customs as a subconscious means of ensuring the members' survival in the alien environment. The island might be squalid and poverty stricken but it was a haven.

Despite the cushion against cultural shock provided by the ethnic community, during the first year many people thought about going home. Few could afford the return fare. In time they got used to the new way of life and "made the best" of their situation. If life were grim for them, their letters home concealed their disappointment. Out of pride and to save face they refused to admit that they were no better off for emigrating, and that, in some cases, they were worse off. They upheld in their letters the given image of America and Lowell, so that they encouraged relatives and friends to emigrate also.

All the nineteenth century immigrant groups relied on religion to bind together the parts of the ethnic community. In an alien environment, where the law, the courts, and the police seemed hostile, the church exercised the only acceptable public authority, and priests of necessity became the community's respectable leaders. Irish Catholic priests were at work in the Paddy Camp Lands years before there was a church building. They said Mass, heard confessions, baptised, and celebrated marriages and funerals. They regularized life for a people living in impermanence and housed in shanties, shacks, and tents. Before most of the Irish were able to move out of their slum, they made sure that their church had a permanent building. St. Patrick's Church, a wooden structure dedicated in 1831, had its foundation laid by Cummiskey and a crew of volunteers. It was built and paid for by the Irish community, which already operated a school teaching four Rs instead of just three. The Catholicism of the Irish set them off from the Protestant natives and helped them preserve their identity, but it also provided bigots with the excuse they needed to persecute and exploit them.

The early churches were missionary in character. The ethnic communities felt beleaguered in Lowell. Even if their religion was already established in Lowell, other ethnic groups usually controlled it. The newcomers felt the need to set up their own churches. This was not an easy task. The first group to try, the French-Canadians, resented Irish domination of the Catholic Church in Lowell. The priests spoke English, services seemed different; the customs were strange. The diocese of Boston, itself Irish-controlled, at first failed to respond and provide a French priest. This failure of the Catholic hierarchy to adapt to a church

composed of ethnic communities happened elsewhere in the
United States in the nineteenth century. Only in 1868 were two
Oblate priests, Lucien Lagier and André Marie Garin, sent to
Lowell to serve the French-Canadians. Within days of his arrival
Father Garin had bought a vacant Unitarian church on Lee
Street; a few weeks later he had collected a three thousand dollar
down-payment for it from his enthusiastic parishioners. This was
the beginning of St. Joseph's Church, the first of many French-
Canadian Catholic institutions in Lowell.

The Polish experience with the Catholic Church was similar
to that of the French-Canadians, but ironically it was against the
French language church that the Poles reacted. Most Poles in the
1890s went to mass at St. Joseph's Church, where the sermons
were often in French and where there was a degree of French-
Canadian chauvinism. Some Polish people distrusted the
priests; in any case, most felt uncomfortable in a foreign church.
Establishing a separate Polish church, however, presented difficulties. Again the problem was Irish domination of the hierarchy. The fervor of Polish nationalism, suppressed in the
homeland, demanded that religious life be deeply rooted in
Polish history and custom. Already in the 1890s a clash had taken
place in Scranton, Pennsylvania, between Polish Catholics and
the hierarchy. The result was a schism and the formation of the
Polish National Catholic Church, which used the Polish language in the rite but left dogma mostly unaltered. In 1901 some
frustrated Polish Catholics in Lowell set up a branch of this
church, St. Casimir's, and a school which emphasized Polish
language and history. Money for the church came from both
Lowell and Scranton Poles. Here was a radical reaction to the
difficulty ethnic groups experienced in setting up national par-
ishes in areas where they were a small minority in the American
Catholic Church. It is a demonstration that a thousand-year-old
religious tradition can collapse in a new situation when the local
representatives of the larger institutional church are inflexible
and unable to maintain in practice the church's claim to uni-
versality.

St. Casimir's Church was the product of the two strongest
forces working on the Poles, their religion and their sense of
nationality (they would say patriotism). In 1901 for many Lowell
Poles, nationalism won out over the ancient religion, but the
creation of the schismatic church split the community. Soon the
Poles who remained loyal to the Roman Catholic Church had

their own parish. It was situated not in Centralville, where most Poles lived, but across the river, in the city proper. Religion thus for the first time failed to unify an ethnic group in Lowell, and in fact produced two Polish communities. Religious schism as always produced social schism. This did not mean that the Poles diffused quickly into the general population. Assimilation for them was just as slow as it was for every other group, because for the first two generations the integrity of the communities was maintained. Nationalism replaced the single religion as the community bond.

Not all Catholic nationalities had trouble with the hierarchy. The Portuguese were lucky in all parts of the diocese. In 1869 Archbishop Williams imported a priest from the Azores to minister to the Portuguese in New Bedford. By the time Lowell had a large Portuguese community, the Catholic Church was able to respond, and in 1907 Archbishop O'Connell dedicated St. Anthony of Lisbon parish. This parish was governed from 1911 to 1924 by an exiled Portuguese bishop, Henry Joseph Reed da Silva.

Lowell's Spanish-speaking immigrants are nominally Catholic. Two priests who speak Spanish serve them. Attendance at Mass is fairly low, mostly because they were unchurched in their homeland. This is due to a long tradition of anti-clericalism in Puerto Rico and Latin America, and to the survival of spiritism, a pagan cult which has taken on the vocabulary of Christianity. There are even two witches in the Lowell community. The Roman Catholic priests have to be missionaries first, and then social workers and interpreters. Protestant missionaries from a variety of fundamentalist churches compete, and have set up small churches, mostly of the storefront variety.*

The Orthodox Greeks faced no problems with a hierarchy in setting up a church in Lowell, although they were hindered as were other groups before them by a lack of money. Even though there was a permanent priest starting in 1895, services had to be held in a variety of halls not really suited to the purpose. Not until 1906 could the Greek community finance a proper church building. Designed by a Boston Irish architect dispatched to

---

*The black population of Lowell is small, estimated at between fifteen hundred and eighteen hundred persons. They live mostly in Lower Belvidere, and in the area around Central and Lawrence Streets. There are two black churches, both Protestant, the Pentecostal Church and the African Methodist Church. A women's association, the Black Genesis Foundation, is in 1976 the leading active community organization.

Holy Trinity Greek Orthodox Church. Photograph by A.L. Eno, Jr.

Istanbul to study the style, this church, Holy Trinity, was a statement by the Greeks of their culture. It was in the Byzantine style, complete with decorated interior and topped by a large glittering golden dome, fronted by two smaller ones. Like St. Anne's Episcopal Church, Holy Trinity seems, much more than the neo-Gothic Roman Catholic churches, to be an authentic part of the old world transferred to Lowell. It summons up the atmosphere of the eastern Mediterranean even when there is only the wan, North American winter sun to reflect off its cream colored bricks and golden domes.

Construction of the church building turned out to be only a first hurdle; at least twice in its early history Holy Trinity Church barely escaped financial disaster. In 1920 parishioners prevented a mortgage foreclosure by taking an emergency collection. During the Great Depression in 1934 only the intercession of Christos Laganas, a successful shoe manufacturer, saved the church when it found itself in a similar situation. The second crisis may have come about because in 1924 and 1928 a large part of the congregation withdrew, leaving Holy Trinity with a reduced membership just as the economy broke down.

Like the Polish religious community, the Greek one also split. In 1923 Holy Trinity Chrch refused to abandon the Julian calendar for the Gregorian as the church in Greece and the American archdiocese had directed. The bad feeling created in the congregation by this was exacerbated a year later when the community split over the deep feelings unleashed by a political crisis in Greece. The supporters of Prime Minister Venizelos could no longer get along with Lowell's pro-monarchical Greeks, and consequently the Greek Orthodox religious community divided. The new Church of the Transfiguration was the result. Yet another schism occurred in 1928 and produced St. George's Church. Like the Irish who sent money to Sinn Fein and like the Poles who supported the movement for Polish independence, the Greeks were more emigrants than immigrants. The situation in the homeland was at once more real and more important to them than affairs in their adopted land.

Beginning with the Irish, the priests, at least for the first generation and usually into the second, were born in the home country. In order to be accepted they needed to speak the language and hold in common with parishioners the familiar customs, traditions, and prejudices. The original need of the immigrants to base the ethnic island on the national religion dictated this. As long as the priests were foreign-born, community leadership stayed strongly tied to the fatherland. Each recruit was a political and cultural refreshment, a check on the tendency to alter or abandon custom. The priest also had to function as an intermediary between his parishioners and civil authorities or employers. He was often the first person to acquire status outside the ethnic community. This was frequently a burden, but a Father John Mahoney or a Father Garin managed it. They became acknowledged leaders in the city.

From the churches sprang the benevolent societies, whose prototype was the Hibernian Moralizing and Relief Socety of 1833. The French-Canadians began with the Union St. Joseph, and followed it after 1889 with the larger Corporation des Membres de l'Association Catholique. The Poles set up their Spojnia and Polish-American Club. While the Greeks in 1894 founded the Washington-Acropolis with the aim of preserving their religion and tradition, they tended to set up their benevolent societies in order to cater to regional loyalties. The Portuguese-American Club came closer to the Irish and French-Canadian model by drawing a community-wide membership. So too did the Jewish Twenty-five Cent Society, which provided its membership with a doctor. The Jews also operated the Workmen's Circle which paid the unemployed person ten dollars a month. As rent in the decade after 1900 averaged $1.25 a week, this sum provided subsistence for the out-of-work. Lowell's newest immigrants run a Spanish-American Center, and UNITAS, a federally funded association. Both try to help the newcomer find jobs and housing.* UNITAS works under the leadership of an Oblate priest, Father Daniel Crahen, who also has sponsored the establishment of a credit union and a used clothing and furniture store.

These organizations offered (and, in some cases, continue to offer) the immigrant a cushion against loneliness, and often against disaster or destitution. They were mostly mutual-aid societies providing relief, group insurance, and a meeting place. They were, like the church, a place where the respectable strands of community life came together, and where successful laymen, like Hugh Cummiskey or J. Henri Guillet, found scope for social leadership. The societies sponsored dinners, fêtes, plays, picnics, and parades, where the immigrants could indulge

---

*The Spanish-speaking minority (Colombian, Mexican, Cuban, but largely Puerto Rican) is Lowell's most rapidly growing population. It numbers around eight thousand. This immigration has taken place over the last fifteen years.

their nationalism on celebration days held to honor patron saints or national heroes like St. Patrick, St. Jean Baptiste, and Casimir Pulaski. In time, the societies multiplied and specialized to serve fractions of the community, but they always tended to maintain their ethnic exclusivity.

For the male immigrant worker, there existed other meeting places besides churches and social clubs. The most idiosyncratic and characteristic example was the Greek coffee house, a village social institution transplanted to Lowell. Strung out along Market Street, the coffee houses numbered about thirty at the height of their popularity, which interestingly enough came only after Greek women had arrived in large numbers and home life had been regularized. Individual houses tended to be frequented by people from a small region of Greece. In the coffee house the immigrant could sit for hours on end, drinking the favored sweet, strong, black coffee, talking in the native language about politics (usually Greek), playing cards, or reading newspapers. The single room was simply set up with chairs around small tables. The place was warm in winter; in summer the entire operation moved to the sidewalk. For the young, single, and poor Greek, the coffee house was one of the few alternatives to the saloon or the brothel for recreation. While the Reverend George Kenngott in his sociological study of immigration in Lowell, primly alludes to "sexual vice" among the unmarried Greeks, arrests for drunkenness among them were relatively few in number, so the coffee house was partly successful as a sobering social institution. Ethnic attitudes toward alcohol are pointed up nicely by the reaction of Lowell's Irish police to the first coffee houses. They could not believe that these were not saloons in disguise and raided them often, finding neither liquor nor gamblers. It took some time before the police could be persuaded that Greek males could gather together to drink only coffee and talk politics for hours.

The more universal male meeting place was the saloon. In ethnic neighborhoods it served as an unofficial social club. If the Acre of early Lowell resembled the Irish districts of nineteenth-century Boston, saloons were numerous and small, run by single families in one room of their tenements. There is evidence to suggest that wives ran the saloons while husbands worked at outside jobs like laboring (although in at least one case the husband was a lawyer). As new groups of immigrants staked out their territory in the city they either set up saloons or frequented

Greek coffee house patrons, 1914. Photograph courtesy of Mr. and Mrs. C. Koumoutseas.

and came to monopolize established ones.* All the nationalities appear in the police-court records of arrests for drunkenness, some (like the Irish) in higher percentages than others (like the English). This disproportion in the records may reflect economic differences, such as the ability to afford bottled liquor, or possession of a pleasant home in which to drink and a wife who tolerated alcohol in the house. Perhaps it just expressed ethnic custom: in some cultures drinking was to be done among people *outside* the home. In any event the statistics show that drunkenness was the ubiquitous scourge of working class families in Lowell in the same way it has always been when poverty dominated life. Before prohibition, beer to take home was sold by the bucket, and rye whiskey was cheap. Kenngott wrote that patronage of saloons was largely limited to young and unmarried men because wages were so low that the married man could not afford to drink. He could not, of course; but he did. As a result temperance movements flourished. From time to time priests administered the "pledge" to the Irish in the city. French-Canadian women posted "La croix tempérance," a black cross, on their walls, and tried to keep alcohol out of the house. "No licence" appeared on the ballot often in the nineteenth century, backed by moralistic prohibition supporters.† For the nineteenth and early twentieth centuries, Kenngott found evidence that alcoholism was the chief reason for husbands deserting or failing to support their families. The husband and father who drank up and gambled away his wages before he reached home every week was no more rare in Lowell than in any other industrial city in the world.

Sometimes an ethnic island created a unique institution in Lowell. Such was Tsagaroulis' drug store. Many of the Greek immigrants could give no set address to their families back home, and the U.S. Post Office found it difficult to deliver letters on which only the city name seemed legible to the postman. The drug store became a sub-post office, a kind of *poste-restante* or general delivery, for the immigrants. The store became a community center, a check-in point for the immigrants; it performed a useful, necessary service, as long as the native language remained the primary tongue of the immigrants and their families.

*This process is at work today in the bars on Central and Charles Streets, where Spanish-speaking and black patrons have eased out an earlier clientele.

†Probably the real reason for placing it on the ballot was political. See Chapter XI.

Language, except in the case of the Irish, defined the ethnic community and reinforced it. There was a close link between religion, nationality, and language. Maintenance of all three retarded assimilation and preserved the ethnic island. The various church schools aided in this effort, as did the understandable reluctance of people to abandon the language in which they had learned to think and in which they invested much patriotic love of the homeland. The French-Canadian Club Richelieu still fines its members twenty-five cents for every slip into English. The ethnic communities preserved their languages in a number of ways.

Newspapers in the native tongue were a consequence of the establishment of fairly large immigrant groups. The French-Canadians had at least twenty-two: *L'Etoile* (1886-1957), a weekly at first, then a daily, was the most successful. The rest tended to be short-lived and of less frequent issue. Foreign language dailies usually had too small a circulation to make them business successes. The Greeks, who also had twenty-two different newspapers at various times, supported only weeklies or monthlies. Other nationalities' efforts at publication were more modest. The Poles had literary societies, and men who corresponded with newspapers back home, reporting on the lives of the immigrants to Lowell. There were French-Canadian, Polish, and Greek writers, poets, and novelists; Irish and French-Canadian song writers. Plays in the native language were performed for most nationalities. The urge to preserve the language started a minor cultural movement in the first two generations of Lowell's immigrants, and was the main reason each group set up its own schools.

In the end the responsibility for maintaining the language fell on the family, the basic unit of the ethnic community. In the first two generations children spoke French, or Greek, or Armenian, or Polish at home, and sometimes parents forbade the use of English. Yet the line could not be held. The state of Massachusetts, after 1901, required any minor not competent in English to attend an evening school to learn the language in order to obtain a work permit. Not every family could pay tuition for the ethnic elementary schools, and some groups like the Greeks and Poles could not afford to build their own high schools. In all these cases economic necessity insured that the children would be forced to learn English. For most nationalities then, the exclusivity of the ethnic community could not extend to the children. Sometimes practicality alone dictated that children would become bilingual. It was not uncommon for a mother with no English to take her child with her when shopping. The child translated and kept her from being cheated. Gradually the old language became the second language because it was a handicap not to speak English. By the time television came along the supremacy of the native tongue had been broken. And television, the most powerful acculturator ever developed, insured by its selling of levelled values and homogenized taste that the non-English languages would lose their currency.

Sentimental attachment to the old languages remains among all the ethnic groups. Even in the third generation children still learn French, or Polish, or Greek, or Lebanese, often in order to talk to their grandparents. Poles at their holidays try to keep the language alive by encouraging small children to recite patriotic poems. Yet there are some signs that the third may be the last bilingual generation as intermarriage and acculturation take place and the ethnic community dissolves.

There was an exception to this pattern of jealous maintenance of the old language. The Jews, who unlike most ethnic groups were anxious to assimilate, quickly picked up English. After 1900 the community even encouraged women to put aside housework to take night classes in English at the Lincoln School. They sent their children to public school and had them learn Hebrew at the synagogue in the afternoons. The children, especially the eldest child, became the invaluable authority on American ways for the parents. The acculturation of the children which other ethnic groups regretted and tried to prevent, the Jews encouraged. They took advice from the eldest child on how to dress, what goods to buy, or what first names to give their later children. The first-born acquired an authority and place in the family not found in Jewish communities in Europe.

Among the foreign-language communities maintenance of a national cuisine was a mark of the ethnic island. The practice began as a natural consequence of coming to a foreign land. There is nothing, except for language, which so continually reminds the immigrant of his submersion in an alien environment as daily contact with strange food. What the traveller seeks out, the immigrant avoids. Whenever possible, people cooked and ate the familiar food. Because American stores could not supply the unusual foods needed by ethnic cooks, Greeks, Poles, Jews, Portuguese, French-Canadians set up grocery stores, delicatessens, butcher shops, and bakeries. In a way they followed the lead of the Irish, who fifty years before began to make a place for themselves in the middle class by becoming victuallers and purveyors to the city. The demands of the national cooking produced, in the case of the Greeks and Poles, supporting farms in the "countryside" in Dracut. The Greeks opened restaurants, some of which have developed a clientele drawn widely from outside the ethnic community.

After the first generation, the immigrants saw in their cooking one way of passing on their national traditions to their children and grandchildren. As the ethnic island lost its isolation, as pressures toward conformity with the American style of life grew and the younger generations moved into the larger community, the ethnic cuisine became more and more restricted to the holiday ritual. It was not that the traditional cooking was abandoned, but that the specialties of the cuisine came to be associated with festivals, when special menus were followed. These holidays were times of reaffirmation, of playing out old customs, when the extended family reinforced its links by a resort to ritual. On Christmas Eve the family feast for the Poles followed a pattern of symbolic acts. It began with all the diners breaking and eating a wafer together, and a solemn mutual embracing of all present, before the meal made up of traditional Polish foods—kielbasa, babka, pierogi, borcht, potatoes, cabbage, and fish—was eaten. The other nationalities placed similar emphasis on the importance of holidays to the family and community. Greek, French-Canadian, Syrian, and Armenian women began the preparation of food days ahead of time. Even in periods of depression and unemployment they made the greatest effort to provide something special to eat, at least at Christmas. The effort was required by tradition, and was habitual. People were scarcely conscious of the cementing social purpose behind the tradition. The celebration alone counted.

The most important protection of the ethnic community's integrity was the marriage of its members to people within the community, even if it meant recruiting a husband or wife in the homeland. Lists of marriages made by the earliest Irish inhabitants show very few out of the community. This pattern seems to have been followed by all the groups subsequently entering Lowell with the exception of the Greeks, who arrived in the beginning without women. A few, therefore, intermarried with other groups. When women began to arrive from Greece in numbers, intermarriage slowed down, but for the men at least, did not cease. Marriage outside the Greek community did not begin for women until the 1940s, and even then was the cause of scandal in the family. In most groups opposition to exogamy was deeply rooted. Religious and national prejudices covered up what was really fear of the outsider. There was no good reason why a Polish man and Irish woman should not marry. But they tended not to, well into the third generation. The prejudicial feelings must be seen therefore as expressions of a behavior pattern by which the community protected its integrity. There is no doubt that intermarriage was the principal solvent of the isolation of the ethnic island.

The first generations resisted assimilation by keeping to the old ways, yet they quickly obtained citizenship. For those who spoke a foreign language, this required that they learn enough English to pass the citizenship test. The French-Canadians set up a series of organizations, among which were the Naturalization Club in 1885, l'Union Franco-Américaine in 1895, the Pawtucketville Social Club in 1897, the Club des Citoyens Américains (CCA) in 1898, and then, just after the city charter change of 1911, they brought all these efforts together in the Permanent Committee on Naturalization, which added a woman's section in 1922 after the passage of the Nineteenth Amendment. This progression demonstrates nicely the political motivation which lay, at least in part, behind naturalization for the French-Canadians. Their numbers grew rapidly after 1885, and they could expect to contest at the polls Irish and Yankee control of the city. A political motive is not so easily discerned among the early Poles, Portuguese, Jewish or Greek immigrants who sought naturalization, and who attended language and citizenship classes at the International Institute. Many of these people, like the Poles, were deeply nationalistic, but they became Americans. Except for Jews from Russia and Lithuania, naturalization was almost a cosmetic process. Americanization tended to cease after the swearing-in ceremony, and few went on to learn any more English. A Greek once explained why: though there were many different nationalities in the mills, they spoke little and seldom mixed after work. Instead they went home into the ethnic isolation of their own communities. In the clubs, saloons, and coffee houses, the serious conversations were about affairs in the homeland; America and Lowell seemed unimportant. What need was there to learn a foreign language? The self-sufficiency of the ethnic community counteracted any pull toward assimilation created by the English-speaking outside world.

For the immigrants the "new world" as it was realized in Lowell was often a deep disappointment. The city was crowded, noisy, and dirty. Early prints of Lowell made it look bucolic, but they never showed the Paddy Camp Lands. By the time of the Civil War, Lowell was a typical nineteenth century industrial city, complete with slums and soot. A Pole remembers arguing with a train conductor who directed him off at the Middlesex Street depot that this dirty place could not be Lowell. So convinced was he of the mistake that he tried to get back on the train, only to be forced off by the conductor. It was disillusioning that "new" and "young" when applied to this country and city did not mean "better."

In the beginning the mills built housing only for the young, Yankee women they employed. Gradually the Irish replaced their tent city with more permanent housing and the area became a neighborhood, Lowell's Irish section, the Acre. Given its start as a shantytown, the Acre never could become in the nineteenth and early twentieth centuries anything better than a slum. The wooden tenement houses, built close together, showed no design for life: sun and air reached only a few of the rooms. Generations of tubercular people spat on the floors and left a killing bequest to those who followed them into the buildings. There was no attention to sanitation and well into the twentieth century many of the buildings had no sewerage except "vaults" which seldom were cleaned and often overflowed. In the tiny yards, in the alleys, in the streets, junk and garbage collected. A typical slum, the Acre was infested with disease, misery, and death. The buildings had been inadequate to begin with and did not age well. By the time the Greeks took over the eastern—and oldest—end, the houses in the Acre were by all standards uninhabitable. The underpaid Greeks had no choice but to live there, as close to the mills as possible, while many Irish moved to the better sections of town, opened up by the network of streetcar lines. Thus the Acre served two nationalities consecutively as the location of their ethnic island.

The French-Canadian section, Little Canada, began less haphazardly than did the Acre. It was built on a piece of open land directly northwest of the mills, which was owned by the Locks & Canals Company and used by the city as a dump. The company let out the land to people—usually French-Canadians—who would build and rent tenements on it during a sixteen-year leasehold. This economic arrangement seems to have dictated a style of building which could house many tenants on a fairly small lot. The landlords put up large, three story tenements—called "blocks" in Lowell—usually having twenty-eight four-room apartments. Each unit had two rooms with windows, two without, a toilet but no bath, and each was heated by a kerosene or coal stove. There was no living room, only a kitchen and bedrooms. The highest rents were paid by top-floor tenants who had skylights in the dark rooms and who had to pay less to heat their flats. Despite the French-Canadian housewives' fanatical devotion to house cleaning, the death rate in Little Canada from tuberculosis and infantile intestinal disease was unacceptably high well into the twentieth century. The landlords' approach to the economics of rental property in Little Canada contributed to this situation. The renewable leasehold system created uncertainty in the landlords. They were reluctant to keep the houses in good repair; they held expenses down, and widened profit margins. Little money was invested in the plumbing and heating systems. The twin threats of disease and fire dogged the French-Canadians of Little Canada, adding to the precarious nature of life.

A very high birth rate and constant immigration from Canada increased the size of the ethnic island, and gradually it extended into neighborhoods across the river. On the north side of the Moody Street bridge, Pawtucketville began. Farther east the French-Canadians shared Centralville, the section which began at the North end of the Aiken Street bridge, with a scattering of other nationalities and with the Poles, whose own main community extended down river toward Christian Hill.

As the city absorbed its new immigrants from eastern and southern Europe between 1890 and 1920, the ethnic disricts took their final shape. The newer ethnic islands were smaller and were located on the south side of the Merrimack. There were two small Polish districts on either side of the Concord River near the eastern end of the downtown mill district where the two rivers joined. The Portuguese also occupied two areas. One began about a half mile from the city center on the west bank of the Concord and then ran westward and northward to reach the mill district near the Pawtucket Canal. The Portuguese now share this section with blacks and Spanish-speaking people. The Jews lived in a district on Chelmsford and Howard Streets which bordered on and cut into the middle-class Highlands. The newer Irish sections in the Highlands and the "Grove" area of South Lowell, were made possible by the extension of street railways. In the interstices between these main population islands lived the Yankees, the English, the Scots, the Syrians, the Armenians, the Germans, the Swedes, the Italians, and the rest of the forty or so ethnic groups which filled the city before assimilation and affluence led people into the suburbs.

Some of the nationalities represented in Lowell by very small numbers were at a disadvantage; their lack of a large community increased their chances of being exploited. Around the turn of the century there existed one huge tenement block containing fourteen nationalities and known widely as "Joe Flynn's Wonderland." The name reflected everyone's astonishment that so many groups could live together without mayhem. The isolated ethnic could be victimized easily, as the experience of an Italian family testified. Trying to survive the depression of the 1930s by growing a garden, the family found that it could not keep the neighbors, who, for the most part, were not Italians, from pilfering it. The family's teen-aged daughters worked as domestic help in the middle-class Highlands, and were exploited and underpaid without compunction by their employers. It was a relief to get a job in the mills. This family lacked the support and small protection a substantial ethnic community could have provided.*

Given the low wages in the mills and the immigrants' initial poverty, it is not surprising to find that much of the city's housing was poorly appointed and generally sub-standard. This was especially true in the ethnic islands before World War II. The many large, comfortable Victorian houses, or even pleasant workers' cottages, which in comparison with suburban tract housing now seem to have such variety and appeal to the eye, were beyond the means of the immigrants. Since 1940, public housing, beginning with a project at the eastern end of the Acre bordering on Market Street and taking much of the old Greek section, has replaced some of the worst slums. Urban renewal has demolished others. Yet new housing has been slow in coming. As older sections of the city age they decline into slums, and unfortunately there will be found the ethnic newcomers, the blacks and Spanish-speaking, reliving the experience of those groups which preceded them. They will pay relatively high

*The Italian pattern of immigration led most of them to Lawrence, not to Lowell.

percentages of their income in rent to be tenants-at-will in barely habitable housing.* The economics of poverty are implacable.

Life in the tenements was crowded. Space was limited and people lived in large groups to save money on rent. This was especially true of men sending remittances home to a wife and children or to parents, as well as for young, unmarried people. Before their women arrived, Greek men lived in particularly bad conditions in tenements without baths where the ceiling plaster fell from the laths, while toilets clogged and overflowed. Tuberculosis rates among them shot up so fast that one alarmed coffee-house owner installed showers above his establishment as a public service. What was really needed was a good diet and decent living quarters, something higher wages from the mills might have provided.

It was not uncommon for the more rundown tenements to have only one kitchen. The Poles solved the problem of communal cooking in a variety of ways designed to insure that people ate only the food to which they were entitled. Women who made bread cut initials in the uncooked dough to protect it from pilferage while it cooled on the window sill after baking. An individual's or a family's meat in the common pot had string with a ticket attached to it. This was needed especially among the unmarried Poles, because, except in cases where a group clubbed together to hire one of their number as cook and housekeeper, everyone had to feed himself.

Violence was native to the communities, a product of the pressures of life. In the 1830s and 1840s the Irish pursued old-country clan rivalries with so much vigor that the church intervened. For all groups, after drunkenness, the most commonly cited crime in the late nineteenth and early twentieth centuries was assault. Crimes against property seem to have been fairly rare. A very old and often noticed social process was at work here. The poor tend to take out their frustrations against themselves and one another. Occasionally there was class dislike expressed, as among the Greek workers who were contemptuous of compatriot, "big shot" small-businessmen. One might suspect similar feelings among the Irish and French-Canadians against landlords of their own group who exploited them. On the whole,

*Interestingly the Spanish-speaking had the lowest official unemployment rate in the city during the depression of the mid 1970s. Like the immigrant groups which preceded them, they are at the lowest rung of the economic ladder. They have filled most of the low paying, unskilled jobs, which are almost always available, depression or no depression. Their entry into the housing market seems to have driven a part of Lowell's small black population out of the city.

however, violence was a rite of male society while confined within the ethnic group. It became dangerous when it turned outward against other groups.

Hostility between ethnic groups began with the confrontation between Yankees and Irish in the 1830s. The native population's dislike of the immigrants stemmed from a series of irrational feelings. There was the not very often described, but common, hatred and fear of the poor in society. People reacted to economic pressure, and sought to protect themselves from the encroachment of people below. Prosperity in the mill city did not spread across the population. There were always natives close to the poverty line who regarded the growing number of immigrants as unnecessary competition. There was also the often expressed religious hatred, which in the first half of the nineteenth century concentrated on Roman Catholicism. It emanated from traditional native xenophobia with roots in the religious conflicts of the English Reformation centuries earlier. Conflict between natives and Irishmen was frequent, and at least once broke out into a full scale riot. On May 31, 1831, a group of natives invaded the Acre intending to damage the nearly finished St. Patrick's Church. The Irish had expected trouble, for the women had collected rocks and brickbats in piles near an old stone bridge across the Western Canal, which was the logical entry point into the Acre. The Irishmen ambushed the drunken invaders at the bridge and drove them back to regroup. A second native attack broke before an Irish counterattack. The natives were then chased back downtown by the excited Irish women who pelted them with rocks which they carried in their aprons. It was a rout.

As their numbers increased, the Irish became predominant. Their economic position improved somewhat and their place at the bottom of Lowell's society was taken by a succession of new ethnic groups. These, in their turn, became scapegoats, victims of violence. Their position was made worse by the mill companies which paid the newcomers lower wages than the established workforce, and tried to use them as strike-breakers. The Irish and French-Canadians fought one another. Greeks, leaving the mills at night, gathered in self-protecting groups, and sprinted down the middle of the street to their boarding houses. Laggards were assaulted by the Irish. It is a tradition that only after a lone Greek pulled a knife to defend himself did this pattern break. Thereafter any beleaguered Greek moving his hand toward his pocket made the odds tip in his favor. Nonetheless the petty violence continued as gangs of Irish boys terrorized Greek and French-Canadian children. Targets might be children carrying lunchpails to their parents in the mills, or French-Canadian children carrying home a pot of beans for supper or a bag of coal for the stove. Students at the Greek-American school, wearing a blue frock-like uniform, were especially victimized for their "effeminate" clothing. The chief battle-ground was the North Common where the Greek, French-Canadian, and Irish sections came together. Around 1915 the Battle of the Knives, an almost legendary riot, took place here when Irish youths tried to prevent a Greek mother and child from drinking at a fountain. Schoolboy violence reflected the prejudices learned from adults.

Life in the industrial city wore down the immigrants' spirit. Southern Europeans found the winters cold, and no one liked the stifling, humid, contained heat of the cotton mills in summer. Hard too were the long hours of dull work. Factory discipline with its blacklists and insistence on regular attendance was hard to get used to, but the regulation of life by the clock was the most unpleasant new experience. The immigrant who was accustomed to the flexibility of a farmer, herdsman, or fisherman, now had his days circumscribed by whistles or bells. In the older economies from which he had come the rhythm of the year and of the climate gave periods of respite from hard work. There was room in the work year for festivals and holidays. In Lowell the mills were uneconomical when closed down, so holidays were rare.* By the 1890s even low water time at midsummer on the Merrimack did not close the mills which now had other sources of power. In fact respite came to be dreaded for it meant slack time, mill closings, and no wages.

For most of the first and second generation immigrants, life was lean even in periods of national economic prosperity. When depressions came, disaster followed. Unemployment meant hunger, soup kitchens, and bread lines. As marriages came under great economic pressure, families began to break up. Fathers left; children went on the road. Some children, to help feed their family, begged for day-old communion bread at the bakery. Some people bribed overseers to get a chance at the few jobs available in the mills, and took the lowest pay when they got them. Lowell's inhabitants suffered as much and in the same way as the residents of other industrial cities. In 1936, how-

---

*Perhaps this is why Representative Henri Achin, Jr., pushed the Massachusetts General Court in 1917 into declaring the traditional French-Canadian festival, New Year's Day, a legal holiday in the state.

ever, conditions worsened. The Merrimack River flooded and wrecked many of the ethnic districts on the north bank of the river, particularly Centralville. There followed the usual looting and threat of epidemic disease. Depression made the life of the new people very hard, and the experience of surviving left its mark.

From the beginning some of the immigrants prospered in Lowell, but not by working in the mills. They made their way in service businesses. In this, as in many things, the Irish experience was repeated by later groups. Before 1850 natives dominated the Lowell economy, and the only Irish enterprises—a few saloons, grocery and variety stores—drew their customers solely from the ethnic group. As Irish numbers continued to grow, their businesses increased and emerged in new fields. In 1870 the Irish owned four breweries, various retail stores selling clothing and footwear, many provision, grocery, and variety stores, an ice delivery firm and a coal and wood company. By 1875 the Irish nearly had replaced the Yankees in the retailing business. In the decade of the 1870s they were also operating businesses in such skilled trades as plumbing, cabinetmaking, carriage-making, and carpentry. Presumably these were owned by a new generation of Irishmen, who had risen through apprenticeship in Lowell or elsewhere. By 1890, as the third wave of immigrants flowed into Lowell, the Irish enjoyed the economic dominance of retail businesses formerly held by the Yankees.

Meanwhile the French-Canadians had been arriving in numbers. In 1875 they had two bakeries and a clothing store along with the usual grocery and variety stores. The pattern of their business activity widened with the increase in their population. In the 1880s French-Canadians dominated the blacksmith trade; they were teamsters, painters, and builders. Yet, by 1890, they could not match the variety and extent of Irish economic activity. The Irish foothold in politics and the economy was so established that the other ethnic groups' options were distinctly limited. This was even more true for the Poles and Greeks who arrived later than the French-Canadians. After twenty years of Greek settlement, a business directory of 1911 listed only grocers, fruit dealers, barbers, bakers, shoe-shine parlor operators, and restaurateurs. The Jews did a little better. After only brief careers as mill hands, they went into business for themselves as ragpickers, clothes peddlers, and junk dealers. Because they spoke several languages, they served the other immigrants who lacked English. One family ran a grocery store in the middle of Polish Centralville. Another operated a used jewelry store in Little Canada. Many became quite prosperous; some even became rich. The second generation frequently went into the professions. Successful challenges to Irish control of the mercantile economy would come only much later in the twentieth century. By 1970 business in the city was in quite diversified hands. And in lower Belvidere the Spanish-speaking immigrants try to renew the pattern which began with the Irish. They have opened two grocery stores, but the modern supermarket in the area takes care to stock ethnic food. This competition is a real threat and in other parts of the city two other groceries owned by Spanish-speaking people have failed. This has not discouraged other small businessmen. The city is like a living organism; it has its habits and imposes its rhythms of life on all its inhabitants.

The immigrant city maintained its classic contours until World War II, although the pattern of life began to change as early as 1920. Federal laws passed in 1924 cut back on immigration and set up quotas aimed against southern and eastern European peoples, among others. The population stabilized and then began to decline as the great mills started to close in the 1920s. The streetcars gave way to buses and automobiles in the following decade. New buildings were less frequently started. Almost imperceptibly Lowell had become old: it was a Victorian city filled with old housing and rundown plants.

After World War II social change accelerated. Lowell's ethnics went to college in large numbers and became white-collar workers. They went where the jobs were and the city began to lose its educated younger generation. Many people moved into the suburban towns like Dracut, Tewksbury, Chelmsford, and Billerica. Among all the forces breaking down the ethnic communities, the developing progress of intermarriage was the most powerful. The bilingual French-Canadian mother married to a Greek man and living in Chelmsford will fail to teach her children to speak French. As that happens assimilation will have won out over ethnicity. Lowell's ethnic communities will lose their hold on their people and no doubt they will become, like the mill girls, the objects of nostalgia. But they deserve more serious treatment because Lowell is more a product of the immigrants than it is of the city's enshrined heroes, Kirk Boott, Nathan Appleton, Theodore Edson, or the famous mill girls.

Merrimack Manufacturing Company employees. Group photograph, circa 1880. (Lowell Historical Society)

There exists an old sepia-toned photograph from the 1880s of the Merrimack Corporation's mill hands posed in front of the now demolished mill buildings. The majority of the workers are women. Their appearance and the date suggest that they are mostly French-Canadians, but they could, from their peasant style dress, dark hair, and dark eyes, easily be mistaken for later immigrants from southern Europe. They are surrogates for all the immigrant women before and after them who lived out their ordinary lives of marriage, work, birth, sickness, and death in the mill city. Most of them appear still to be young, and their dark eyes have not yet become dulled. Inevitably many of them would die young and most could look forward to a life of hard work. But the families they began would outlast the mills and be the foundation of a city which Kirk Boott would not have recognized. The new people have made themselves a home.

XIII

Minds among the Spindles:
A Cultural History

By Arthur L. Eno, Jr.

"It is the boast of Lowell," wrote historian Charles Cowley in 1856, "that it has no aristocracy, either of wealth or talent, or of rank or position. It is simply a city of mechanics, who have made the world ring with their achievements in mechanism—nothing more."

The achievements of the mechanics, whether in science, as it was then called, or in technology, as we would call it today, were indeed impressive; they were at the basis of the founding and development of Lowell. Francis Cabot Lowell's "patriotic espionage"* and larceny of the idea of the power loom required the mind of a mathematical genius to reproduce the loom. Lowell was aided in this task by a true mechanic, Paul Moody, whose achievements in perfecting the loom became world-famous. Moody went on to invent or improve most of the machinery used in the Boston Manufacturing Company in Waltham. When the Lowell Experiment began in 1823, Moody was brought to Lowell to head the Machine Shop. In compensation for the loss of his services, and for the use of its patterns and patent rights, the Merrimack Company made a $75,000 payment to the Boston Company. The new city's textile industry had not yet been completely set up when Moody died at fifty-four in 1831.

*This felicitous expression is from Perry Miller's *The Life of the Mind in America*.

At Moody's death, the Locks & Canals Company (which had in the meantime taken over the Machine Shop from the Merrimack Company) replaced him with one of the more colorful figures in early Lowell history. Major George Washington Whistler was a graduate of West Point; after teaching there, he had been engaged in railroad building. In 1833 he resigned his commission to become engineer of the Locks & Canals and head of its Machine Shop. During his brief stay in Lowell, Whistler put his engineering experience to practical use and established a profitable side-line for the Machine Shop: building locomotives. When he left Lowell in 1837 to supervise the building of a railroad from Boston to Albany, and later from St. Petersburg to Moscow, he took with him his three-year old son who was to become a great painter, world-renowned wit, and an even more colorful figure than his father.

Whistler's successor was twenty-two-year old James Bicheno Francis who had come from England as his assistant. For forty-eight years Francis continued as chief engineer and then as consulting engineer of the Locks & Canals. During his long tenure he rebuilt the Pawtucket Dam, erected the Francis Gate (known locally as "Francis' Folly" even though it twice saved the city from destruction by flood) and dug the Northern Canal. With Uriah Boyden he improved the design of water turbines. He also conducted scientific experiments to measure the flow of water for the purpose of making an equitable distribution of the waterpower in the Lowell canals. They were published as *Lowell Hydraulic Experiments* (1855). If Francis' other activities smack of practical technology, the hydraulic experiments savor of scientific research, published for the benefit of engineers and scientists, who were thereby enabled to apply them to practical use, and to establish the science of hydraulics. It was Francis who set the scientific standard of the Locks & Canals and its close connection with engineering and other learned societies in Boston. Francis has not been given the credit he deserves for setting the foundations of present-day Lowell and for being one of the first to set up an industrial laboratory.

Francis resided in Lowell as long as he lived. He was honored by his fellow citizens who elected him alderman and representative in the Massachusetts legislature. But his fame spread far beyond the city limits, and he became a member of the corporation of the newly formed Massachusetts Institute of Technology, president of the American Society of Civil Engineers, Fellow of the American Academy of Arts and Sciences, and the recipient of honorary degrees from Dartmouth and Harvard.

Another early scientist was Samuel Luther Dana, M.D., who gave up his medical practice for industrial chemistry and became the chief chemist of the Merrimack Company in 1826. Until his death in 1868, he applied the principles of chemistry to industrial processes, especially to the printing of cotton textiles. While studying the use of cow manure in printing calicoes, he became interested in the agricultural uses of cow dung and produced the pioneer work in agricultural chemistry: the *Muck Manual for Farmers* (1855), which went through many editions. The work is "respectfully dedicated to the Citizens of Lowell." In later years he investigated the problem of lead in the water mains of the city, and, after performing an autopsy on Dr. Augustus Peirce of Tyngsborough, attributed his death to lead poisoning from the pipes leading from his well.

Warren Colburn, recruited by Boott as superintendent of the Merrimack Manufacturing Company, was a mathematician and a teacher. He had already published his textbook on *Intellectual Arithmetic* (1823), which was republished many times over the course of forty years. While in Lowell, Colburn was as much concerned with giving courses and lectures at the Lyceum and the Middlesex Mechanics' Association as he was with superintending the operations of the Merrimack.

Among the other men of science were Charles S. Storrow, who started his long career in Lowell as manager of the Boston & Lowell Railroad before going to Lawrence as agent of the Essex Company which built the city. Later he was elected mayor of Lawrence. Samuel Batchelder, president of the Hamilton Company, was an inventor of textile machinery, including the dynamometer for registering the power of belt-driven machinery. He wrote *Introduction and Early Progress of the Cotton Manufacture in the United States* (1863), an important source for historians of the industry. Elias Howe worked in Lowell as a machinist before he moved on to invent the sewing machine. Erastus B. Bigelow of the Lowell Manufacturing Company invented a loom for weaving carpets and also published *Remarks on the Depressed Condition of Manufactures in Massachusetts with Suggestions as to its Cause and its Remedy* (1858). Perhaps the most successful inventor was George Wellman of the Merrimack Corporation, who patented the self-top card stripper. With typical short-sightedness, the Lowell corporations refused Wellman's offer of the exclusive right to the invention in Lowell for three thousand dollars. Before his death, Wellman had received more than twenty-five thousand dollars from them in royalties.

The endless list of textile manufacturers and mechanics who produced invention after invention gives credence to Michel Chevalier's statement that the typical American "is a mechanic by nature; in Massachusetts and Connecticut there is not a laborer who has not invented a machine or tool."

As befitted its status as second city of the Commonwealth, Lowell in its early days was a center of intellectual activity not limited to the scientific and technological.

In 1830, Congressman Edward Everett delivered the Fourth of July oration before a large crowd. Over a period of many years, starting in 1836, Ralph Waldo Emerson gave at least twenty-five lectures in Lowell. In 1838 the American Institute of Instruction held a five-day meeting in Lowell, at which the mayor, Dr. Elisha Bartlett, addressed the convention on "The Head and the Heart; or, the Relative Importance of Intellectual and Moral Culture." In 1843 an anti-slavery convention featured a speech by William Lloyd Garrison. In 1851, Everett again spoke in Lowell, this time addressing a meeting of the Middlesex Society of Husbandmen and Manufacturers. Between 1851 and 1867, the Middlesex Mechanics' Association held several expositions, at which prizes were awarded for the best mechanical inventions and works of art, as well as for locomotives, needlework, and patent medicines. Nearly two thousand labor delegates attended the New England Workingmens' Convention in Lowell in 1845. On September 9, 1860, Henry David Thoreau delivered his only lecture in the city. The 1880s saw the founding of a French Protestant College, which later moved to Springfield and became American International College.

For some years after the opening of the factories, Lowell had the air of an enormous Female Academy. Mill girls met in reading and improvement circles; they read their poems and essays and finally published their own magazines. The proliferation of ladies' journals, the *Operatives' Magazine*, the *Lowell Offering*, the *New England Offering*, and the *Ladies' Pearl*, to cite only the best known, indicates a widespread audience during the years 1840 to 1845. Regardless of the literary merit of these publications (and Dickens as well as other foreign visitors was impressed) the fact of their publication is more important than their

LOWELL OFFERING

August, 1845.

"Is Saul also among the prophets?"

A REPOSITORY
OF ORIGINAL ARTICLES, WRITTEN BY
"FACTORY GIRLS."

LOWELL: MISSES CURTIS & FARLEY.
BOSTON: JORDAN & WILEY, 121
Washington street.
1845.

Title page of the *Lowell Offering*, 1845. (Lowell Historical Society) content. And the fact that all of them contained local work—the *Offering* was exclusively written by mill girls—makes them even more significant. Fortunately, a few of the authors were content to write about their every-day life and so made a much more valuable contribution than the general moralistic essays of their sisters. Harriet Martineau, the English philosopher-reformer-writer, was so impressed with the *Lowell Offering* that in 1844 she secured the London publication of a collection of excerpts entitled *Mind Among the Spindles*; she herself contributed an introduction.

While the *Offering*'s mill girls were reading their works at gatherings along the Merrimack, there was, elsewhere in town, along the Concord River, another salon of intellectual activity at "Wamesit Cottage," the home of Jane Ermina Locke. Daughter of a distinguished New Hampshire family and sister-in-law of Lowell's first police court judge, she wrote poetry extensively and had it published, first in newspapers and journals, and later in books. Through her literary contacts, she became aware of the financial difficulties of a far more famous writer than she—Edgar Allan Poe. She invited him to lecture in Lowell. He came in 1848 and lectured on American poets and poetry. His visit followed a lengthy, warm correspondence; on his arrival he was surprised to find, not a young, attractive, nubile poetess, but a rotund, plain matron with sickly children. The romantic Poe was disillusioned, but next door at the "Stone Cottage" of the Richmonds he found what he had anticipated. He promptly fell in love with Mrs. Nancy Richmond,* whom he immortalized in several passionate letters and in one of his last poems, "To Annie." Mrs. Locke was understandably hurt. She wrote Mr. Richmond to let him know what was going on. This naturally ended her friendship with Poe; her wrath was assuaged only by his sudden death less than a year later. She composed a eulogy of Poe, adding it to her previously published odes on the deaths of Washington and of William Henry Harrison, the Whig hero of Tippecanoe.

The later years of the nineteenth century saw a number of published Lowell poets, including Benjamin W. Ball, the poet laureate of the 1876 semi-centennial celebration, Robert W. Caverly, the epic poet of the Merrimack River, and Frederick Fanning Ayer, son of Dr. J. C. Ayer and the only one of the group to settle permanently outside Lowell.

A more popular genre of literature, however, was more

*She changed her name legally to Annie in 1879 after her husband's death.

representative of Lowell's culture. A typical example was Dr. Ariel I. Cummings' novel, *The Factory Girl: or Gardez La Coeur** (1847), which glorified the pure young women who became factory operatives, while at the same time revealing the snobbish disdain in which they were held in some quarters. Typically in these fictions, a loutish, rich young man, presumably well educated, tried to seduce the fair and virtuous, but poor, mill operative, of course without success.The characters followed a real-life pattern of the mill girl working either to pay off the mortgage on the family farm, or, more often, to educate a favorite brother at Harvard. These uplifting stories were expanded versions of shorter works in the *Offering*.

Even more popular were the "scandal" novels: the anonymous *Mysteries of Lowell* (1844) and *A Tale of Lowell: Norton; or The Lights and Shades of a Factory Village* (1849) by "Argus" (not to be confused with *Lights and Shadows of Factory Life* (1843) by a "Factory Girl", which belongs to the earlier category). These latter works have the same general theme as Cummings' *Factory Girl*: the incorruptibility and nobility of the factory operative, untouched by the futile attempts on her virtue by men of the "better sort." In the "scandal" novels, however, the descriptions were more racy, the attempts more frequent, and the escapes more narrow.

A still later type of literature of Lowell is the mystery or adventure story, predecessor of the twentieth-century pulp magazines. Examples of this type are *The Factory Detective; or the Mystery of the Merrimack Mills*, by the author of "The Rink Detective," published in New York in 1886; and *Dan Hayes' Greatest Case, or the Mystery of the Central Bridge Fire* by George W. Goode, published locally in 1887, and based upon an actual conflagration. Here again appeared the virtuous mill girl whose seduction was not accomplished, but who suffered drugging and abduction while her fiancé was mugged and as a result suffered from amnesia. Along with these contemporary themes there was a nineteenth century touch: the bank robbers setting out to rob a Lawrence bank, and the detective pursuing them, travelled down the Merrimack River in rowboats.

This type of literature was not limited to the English speaking. There have survived at least two similar works in French by Lowell authors about Lowell murders; one of the stories,

---

*The doctor's literary ability is somewhat greater than his knowledge of French grammar.

Bélanger ou l'Histoire d'un Crime (1892) by George Crépeau, features an exciting chase across Beaver Brook.

The "Yankee El Dorado"—as Harriet Robinson called Lowell—was a great magnet attracting foreign visitors, novelists, sociologists, reformers, and travellers, as well as American politicians and presidents, all anxious to inspect this marvelous new phenomenon—an earthly workers' paradise. The novelty, and the wages, also attracted young men and women from rural New England anxious for the opportunity to work, learn, and make money.

The growing population and wealth attracted others: Lowell was invaded by phrenologists, mesmerists, and fortune-tellers. Millerites in Lowell predicted the end of the world in 1842 (and then, after 1842, reset the date). Amelia Bloomer's ideas of women's dress resulted in a "Bloomer Ball" in 1851. Temperance advocates also abounded, although most of the members of the Cold Water Army were probably natives. Even John Greenleaf Whittier came to edit his abolitionist newspaper, the *Middlesex Standard*, in 1844 and 1845, hoping to convert the Cotton Whigs at all levels of the textile industry into Conscience Whigs, Free-Soilers, and Abolitionists. Louis Kossuth, hero of the 1848 Hungarian revolution, came seeking support for his country.

For good or ill, all came to take something away from the city, to exploit the resources of waterpower, of people, or of money; and, after taking, they left. But they were not the only ones taking from the city. As Ben Butler phrased it, "Our City has been a hive of industry and as a rule the honey has been gathered by others." Not only did most of the dividends go to non-resident owners, but even the wages of the operatives went out of town, at first to their New England homesteads or to their brothers' colleges as tuition payments, and later to foreign homes in the Old Country. And when their bodies became sick and worn out, the operatives too left Lowell forever.

Prominent in the exodus as well were the artists, painters, and writers, who found the climate unfavorable for their art. Both the leading artist and writer had to find fame beyond the city limits.

James Abbott McNeil Whistler, born here while his father was engineer for the Locks & Canals, left Lowell at the age of three. He was without doubt a Lowell native, but hardly, in view of his early departure, a Lowell artist, and he always denied his birthplace. Recognition came only after Whistler had left his

James A. McNeil Whistler, 1834-1903. Cartoon from *Vanity Fair*, March 8, 1873. (Private Collection)

native country to become a resident of Paris and London, and the author of a satirical book whose title epitomized the artist's life: *The Gentle Art of Making Enemies* (1892). Despite his denials, the precursor of the impressionist school of painting was born in Lowell on Worthen Street, in a house now named for him, but which had been built for Paul Moody, and which was later long occupied by James B. Francis. The records of St. Anne's Church show that he was christened there on November 9, 1834.

Lowell's most celebrated and influential writer was born almost a century later. Jack Kerouac was the son of Catholic French-Canadian parents; by heredity he was completely different from Whistler, but like the painter, he rebelled against the bourgeois world. His first novel, *The Town and The City* (1950), was in large part the story of Lowell (called "Galloway" in the book). After his Beat period, exemplified by *On The Road* (1955), Kerouac returned in his books to his native city and wrote of his youthful experiences in *Maggie Cassidy* (1959), *Dr. Sax* (1959), and *Visions of Gerard* (1958). In 1966 he returned to Lowell, but the reality apparently did not match the recollections of his rich imagination and he left again after a few years. He died in Florida in 1969.

In his works, Kerouac expressed perhaps better than anyone else Lowell's hostility to art and literature. He became the leader and prophet of a new school of writing only after he had left the city.

Lowell was the starting point for other artists. David Neal (1837-1915) is probably second to Whistler in renown, albeit a distant second. He left early for Munich where he spent most of his time painting portraits and classical subjects in the traditional style. William Preston Phelps was a sign painter in Lowell who aspired to greater things and went to Europe to study painting with the financial help of some friends (including Mrs. Annie Richmond). On his return, he painted several Lowell scenes until he removed to Chesham, New Hampshire, where he became famous as the painter of Mount Monadnock.

Margaret Foley had been a mill girl and a contributor to the *Lowell Offering*. She became a fine sculptress, specializing in cameo bas-reliefs. She too left Lowell, went to Boston to open a studio, and finally settled in Rome.

Other artists followed the exodus to Boston, among them Lester G. Hornsby, a fine etcher in the style of Whistler, and Alfred Ordway, founder of the Boston Art Club.

Jack Kerouac, 1922-1969. Sculpture by Mico Kaufman. Courtesy of Mrs. Charles G. Sampas. (Photograph by Peter Schell)

In contrast to these, a well known artist remained here. Thomas Bayley Lawson came from Newburyport in 1842 and for the next forty-five years, in his studio above the Institution for Savings, painted portraits of almost everyone of note in the city. He also did a portrait of Daniel Webster from life (and copied it many times). He was commissioned by the city to paint portraits of most of the early mayors. His detailed register listing more than 360 portraits and the price received for each has survived. Lowell society obviously beat a path to his studio; Lawson earned a well deserved local fame, but is not reckoned among the outstanding portraitists of the country.

The same pattern prevails among the authors. Like Kerouac, those who achieved the greatest renown left the city before attaining it. Lucy Larcom is perhaps the best known, as well as the most typical. Her poems, published in the *Lowell Offering* and praised by Whittier, gained her a modest reputation in her adopted city. In 1845 Larcom left Lowell and the cotton mills for the Midwest, where she became a teacher. Her major mill poem, *An Idyll of Work*, was published in 1875, long after she had left the mills. Her writings (prose as well as poetry) grew in number and made her famous by the time she published her autobiography, *A New England Girlhood*, in 1889, four years before her death. Her colleagues on the *Offering*, Harriet Hanson Robinson, Harriot F. Curtis, and Harriet Farley, produced their major works after leaving Lowell. Robinson's *Loom and Spindle* is the most memorable — a fond, nostalgic reliving of her days as a mill girl, written in Malden in 1898. In the last chapter, she retells her experience in speaking to a group of mill girls in Lowell shortly before writing her book. As she was speaking to the audience and questioning the young women, she realized that the life of the operative had changed drastically since she had been in the mills, and that the operatives no longer had the joy and hunger for learning of the earlier days; drudgery and weariness had become the order of the day.

The other two alumnae of the *Offering* produced novels in their post-Lowell days. Harriet Farley's later work probably cannot equal her stirring editorials in the *Lowell Offering*, in which she battled all the critics of the paper, on the one hand attacking Orestes Brownson for his supposed libel of the factory girls, and on the other, defending the magazine against Sarah Bagley's accusations that the editors were the dupes of the mill owners and were guilty of misrepresentation for not writing about the sordid side of factory life.

Lucy Larcom, 1824-1893. Photograph courtesy of Lowell City Library

One twentieth century author did remain in Lowell and achieved more than local recognition. Philip S. Marden had a distinguished career as editor of the *Courier Citizen*. He later published collections of his notable "Saturday Chat" columns from that newspaper.

The anti-intellectual atmosphere of Lowell was commented on by one of her most important literary visitors—the Quaker poet of the Merrimack valley, John Greenleaf Whittier. From his stay in Lowell as editor of the *Middlesex Standard* came a series of newspaper articles later published in 1845 as *Stranger in Lowell*—the most literary of the descriptions of Lowell by domestic visitors. In 1844, in a letter to Ann Elizabeth Wendell, Whittier wrote: "Tell E. L.* that even her 'fine frenzy' would suffer in such a place as Lowell; and that a residence of six months amidst the din of the shuttles would drive everything like poetry out of her head, as effectually as out of mine."

Emerson agreed that Lowell was not literary, but technological. In his journal he wrote with grudging admiration:

> An American in this ardent climate gets up early some morning and buys a river; and advertises for twelve or fifteen hundred Irishmen; digs a new channel for it, brings it to his mills, and has a head of twenty-four feet of water; then to give him an appetite for his breakfast, he raises a house; then carves out, within doors, a quarter township into streets and building lots, tavern, school, and the Methodist meeting house—sends up an engineer into New Hampshire, to see where his water comes from, and after advising with him, sends a trusty man of business to buy of all the farmers such mill-privileges as will serve him among their waste hill and pasture lots, and comes home with great glee announcing that he is now owner of the great Lake Winipiseogee, as reservoir for his Lowell mills at midsummer.

> They are an ardent race, and are fully possessed with that hatred of labor, which is the principle of progress in the human race, as any other people. They must and will have the enjoyment without the sweat. So they buy slaves, where the women will permit it; where they will not, they make the wind, the tide, the waterfall, the stream, the cloud, the lightning, do the work, by every art and device their cunningest brain can achieve.

If the air of Lowell was not friendly to artists and authors, it seems to have been more favorable to the professions. Doctors, lawyers and politicians thrived: many of them even achieved distinction without leaving the city.

*Possibly Lucy Larcom's elder sister Emilie; the Larcoms were friends of Whittier and his sister.

Shortly after the founding of the mills, several young physicians arrived. Samuel L. Dana had given up the practice of
medicine to become the Merrimack Company's chief chemist.
But John O. Greene, Elisha Bartlett, and Elisha Huntington
came as practicing physicians and found fame.

Six days after arriving in East Chelmsford, Greene had as his
first patient Kirk Boott, who had been thrown out of his carriage
while descending a hill. Fifteen years later, in 1837, Greene
again attended his first patient, for the last time, when Boott was
fatally stricken in his chaise near the Merrimack House. Greene
was elected to the first school committee of Lowell and was
re-elected for fourteen years. Speaking at the semi-centennial
exercises in 1876, he was one of the longest survivors of the
original "old residents." In his long practice he enjoyed the
respect of numerous patients and fellow-citizens.

Elisha Bartlett started practice in Lowell in 1827. Nine years
later, at the age of thirty-two, he was elected the city's first mayor
—a great honor because, as his eulogist pointed out, there will
be only one first mayor in the city's history. Prior to his election,
Bartlett had edited an early medical journal, *Medical Literature
and American Medical Students' Gazette* (1832). After his two
terms as mayor, he published his famous contribution to the
"Battle of the Books": *Vindication of the Character and Condition of the Females Employed in the Lowell Mills* (1841), a reply
to Orestes Brownson's critical article on "The Laboring Classes"
in the July, 1840, issue of *The Boston Quarterly Review*. After
leaving Lowell, he was a professor in several medical schools,
including Dartmouth and the College of Physicians and Sur-
geons in New York.

Even more honored by his fellow citizens was Dr. Elisha
Huntington, who was elected mayor eight times between 1840
and 1858, a record never equalled. In 1852, Huntington was
elected lieutenant-governor of Massachusetts, one of two Lowell
men to hold that office.*

Another early physician, who achieved international renown,
was Gilman Kimball. After studying surgery in Paris, Kimball
came to Lowell in 1830, and became head of the Corporation
Hospital when it was founded in 1840. He specialized in
gynecology, an appropriate specialty in the City of Women. He

---

*The other was John Nesmith, industrialist, inventor, and developer of Belvi-
dere, who served in 1862.

pioneered several types of gynecological surgery, which were daring for the time, and which spread his fame to Europe.

Lowell has had at least its share of historians, starting with the Reverend Henry A. Miles who wrote *Lowell As It Was and As It Is* (1845). Despite its intense pro-mill bias, this is a fascinating and valuable work. It is the chief source of information about the Lowell Moral Police, the system of paternalistic control devised by the mill owners to protect the morals of the mill girls and to allay the fears of their parents.

The Herodotus of Lowell was Charles Cowley, lawyer, Civil War paymaster, editor, pamphleteer, and corporate reformer. His *History of Lowell* is the source of most information about the history of the city until 1868, the book's date of publication. Although the later years are treated merely in a chronological listing, there are many passages where Cowley lets his indignation show. When reporting how the floor of Huntington Hall collapsed during an oration by Rufus Choate where there were assembled "nearly all the Lowell politicians of all parties," Cowley comments that [their] "loss would have been an infinite gain." His judgment on the decision of the Lowell corporations at the beginning of the Civil War to sell their cotton and close down their factories was even more vitriolic: "under a mistaken belief that they could not run their mills to a profit during the War, [they] unanimously, in cold blood, dismissed ten thousand operatives, penniless, into the streets! . . . . This crime, this worse than crime, this *blunder*. . . ."

More sociologist than historian was George F. Kenngott, a Unitarian minister whose Harvard doctoral thesis was published as *The Record of a City* (1912). Kenngott treats of immigration and the life of the immigrant workers which Cowley in 1868 could only have imagined.

The latest published local historian was also the most prolific. Frederick W. Coburn published his three-volume history in 1920. The most recent general history, it is marred only by the one-and-a-half volume "biographical section" of paid biographies and by the traditional neglect of the mill operatives except as participants in parades for visiting presidents and as writers in the *Lowell Offering*.*

Journalism is a profession which flourished in early Lowell,

*Although they were not written by local historians, mention should be made here of John Coolidge's *Mill and Mansion* (1942) and Hannah Josephson's *The Golden Threads* (1949), both excellent works.

where at one time there were as many as a dozen daily, tri-week-
ly, and weekly newspapers being published. They represented
all views: from the *Lowell Journal* (which later became the
Courier-Citizen) speaking for the establishment, through the
Advertiser, which "always supported the democracy" (although
the Democrats failed to support it and it disappeared), to the
Voice of Industry, a powerful and well written labor newspaper
campaigning not only for the ten-hour day, but also
simultaneously for women's rights, suffrage and the abolition of
slavery. There was also a libelous sheet known as *Life in Lowell.*

The *Voice* was published in Lowell for several years, at one
time as the official organ of the Lowell Female Labor Reform
Association. Its editor for a time was another literary mill girl,
Sarah G. Bagley, who never received the recognition she deserved. Leaving the mills in 1846, she became the first woman
telegrapher and was in charge of the Lowell office of Samuel
F. B. Morse's Magnetic Telegraph. After this, no trace of her life
(or death) can be found. Although she had submitted stories to
the *Offering* (and had some published), she felt that the *Offering*'s editors had been duped by the mill owners to "gloss over
the evils, wrongs, and privations of factory life." When the *Offering* finally ceased publication, Bagley wrote that on the whole it
had done more harm than good. With such jibes at Lowell's
beloved symbol, it is little wonder that Sarah Bagley's name has
disappeared and that not one copy of the *Voice of Industry* is
known to have survived in Lowell.

The most literary newspaper was *Vox Populi* which continued for many years, publishing articles by Ben Butler and
other young anti-establishment lawyers. The *Vox* always prided
itself on its literary style; nevertheless, it also perished.

A journalist who worked in Lowell (and married Harriet
Hanson, one of the literary mill operatives) was William S.
Robinson, who edited newspapers in Lowell, Concord, and
Boston. He wrote satirical profiles of political figures under the
pen-name of "Warrington." For many years he served as clerk of
the Massachusetts House of Representatives; he was finally oust-
ed by the efforts of Ben Butler, with whom he had carried on a
lifetime feud begun when Robinson wrote a critical report of one
of Butler's early court victories.

The legal profession also produced many men of distinction.
Before Lowell was founded, Ashahel Stearns practiced law by

the Pawtucket Falls. He left in 1817, before the arrival of the mills, to become the first professor of law at Harvard's newly founded law school.

In the early days of the city, there was a distinguished group of practitioners. Wendell Phillips, the great abolitionist, studied law in Lowell in the office of Thomas Hopkinson, a partner of Luther Lawrence. John P. Robinson, acknowledged to be the greatest of them all, was slightly immortalized by James Russell Lowell for his political unorthodoxy in abandoning Governor George N. Briggs, the Whig gubernatorial candidate in the 1847 election, to vote for Caleb Cushing.* Robinson had studied law in Daniel Webster's office, and was reputed to be the best classical scholar in Lowell. After a distinguished legal and political career, which included serving as representative and state senator, Robinson died tragically in the McLean Asylum for the Insane in Somerville.

One of the early corporation attorneys was Seth Ames who went on to become a justice of the Supreme Judicial Court of Massachusetts. Another, Josiah G. Abbott, became one of the first appointees to the newly created Superior Court, but resigned to practice law and later refused appointment to the Supreme Judicial Court. William S. Gardner, who had practiced law in Lowell for many years, served as justice of the Supreme Judicial Court from 1885 to 1887. Lowell's only other Supreme Court justice was Stanley E. Qua who was also, from 1947 to 1956, the only Lowell lawyer to serve a chief justice of that court. William A. Richardson, one of a trio of lawyer brothers from Tyngsborough who practiced in Lowell, became chief justice of the United States Court of Claims in Washington, after serving as secretary of the treasury in the administration of President Grant.

Without doubt, the most famous Lowell lawyer was Benjamin Franklin Butler. His career as a politician, Civil War general, and governor of Massachusetts has obscured his greatness as a lawyer. During his many years of law practice (which continued

---

*"But John P.
Robinson he
Sez he wunt vote for Guverner B.

       *   *   *

So John P.
Robinson he
Sez he shall vote for Gineral C."

Lowell, *The Biglow Papers*, III, 5, 19.

without interruption during his terms as congressman and even during his one-year term as governor), he maintained an exhausting schedule, with offices in both Lowell and Boston and later in Washington as well. In his peak years, he appeared on one side or another of a large percentage of the cases decided by the Supreme Judicial Court and reported in the Massachusetts Reports; in addition, he argued many cases in the United States Supreme Court, one of the less successful of which was his argument for the government in *Ex Parte Milligan*.*

He early achieved fame locally as an advocate for mill operatives whose wages were being unlawfully witheld by the corporations. One such operative retained Butler to collect her wages by attaching the great water wheel of the Merrimack mill. Butler succeeded in collecting the wages without legal action; however, he did not disabuse his client from thinking that he had attached the millwheel, and his reputation was made. His success brought down on him the lifetime enmity of all the mill establishment.

Successful as he was as a lawyer, Butler's fame came primarily through politics. He attended the Democratic National Convention in 1860 and cast fifty-seven ballots for the nomination for president of Jefferson Davis, who, a few years later, after Butler's capture of New Orleans, declared him an outlaw and placed a price on his head. In the Civil War, he was one of the first generals to reach the capital with troops; he quickly subjugated Maryland, thus assuring a line of supply between the industrial north and Washington. Because of this service, he was promoted to major general and became the senior ranking of the "political generals" who were so numerous in the Union Army. Before he was cashiered, he had brought order to captured New Orleans, had threatened Richmond (and bungled the opportunity to take it), and had anticipated the Emancipation Proclamation by declaring the slaves of rebels to be "contraband of war" and enlisting them in the Union Army. One of the many ironies of his long career was his refusal to accept the vice-presidential nomination for Lincoln's second term unless the president guaranteed to die within three months of the inauguration. If Butler had not been so cynical, he might well have been president of the United States without having to run an abortive campaign as the People's party candidate in 1884.

*Holding that President Lincoln had no right to have Milligan, a citizen of a free state, tried by a military court, and that the right to a trial by jury could not be denied him.

After the War, Butler was elected to Congress as a Republican for five terms. A Radical Republican, he was one of the Board of Managers of Andrew Johnson's impeachment. He also voted for the first civil rights bill enacted by Congress and supported women's suffrage many decades before it became law.

In 1871, Butler began a quest for the governorship of Massachusetts, first as a Republican, then as a Democrat. He was finally successful and served a stormy one-year term in 1882-83. During his term, because another of Butler's old enemies, Judge Ebenezer Rockwood Hoar, was chairman of the Board of Overseers, Harvard University abandoned its tradition of awarding an honorary degree to the governor in office and established its present policy of extremely selective awards.

After his defeat for a second term, Butler gave up active politics (except for his one presidential campaign as a third-party candidate) but continued his extremely busy and lucrative law practice. He relaxed on his yacht, the *America,* which he had bought from the Navy Department, and which gave its name to the America's Cup racing trophy; and he published his autobiography, *Butler's Book* (1892).*

He died in 1893, still the center of controversy, the favorite target of cartoonists like Thomas Nast, but with a huge constituency of his fellow citizens, blacks, women suffragists, and a few journalists like Charles A. Dana of the *New York Sun* who wrote:

> For the last quarter of a century at least, Benjamin F. Butler has stood out as the most original, the most American and the most picturesque character in our public life. He had courage equal to every occasion; . . . . . . his intellectual resources were marvelous; his mind naturally adhered to the poor and the weak; and his delight was to stand by the underdog in the fight. In these qualities he was a great and exceptional man. . . . . But was he great in everything? . . . No man attains to that height, and no man ever scorned the impostures of sham goodness and unattainable perfection more than Benjamin Butler. He was no pretender and no hypocrite. He lived his life, a life of energy and effort, of success and of failure and he has passed to the allotted reward while we who remain may well be grateful to heaven that such a man has lived.

In the year of Butler's death, a second Lowell lawyer was

---

*Another major Lowell autobiography was *Recollections of Seventy Years* (1934) by William Cardinal O'Connell, a prince of the Catholic Church who was born in Lowell and who was a mill hand for one morning, until he quit in disgust. O'Connell did not share Nathan Appleton's view of the pleasures and benefits of factory labor.

elected governor of Massachusetts. Frederic T. Greenhalge was born in England and as a boy of twelve came to Lowell with his father who was to head the Merrimack Print Works. Graduate of Harvard, mayor of Lowell, and congressman, Greenhalge was elected governor three times, but died early in his third term.*

Such was the contradictory story of Lowell: it was, on the one hand, a place of intense intellectual activity and a magnet attracting visitors from afar; on the other, a typically grim industrial city smothering native artistic genius. Perhaps this is the story of every American city, as well as of the nation itself.

During the decade in which the two governors from Lowell died, there were founded two institutions of higher education: in 1894, Lowell Normal School, which eventually became Lowell State College, and, in 1895, Lowell Textile School, which for decades was world renowned as the outstanding school for textile education. More than three-quarters of a century later, both institutions were merged into the University of Lowell. Today the activities of the university, the efforts to establish in Lowell the nation's first Urban National Cultural Park, and many other current projects are reminiscent of the bustle of the early days of Lowell.

Perhaps these activities will produce a cultural renascence and make Lowell once again a factor to be reckoned with; perhaps even, finally, they will prove the truth of its municipal motto: ART IS THE HANDMAID OF HUMAN GOOD.

*The only other Lowell resident to become a governor was Charles H. Allen, appointed governor of Puerto Rico by President McKinley in 1900.

XIV

The Outsiders' View:
Visitors to the Industrial Showcase

By Robert Dugan

Lowell, with its steeple-crowned factories, resembles a Spanish town with its convents; but with this difference, that in Lowell, you meet no rags nor Madonnas, and that the nuns in Lowell, instead of working sacred hearts, spin and weave cotton. Lowell is not amusing, but it is neat and decent, peaceable and sage. Will it always be so? Will it be so long?

So wrote, in 1836, Michel Chevalier, the French political economist sent to the United States by Thiers, minister of the interior under King Louis Philippe. Chevalier was charged with studying American industry and came to Lowell on June 12, 1834. Out of his visit came two chapters on Lowell and the mill girls in his *Society, Manners and Politics in the United States*. He was most impressed with the female operatives and, as he watched them pass in the streets, said to himself, "This, then, is not Manchester [England]."

When, many years later, Prince Jerome Napoleon Bonaparte visted the United States, Chevalier urged him to visit Lowell to see the mill girls. On September 21, 1861, the prince, accompanied by his wife, Princess Clothilde, arrived for the grand tour. Seated in a barouche, the visitors were driven through the principal streets to get an overall view. But the celebrated mill girls were nowhere to be seen. As Charles Cowley reported:

More than a quarter of a century had elapsed since Chevalier's visit; the New England girls on whom he then gazed so admiringly, had passed away; and their places now filled by a motley crowd of American, English, Scotch, Irish, Dutch and French Canadians, who were hardly likely to arouse the exquisite poetic sentiment which Chevalier felt for the factory-girls of 1834.

When, in 1867, Napoleon III appointed Chevalier to organize the International Exposition in Paris, the aging Chevalier thought it would be a fine idea to have some of the Lowell mill girls demonstrating their power looms. He asked a Boston friend to try to arrange it, only to learn that there were no more demure farm girls left in Lowell. In fact, on the very day the exposition opened, the Lowell spinners went out on strike for higher wages.

Chevalier was one of a long line of foreign observers to visit Lowell. The first to write of his visit was Captain Basil Hall of the Royal Navy who came to Lowell in 1827, the year after its incorporation and five years after the founding of the mills. At such an early date, the captain was already impressed with the neatness of the workers and the cleanliness of the city — a refrain which was to endure through Trollope's visit during the Civil War.

English writer and social reformer Harriet Martineau visited the United States between 1834 and 1836. Spending several months in Massachusetts, Martineau had a chance to visit Lowell and commented on some aspects of life here in her *Society in America*. Writing in general terms on manufacturing, she pointed to Lowell as an example of an industrial system in which the operatives were well off. She also believed that the factories and boarding houses relieved suffering from poverty for the rural girls by providing for their care.

An English novelist, Frederick Marryat, made a trip to the United States in 1837. During his stay, he visited Lowell and wrote about it in his *A Diary in America*. Marryat had come to Lowell doubting the glowing reports of Miss Martineau; he proved his doubts, at least to his own satisfaction, when he heard one American female swearing most proficiently. He wrote that two days at Lowell convinced him that human nature was the same everywhere.

In January, 1842, came the most distinguished English man of letters to visit Lowell, Charles Dickens, who devoted a chapter of his *American Notes* to his favorable impressions of Lowell. Again, he was impressed with the cleanliness (and the newness)

Casey and Meehan take care of most of the patronage demands of the French, but they openly courted French votes. Casey became mayor in 1904 and 1905 but was defeated in 1906 and 1908 by a split in the party over his use of the police board to obtain campaign funds. This raised the temperance issue once more to the benefit of the Republicans.

Casey's successor as Democratic mayor, John Meehan, did not repeat his predecessor's mistakes. Meehan was the ablest politician in the Democratic party since Butler and Donovan. He quickly reunified the party and deftly avoided the liquor-law issue. In two years the Republicans believed their party was finished as a force in municipal politics. Meehan was aided in his organizational work by another upcoming young Democrat, James E. O'Donnell, Jr.

Born in Lowell in 1875, Meehan resided in Ward Two in the city center, and worked as an accountant for a construction company. He was principal of the Butler Night School where mill workers could learn to read and write. In 1906, he served the first of three terms as state representative. Meehan won a primary fight with O'Donnell for the mayoral nomination in 1909 with a strong vote from the workingclass French sixth ward. In the election campaign he worked hard to reunite the party, concentrating on the other French ward. So large was his vote for mayor in 1909 that the *Courier-Citizen,* the Republican daily, mourned that the city would never again see another Republican mayor. In 1910, Meehan repeated his success with a landslide victory, demonstrating the durability of the Democratic coalition with the French voters, especially those in Ward Six. The Democrats had reserved two places on their aldermantic ticket for French-Canadians, Joseph Jodoin, and Hercule Toupin, who carried most of the 1882 registered Republican votes in the French wards. The Board of Aldermen went nine to zero Democratic, Democrat Edward Foye became purchasing agent, and the Democrats on the Common Council in combination with the aldermen controlled all city appointments.

The crushing defeat in 1910 convinced the Republican leadership that their party was in shambles, and they moved to revive interest in municipal reform. The immediate motive was to prevent the Democrats from becoming the only viable political force in the city by changing the rules of the political game. Long term dissatisfaction with growing city indebtedness and rising taxes, the liquor scandals, and the takeover of city jobs by Democrats provided wide support for a municipal reform movement, organized and directed in 1911 by a group of lawyers in the Lowell Board of Trade.

The Board of Trade proposed a new city charter in 1911. A four-member commission and mayor elected at-large would conduct the affairs of the city much as a board of directors conducted the affairs of a corporation, an analogy which the reformers emphasized. Each commissioner would be responsible for the operations and finances of a separate city department. Wards would be abolished as representative units; political party designations would end. Elections would be non-partisan and city-wide. The School Committee was to be elected at-large, again eliminating a representative from each ward. Recall, referendum, and initiative procedures would replace annual elections but beginning the process required the signatures of twenty percent of the voters. The liquor licensing and enforcement functions of the police board would be separated.

The proposed charter struck deeply at the power of the Democrats in the city. The ward system was the foundation of Democratic representation on the Common Council, the School Committee, and in the state legislative districts. The dual functions of the police board provided campaign funds. Meehan and the Democrats saw the reform proposal as a direct assault on their strength and success as a party, and they struggled fiercely to defeat it. Hecklers at pro-charter rallies claimed the reform was anti-democratic elitism and a conspiracy of business interests against the working man. Meehan testified at the legislative hearings on the proposal in March, 1911, that the charter was backed by men who have "dinner" against men who have "supper." He described Lowell as a city which needed the ward system to represent its different neighborhoods and nationalities. Nonetheless, the Republican-controlled legislature voted approval, and the charter proposal came to a vote in Lowell in the November elections.

The strategy of the Democrats was to turn out a heavy vote against the charter based on the landslide vote of the preceding year. It became evident however that the French community would split on the charter issue; L'Etoile and middle class French lawyers, small businessmen, and doctors came out strongly for the charter change. Their spokesman, Dr. Joseph E. Lamoureux, argued in a column in L'Etoile called "Oui ou Non?" that the political influence of the French would increase with the new charter because the influence of the Irish, whose power lay in the wards, would decline. Meehan and the Democrats attempted to counter Lamoureux by taking political ads in French in *L'Etoile* to argue that the French risked the loss of all representation in the city government and on the school committee in non-partisan at-large elections.

The middle-class voter was the major target of the proponents of charter reform. The old system, they explained, was corrupt and expensive, directed by men who made politics a profession. The new city charter meant efficiency, reduced expenditures, lower taxes, and a more business-like conduct of city programs. Meehan and the Democrats worried about the impact of these arguments on middle class Irish voters. One major defection was James E. O'Donnell, Jr., who announced his neutrality on the charter question and his intention to run for mayor whichever system won in November.

O'Donnell was born in Lowell in 1875, the son of a well known undertaker in the Irish community. He attended Boston University Law School and was a typical middle class professional man, yet he had a political sense. O'Donnell saw that the middle class Irish vote would desert the party on charter reform in the election on November 7. The vote on the charter in the regular elections divided along class lines. The Yankee middle class wards voted heavily for the charter. The French wards split, as many had predicted, with the working class, "Little Canada" Ward Six voting against the charter, and the more affluent Ward Seven in Pawtucketville, across the river from the mills, voting for the charter. Traditionally Irish, Democratic, and working class wards Two, Four and Five voted heavily no; but wards Three and Eight in the Highlands, an area where middle class Irish families were moving away from the central city, and which voted Democratic on all other issues, provided the winning margin for the charter. The charter reform carried by a 1294-vote majority at the same time as Democratic Governor Eugene Foss carried the city by 2381 votes. The defection of middle class Irish votes was obvious; Meehan's work and hopes were smashed.

The primary to nominate candidates for mayor was a curious affair. Although formally non-partisan, everyone in the city knew that O'Donnell would be the Democratic candidate after he defeated primary opponents in the party too closely identified with Meehan and the old system. The Republicans, however, had a problem in the primary. None of the reformers were interested in interrupting their professional lives to take on the mayor's office. Dr. Lamoureux, for example, refused to disrupt his medical practice. The pro-charter groups decided to back Colonel Percy Parker, an ex-West Point officer and Indian fighter, who lived on his investments in banking, real estate, and trolley lines. His manner was stiff and condescending; his only political experience was on the Park Commission. Backed by the solid Republican vote, Parker won the nomination. Another major result of the primary vote was to eliminate all French-Canadian candidates for the commission or the School Committee; none would appear on the ballot.

O'Donnell concentrated on unifying the Democrats and winning the loyalty of Meehan's supporters. All of the old line Democrats knew that if they could elect three members of the commission, they would control the city government. O'Donnell's neutrality on the charter question enabled him to appeal to middle class Irish voters, and he relentlessly campaigned in the French wards, walking the streets and tracking down voters. In contrast, Parker merely allowed himself to be driven through the French neighborhoods in an expensive touring car, nodding occasionally to passersby.

On election day O'Donnell and the Democrats won control of the commission and the school committee, capturing the city government under the new charter. This decisive shift to Irish Democratic control reduced to insignificance all other political forces in the city. The Democratic wards delivered heavily for O'Donnell, who led the balloting, and for two other Irish Democrats, Lawrence Cummings and James E. Donnelly. Their three votes controlled the commission. All four Irish Democrats nominated in the primary were elected to the school committee with the only other place going to Yankee John Jacob Rogers. This was an historic and impressive reversal of control typifying the decline of Yankee power in municipal politics. One of the major factors in the school committee election was the massive registration of women voters under an 1870 state law which permitted women to vote in school elections. Organized mostly by Irish Democratic candidates for school committee, women registered by the hundreds. When each ward was guaranteed a representative on the school committee, their votes were not needed. In an at-large election they were vital. The day the books closed before the election, women voters had increased by 5435 or an increase of six hundred percent.

The Democrats in the city literally went wild over the election.

The vanguard of a cheering crowd of ten thousand led by a brass band unhitched the horses from O'Donnell's carriage and drew him through the streets of the business district. Red torches and roman candles lit up the scene until supplies in local shops were exhausted. The cheering became deafening in front of the *Low-ell Sun* building in Merrimack Square. The *Sun*, owned by John H. Harrington, had endorsed Parker, and the crowd jeered. After many speeches and many ovations O'Donnell, bursting with satisfaction and joy at the returns, finished the celebration by singing several vaudeville tunes.

The Yankees were silent, the French deeply resentful. *L'Etoile* now saw that Mayor Meehan had been right:

> Now that the candidates are elected at-large how can the French or any minority group hope to hold the balance of power which was the only weapon we had. . . . We must say with bitterness that for the present the political influence of the French-Americans is finished under the new charter.

Charter reformers had organized in 1911 to prevent the Democrats under Meehan from enjoying a powerful coalition with the French. The result was to eliminate both Yankee and French influence in the city's political life and to deliver municipal politics into the hands of the Irish.

After 1911 the shift to Irish Democratic political strength in the city was capped by the adoption of a strong mayor, Plan B charter* in 1924 and by an astounding turnout in the 1928 elections. The key element was the presidential candidacy of Irish Catholic Al Smith of New York on the Democratic ticket against Republican Herbert Hoover. Local party workers, their relatives, and youngsters more than doubled the registration of Democratic voters in Lowell. This enormous new registration became the source of a new generation of Democratic leaders with a very large constituency in the city.

Smith and the Democrats, local and state, swept Lowell in the elections of 1928. Hoover carried only two of the city's wards, and Smith won the city by 10,000 votes. The election, in which an amazing 93.5 percent of the voters turned out, laid the basis for Franklin D. Roosevelt's victories in Lowell starting in 1932.

The city's Democratic party fared much less well during the years of the Depression and the New Deal. Many of the textile mills had departed en masse in the late twenties, and some of the mill owners decided to tear down the brick structures instead of paying property taxes on the buildings. The mills literally began

*Plan B is one of several standard charter forms provided by the General Laws of Massachusetts.

to disappear, while the value of the inner city property declined quickly. Falling tax revenues and general helplessness in the face of economic difficulties paralyzed the city government. Republican leadership, bent on economy, returned to city hall. Democrats on the council worked hard to get the unemployed on relief and on city work, partially financed by federal WPA money and partially by borrowing from the state. However in 1938 almost forty percent of the population of Lowell still received some kind of relief. The stagnant economy of the 1930s greatly increased the value of political jobs, which produced serious factionalism among the Irish Democrats. This factionalism reached a critical point during the early 1940s resulting in a change from the strong-mayor, Plan B government to the city manager-council government of Plan E.

In the 1939 elections former city laborer and state representative George T. Ashe got the backing of Democratic ex-mayor James J. Bruin to recover control of the mayor's office from the Republicans. Organization and money for rallies and radio speeches plus Ashe's image as a workingman's candidate helped him win easily against Republican warhorse Thomas H. Braden. The key issue of the campaign was Ashe's promise to cut both city spending and the tax rate, taking the economy issue from the Republicans. Cuts in city spending, however, struck at the political base of the local Democratic party which depended heavily on the bloc votes of city employees and on patronage for the unemployed. The new mayor quickly found himself in angry conflict with his own party's leaders. Furthermore, Ashe was unable to cut taxes sufficiently to please the Taxpayers' Association, and he therefore risked alienating the anti-tax forces which had backed him in 1939.

In an effort to regain the support of the Taxpayers' Association for another mayoral try in 1941, Ashe pushed a departmental merger plan to place all city employees under one head and thus eliminate all department heads. This, he argued, would increase efficiency and decrease expenditures. Enraged city employees hired Bruin as their attorney to fight the plan. The city council defeated the idea, but it was good politics for Ashe to advocate among economy minded voters.

Meanwhile the mayor moved to undercut Bruin's hold on city employees by supporting expansion in the Water Department and by using WPA funds to raise the salaries of city workers. Shut off from Bruin's sources of support in the local party, Ashe built his own campaign treasury and organization. In August, 1941, with employment rising from defense contracts in the area, the incumbent mayor could announce a $5.60 tax cut in time for the September Democratic primary against William C. Geary who was backed by Bruin. Ashe won narrowly and again faced Braden whom he defeated but by a much smaller margin than in 1939. The fight with the Bruin Democrats nearly cost Ashe the election.

The re-elected mayor faced immediate trouble. He had alienated the regular Democratic party which controlled local campaign financing. He needed to raise money for his own political organization. Then in February, 1942, a Middlesex County grand jury began to investigate scandals in the City Water Department and in city purchasing. In April Ashe was indicted on one count of conspiracy to defraud dealing with kick-backs on city purchases and on one count of bribery arising from school renovation contracts. While the trial proceeded, a movement organized in Lowell for a new city government to eliminate the strong mayor and replace him with a city manager who would use the mayor's powers efficiently and with no attention to politics. Mayor Ashe was convicted on both counts in November, 1942, and the strong-mayor system in Lowell was on its way out.

The movement for the adoption of Plan E was headed by Harvard educated Yankee lawyer, Woodbury F. Howard. City government under Plan E would consist of nine councilors elected at-large by proportional representation. The majority of the councilors would then select a city manager to administer the city. Howard deftly got backing for the new charter from those groups discouraged from political activity under the old charter. The committee for Plan E featured prominent Greek, French, and Yankee names plus several Irish ones along with a lone Polish name. The reform movement implicitly opposed ethnic divisions and explicitly condemned partisan politics.

A special election was held in November, 1942, to vote on the new charter. Despite the strong opposition of the city employees led by Hubert L. McLaughlin, former city solicitor under Ashe, and from the local Democratic leaders, Bruin and Geary, the new charter won by a small margin. The victory margin came from heavy voting in French Ward Six and in Republican Ward Eight with significant support from traditionally Democratic wards, indicating strong disenchantment with the Ashe conviction and the local party.

Woodbury Howard became mayor in 1943 because of his iden-
tification with Plan E and the election of four other reform councilors who voted for him. The key choice of city manager, however, went to ex-city treasurer, Democrat John J. Flannery, the
personal candidate of Councilor Joseph J. Sweeney who as acting mayor had replaced Ashe. On the vote to choose the manager,
reform sentiment vanished and the Democrats won on a straight
party vote, five to four. Woodbury Howard and the Republicans
on the council continued to advocate reform in city government
and oppose moves by Bruin and Geary to get rid of proportional
representation. Howard, however, lost his bid to be mayor again
in 1945 and ended his career on the council in 1950.

An integral feature of the new Plan E charter was proportional
representation, a weighted system of voting in elections which
favors minority group participation in city affairs.* The PR system increased the power of groups which had formerly played a
limited role in city politics. The most noticeable new groups
were the Greek-Americans and the Polish-Americans. By 1950,
most major ethnic groups in Lowell—Yankees, Irish, French,
Polish, and Greeks—were represented on the city council by
Hockmeyer, Callery, Ayotte, Janas, and Eliades, among others.
Until PR was dropped in 1958, the Irish held four seats, picking
up another when the Yankee representative failed to get elected,
the French held two seats, the Poles one (beginning in 1947) and
the Greeks one (beginning in 1949).

In response to persistent efforts by Democrats locally and
through the state legislature, a referendum on PR was placed on
the ballot in November, 1955 allegedly to end the complications
in the system's method of ballot counting. In a council vote
which precipitated a two-year court fight, and a new referendum
in 1957, five council members (the Irish and Polish councilors)
voted to waive a state requirement that all voters be mailed
notices of the referendum, a move which demonstrated hostility
to PR. Against the waiver and in support of PR were two French
votes, one Yankee, and one Greek vote. The electorate voted
strongly against PR in the disputed election, but Councilor
Samuel A. Sampson brought a suit in Superior Court which

*The proportional representation system permits a voter to cast a ballot for as
many candidates as he wishes from a long ballot, by numbering the choices. After
all ballots are counted, the candidate with the lowest number of first place votes
is eliminated and his ballots are distributed to the next choice on the ballot. The
process is repeated until the requisite number of candidates is elected. The
process is time-consuming and it often took several weeks to decide the
election—one of the arguments used to defeat the voting system.

"Council Meeting, Plan E Style." Cartoon by George Gagan. *Lowell Sunday Telegram*, November 21, 1943. Courtesy of Lowell Sun Publishing Company.

invalidated the election on the grounds of violation of state election laws by failing to notify the voters by mail.

The fight over PR began again in November, 1957. It involved a tussle between the League of Women Voters who supported PR and anti-PR Irish-American councilors who directed the city solicitor to stop the League from campaigning for PR from a booth owned by the city in Kearney Square. The booth was dismantled. In the referendum vote, PR was defeated again by a wide margin. Anti-PR forces carried a substantial vote in the Greek stronghold in Ward Two while the majority of Greeks, Yankees, and French voted to retain PR. In the next election Irish candidates took seven council seats, thereby dominating the city government. Minority group representation in city politics was by no means eliminated by the defeat of PR, but it was definitely limited, and the crucial votes to choose the city manager were held by the Irish councilors. This pattern of Irish strength in at-large elections and the choice of city manager remains the distinctive feature of local politics.

Prior to 1975, with the exception of the 1875–77 term, the congressional representatives from the Lowell district since the Civil War have been Republican.* Many of them were residents of the city: Benjamin F. Butler (1877–79); Frederic T. Greenhalge (1889–91) later governor of Massachusetts; Butler Ames (1903–1913) the grandson of Ben Butler; John Jacob Rogers (1913–25) whose widow Edith Nourse Rogers succeeded him in 1925 and held the seat until 1960, followed by F. Bradford Morse (1961–72) and Paul W. Cronin (1973–74). Paul E. Tsongas, the district's first Democratic representative since 1877, was elected in 1974. Success in the congressional elections was aided by persistent factionalism within the district's Democratic party, largely a tug-of-war between Lawrence and Lowell Democrats over the party's nomination. Most Republican representatives also paid close attention to the particular needs of the city through depression and war. The best example of this was the remarkable career of Edith Nourse Rogers who served the district ably and far longer than any other representative. Although labor and ethnic issues dominated municipal politics and the city voted solidly Democratic in presidential elections after 1924,

*In 1872 the congressional district had been redesigned to place both Lowell and Lawrence in the same district. The exception to Republican rule came two years later when Democrat John K. Tarbox defeated James C. Ayer of Lowell in a heavy Democratic vote. Only three Democrats have ever represented Lowell in Congress: Gayton Osgood (1833–35), Tarbox (1875–77), and Paul E. Tsongas (1975–   ).

Yankee Edith Rogers consistently convinced the voters of Lowell to split their tickets and give her an unparalleled personal following for over thirty years.

Edith Nourse was born in Saco, Maine, in 1881, the daughter of a Yankee mill company executive. The family came to Lowell when she was a young girl. She attended the Rogers Hall School and a finishing school in Paris where she was captivated by French culture. But Edith Nourse also acquired from her father a thorough knowledge of textile mills and their financial, labor, and trade problems. In 1907 she married the son of another Lowell textile executive, John Jacob Rogers. Her deep love of western European society and her interest in the problems of textile manufacturing in New England would be two formative experiences in her political life.

In 1917 Edith and John Rogers (he had been elected to Congress in 1912) involved themselves deeply in World War I. They both toured the French war zone and she worked for the YMCA and the Red Cross caring for the wounded. In 1918, they returned to Washington where Rogers enlisted. She continued her work at Walter Reed Army Hospital until 1922. Her work with World War I veterans made her and Rogers popular with veterans' organizations which became politically powerful after the war. In the 1920s she served without pay as an inspector of veterans' hospitals, and her work was recognized and supported by three Republican presidents. When her husband died in March, 1925, the state Republican party insisted she succeed him. She expected to serve only for a few years but found she greatly enjoyed the life and the work. She spoke her mind on the floor of Congress and dealt aggressively and perceptively with national issues. Her secure Yankee background, travel, and education as well as the unshakeable political base in her district made her a formidable representative.

Congresswoman Rogers was a liberal and an internationalist, typical of successful Republicans of the northeast. She voted for most of the key New Deal programs of the thirties—the Wagner Act which protected union organization, the Social Security Act of 1935, and the minimum wage law of 1938—in line with the needs of her Lowell constituents, if not with the Republican leadership. However, she strongly opposed the Roosevelt administration's program of flexible and negotiable tariff rates. In 1938, fearful of competition in shoes, she attacked a trade treaty with Czechoslovakia and insisted on high tariffs on all textiles coming from Japan. Her attachment to her happy days in Paris and her work in World War I made her an early opponent of Hitler. In 1937 she voted to amend the neutrality legislation which prevented Roosevelt from demonstrating opposition to German and Japanese expansion and later she became an active supporter of the United Nations.

During World War II Edith Rogers served on both the Veterans' Affairs Committee and the Armed Services Committee;* she sponsored major legislation including bills for a Women's Army Corps in 1942 and for a G. I. Bill of Rights which granted housing, education, and medical benefits to veterans. Her busy staff spent hours each day on constituents' problems, particularly the needs of armed-service widows. She subsequently introduced legislation to grant pensions to war widows. Defense contracts awarded to Lowell businesses greatly improved the local economy. All of her activities were well publicized in the district; she was a good politician and unbeatable at election time. Representative Rogers died of a heart attack at the age of seventy nine in the midst of her re-election campaign of 1960.

The voters of Lowell were devoted to Republican congressional representatives, but less so to Republican candidates for president especially since the 1920s. The magnetic spell of Civil War Republicanism lasted until 1892 when Lowell voted for ex-President Grover Cleveland. The 1896 election, however, shattered the Democrats over the issue of the gold standard for the dollar, and William McKinley swept the city. The city continued to vote Republican for president until the 1912 elections, when the Republicans split and ran two candidates, both former presidents. While William Howard Taft and Theodore Roosevelt both did well, they divided the Republican vote locally as they did nationally, and Democrat Woodrow Wilson carried Lowell in 1912 and 1916. This forecast a strong trend away from the Republicans in the mid 1920s.

After the turmoil of American involvement in World War I the conservative candidates of the Republican Party seemed attractive to Lowell voters, but in 1924 the electorate showed a strong

---

*She also served on the House Foreign Affairs Committee and on the Civil Service Committee, two very important assignments. Democratic strength in Congress in the 1930s greatly reduced the number of Republicans in the House and good committee assignments were available. When the Republicans won the Ninetieth Congress in 1946 during the Truman administration, Rogers had to choose between chairing the Veterans' Committee or continuing on Foreign Affairs. She chose the veterans and remained the ranking Republican member until her death.

interest in the reform-minded Progressive party candidate, Robert LaFollette of Wisconsin, although voting was light. After the 1924 campaign there was an unprecedented increase in the numbers of voters in the city (38.4 percent) and the beginning of a massive voter realignment. The 1928 campaign of Irish Catholic Al Smith of New York began the pattern of landslide Democratic victories in Lowell which lasted through 1972. In national party politics, even in the controversial 1948 and 1972 elections and during the Eisenhower years Lowell was a solid Democratic city.

The two major influences that explain why Lowell was a Whig-Republican city in the nineteenth century and a Democratic city in the twentieth were, first, the economic power of the textile mills and, later, the impact on politics of the multitude of ethnic groups that came to work in the mills. While the power of the textile interests was balanced in part by the old settlers and the Irish Democratic organization faced anti-tax and anti-corruption "reform" groups, the prevailing pattern in the city mirrored its textile industry—the mills—and its immigrant people—the multitudes.

XII

The New People: An Introduction to the Ethnic History of Lowell

By Peter F. Blewett

The new people, the immigrants, have always been a part of Lowell. On April 6, 1822, a labor contractor named Hugh Cummiskey led thirty Irish laborers to the vicinity of Pawtucket Falls. They had walked up from Charlestown along the Middlesex Canal to begin the work of deepening the existing Pawtucket Canal and digging others which were to channel the water to power cotton mills. They were met by the lordly Kirk Boott, who gave them tools and bestowed on them a little money for their "refreshment." This was about as much provisioning as they would get from their employers, the mill owners, who set up no living quarters for them, and had no intention of making this foreign born group a part of the mill town's work force. Their plan called for the employment of young, native born women in the cotton mills. The Irish were initially necessary but extraneous and perhaps unwelcome in the long run.

In the 1820s and 1830s Lowell was a boom town. New factories, a railroad, boarding houses, even a stately home for Kirk Boott were built, and the Irish stayed on to provide the labor. They lived, segregated, in a shantytown, variously called "Paddy Camp Lands," "New Dublin," or "The Acre," on property over which the companies chose not to exercise control. And so, before it was even finished the planned city of Lowell had its first slum. As early as August, 1822, long before the mill girls began to arrive, the Irish had established families living in the new town. They increased in numbers, attracted by the opportunities for work, and became an important element in the population. The mill agents were forced to deal with them; hence in the name of good discipline Boott provided the land for a Roman Catholic Church whose priest would, he hoped, keep the Irish in order.

The possibilities for work drew most of the new people to Lowell. From England and Scotland came experienced textile hands and masons. From Quebec province in 1841 a blacksmith arrived, followed four years later by the first French-Canadian carpenter, and then, over the next fifteen years, by the first wave of their countrymen drawn away from the poverty of the farms. In the late 1840s more Irishmen, potato famine refugees, arrived, just as the mill girls began to fail as a docile work force. They were hired by the companies as operatives at lower wages, and a pattern became set. Each new ethnic group entering Lowell rehearsed this experience with the mills, as its appearance in the city allowed the managers to undercut the existing wage structure.

Once the mill managers recognized the profit potential of low-paid immigrant labor for whom they did not have to provide subsidized housing, they began to recruit intensively. The same method which drew rural, Yankee women applied to Quebec farmers. French-speaking recruiters toured eastern Canada, especially after 1865, and convinced the inhabitants that Lowell offered high wages and good jobs. As a consequence, thousands of French-Canadians came to Lowell, leaving behind the deadend of small farms, harsh climate, overpopulation, and land hunger. By 1900 they composed about a fifth of the city's population.

In the nineteenth century the population of Europe rapidly expanded especially in the agrarian countries. There came to be more people than the land could support. Vast patterns of migration developed, at first from the farms into the cities, but inevitably out of the homeland and into the undeveloped parts of the world. Lowell, like the rest of the United States, was the destination of large numbers of migrants driven from Europe by a great depression during the last third of the nineteenth century. They could generally be classified as peasants, either farmers or herders; most were young; few had saleable skills. In short, they

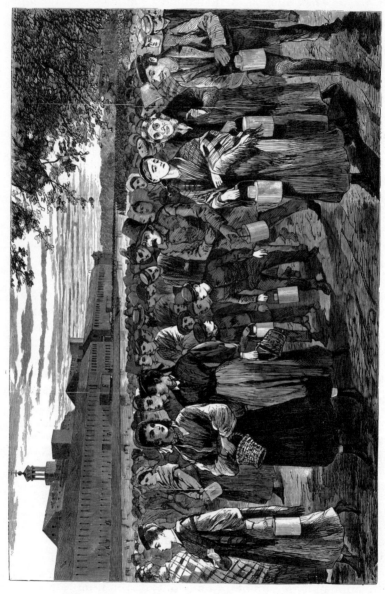

"Bell Time." Workers leaving the mills. By Winslow Homer. *Harper's Weekly*, July 25, 1868. (Lowell Historical Society)

were ideal for the work force in the mills. Whether it was Poland, Portugal, Greece, or Russia that they left, the prime motive was economic. Some, like many of the Poles and Greeks, intended to work, to save, and to return home, perhaps to buy land. A few did, but most, like the Irish, came and settled almost inadvertently. Sometimes political oppression, religious persecution, or the need to evade conscription into a foreign overlord's army, set people on the road which led to Lowell. Once a few people of a nationality became established, they acted as magnets drawing in relatives, friends, and fellow villagers. An eastern industrial city like Lowell with its demand for low-wage, initially unskilled, labor was a natural place for the impoverished immigrant to stop. Even after the cotton mills died, the pattern remained and was replicated—so strong was the web of ethnic connection back to the homeland.

The actual journey to Lowell was slow and hard. Irishmen often tried their luck first in the industrial cities of England, then pushed on to America, pausing in port cities like New York, Boston, Quebec, or Montreal before reaching Lowell. While most French-Canadians came by train, some walked from Quebec. The late nineteenth century immigrants from Europe travelled a longer distance. Because most of the immigrants were young, the trip was a wrenching initiation into the world. It was an experience perhaps more fearsome than exciting or promising. They came from rural home villages, which few of them had previously left, even for short trips. Sometimes this meant a more difficult break even than leaving relatives and friends. For one teenaged Polish widow it meant leaving behind a young son, who sentiment insisted would join her in time, but whom reality told her she would never see again. Once aboard the train the immigrants were on a journey into an alien world. After contending with the bewildering "foreign-ness" of the port city of Bremen, Hamburg, or Liverpool, they faced the singular experience of the long sea voyage. Travelling by Belgian or English ships could be quite comfortable, but the usual experience on ships of other flags was dismal. Few had cabins and people were crowded into unpartitioned below-deck quarters, where all their human activities were carried out for as long as a month. The food was usually poor, and except in mid-summer, the weather on the ocean was bad. One Polish girl, travelling alone, experienced days of terror on a ship hove-to at sea waiting out a storm. Sixty years later she could remember still the experience of lying among hundreds of strangers in the claustrophobic below-decks as the ship, its bow facing into the wind, rose and dipped with every huge swell.

The European imagination perceived the United States as an economic Land of Oz. This image was shaped by agents for steamship lines, travel writers, labor recruiters, journalists, and, perhaps most important of all, by immigrants writing home. The newcomer came with exaggerated hopes. Sometimes experience confirmed promise. As one Greek remembered: "When I come to Staten Island [sic], when I come out, I found a dime on the street. Jesus, I said, Christ's sake, I just come here, I begin to get rich now!" For most of the immigrants, though, disillusionment began at Ellis Island. There were long lines, cursory but arbitrary medical checks, and sometimes rancorous dealings with officials. The place acquired a bad reputation. Here people lost ancient family names because officials could not spell or understand them. Poles were infuriated by this; Jews often did not mind: many would change their names when they became citizens. Here a little girl, who had red-rimmed eyes from crying all night, could be diagnosed as tubercular and prevented from landing. She would be detained until her mother could travel from Lowell to rescue her from the bureaucracy. Here the immigrant's dream could crash as the sick person was forced to return to Europe.

Many of the immigrants of the 1890s and early 1900s came through to Lowell consigned to relatives, wearing tags sometimes inscribed with simply the city's name as a guide for ticket sellers and train conductors. The Jewish community in Lowell maintained someone at the Middlesex Street depot to meet all trains. He greeted the newcomer in Yiddish, elicited the name of the person's relatives in Lowell, and directed him to them. Within days a relative, or *landtzman*, a person from the same area of the old country as the newcomer, helped him to find a job. All the ethnic groups beginning with the Irish provided lodging and help for the newcomers: no matter that a French-Canadian family of twelve was crowded into a four-room tenement in "Little Canada;" it somehow accommodated the new arrivals. This sense of community obligation was perhaps the most powerful social accomplishment of the immigration period, and represented the maintenance of an old agrarian social attitude in the new environment of a foreign industrial city. To many immigrants this aid meant survival—emotional as well as physical or material. Each ethnic group created its island of separate culture, language, and customs as a subconscious means of ensuring the members' survival in the alien environment. The island might be squalid and poverty stricken but it was a haven.

Despite the cushion against cultural shock provided by the ethnic community, during the first year many people thought about going home. Few could afford the return fare. In time they got used to the new way of life and "made the best" of their situation. If life were grim for them, their letters home concealed their disappointment. Out of pride and to save face they refused to admit that they were no better off for emigrating, and that, in some cases, they were worse off. They upheld in their letters the given image of America and Lowell, so that they encouraged relatives and friends to emigrate also.

All the nineteenth century immigrant groups relied on religion to bind together the parts of the ethnic community. In an alien environment, where the law, the courts, and the police seemed hostile, the church exercised the only acceptable public authority, and priests of necessity became the community's respectable leaders. Irish Catholic priests were at work in the Paddy Camp Lands years before there was a church building. They said Mass, heard confessions, baptised, and celebrated marriages and funerals. They regularized life for a people living in impermanence and housed in shanties, shacks, and tents. Before most of the Irish were able to move out of their slum, they made sure that their church had a permanent building. St. Patrick's Church, a wooden structure dedicated in 1831, had its foundation laid by Cummiskey and a crew of volunteers. It was built and paid for by the Irish community, which already operated a school teaching four Rs instead of just three. The Catholicism of the Irish set them off from the Protestant natives and helped them preserve their identity, but it also provided bigots with the excuse they needed to persecute and exploit them.

The early churches were missionary in character. The ethnic communities felt beleaguered in Lowell. Even if their religion was already established in Lowell, other ethnic groups usually controlled it. The newcomers felt the need to set up their own churches. This was not an easy task. The first group to try, the French-Canadians, resented Irish domination of the Catholic Church in Lowell. The priests spoke English, services seemed different; the customs were strange. The diocese of Boston, itself Irish-controlled, at first failed to respond and provide a French priest. This failure of the Catholic hierarchy to adapt to a church

composed of ethnic communities happened elsewhere in the
United States in the nineteenth century. Only in 1868 were two
Oblate priests, Lucien Lagier and André Marie Garin, sent to
Lowell to serve the French-Canadians. Within days of his arrival
Father Garin had bought a vacant Unitarian church on Lee
Street; a few weeks later he had collected a three thousand dollar
down-payment for it from his enthusiastic parishioners. This was
the beginning of St. Joseph's Church, the first of many French-
Canadian Catholic institutions in Lowell.

The Polish experience with the Catholic Church was similar
to that of the French-Canadians, but ironically it was against the
French language church that the Poles reacted. Most Poles in the
1890s went to mass at St. Joseph's Church, where the sermons
were often in French and where there was a degree of French-
Canadian chauvinism. Some Polish people distrusted the
priests; in any case, most felt uncomfortable in a foreign church.
Establishing a separate Polish church, however, presented difficulties. Again the problem was Irish domination of the hierarchy. The fervor of Polish nationalism, suppressed in the
homeland, demanded that religious life be deeply rooted in
Polish history and custom. Already in the 1890s a clash had taken
place in Scranton, Pennsylvania, between Polish Catholics and
the hierarchy. The result was a schism and the formation of the
Polish National Catholic Church, which used the Polish language in the rite but left dogma mostly unaltered. In 1901 some
frustrated Polish Catholics in Lowell set up a branch of this
church, St. Casimir's, and a school which emphasized Polish
language and history. Money for the church came from both
Lowell and Scranton Poles. Here was a radical reaction to the
difficulty ethnic groups experienced in setting up national par-
ishes in areas where they were a small minority in the American
Catholic Church. It is a demonstration that a thousand-year-old
religious tradition can collapse in a new situation when the local
representatives of the larger institutional church are inflexible
and unable to maintain in practice the church's claim to uni-
versality.

St. Casimir's Church was the product of the two strongest
forces working on the Poles, their religion and their sense of
nationality (they would say patriotism). In 1901 for many Lowell
Poles, nationalism won out over the ancient religion, but the
creation of the schismatic church split the community. Soon the
Poles who remained loyal to the Roman Catholic Church had

their own parish. It was situated not in Centralville, where most Poles lived, but across the river, in the city proper. Religion thus for the first time failed to unify an ethnic group in Lowell, and in fact produced two Polish communities. Religious schism as always produced social schism. This did not mean that the Poles diffused quickly into the general population. Assimilation for them was just as slow as it was for every other group, because for the first two generations the integrity of the communities was maintained. Nationalism replaced the single religion as the community bond.

Not all Catholic nationalities had trouble with the hierarchy. The Portuguese were lucky in all parts of the diocese. In 1869 Archbishop Williams imported a priest from the Azores to minister to the Portuguese in New Bedford. By the time Lowell had a large Portuguese community, the Catholic Church was able to respond, and in 1907 Archbishop O'Connell dedicated St. Anthony of Lisbon parish. This parish was governed from 1911 to 1924 by an exiled Portuguese bishop, Henry Joseph Reed da Silva.

Lowell's Spanish-speaking immigrants are nominally Catholic. Two priests who speak Spanish serve them. Attendance at Mass is fairly low, mostly because they were unchurched in their homeland. This is due to a long tradition of anti-clericalism in Puerto Rico and Latin America, and to the survival of spiritism, a pagan cult which has taken on the vocabulary of Christianity. There are even two witches in the Lowell community. The Roman Catholic priests have to be missionaries first, and then social workers and interpreters. Protestant missionaries from a variety of fundamentalist churches compete, and have set up small churches, mostly of the storefront variety.*

The Orthodox Greeks faced no problems with a hierarchy in setting up a church in Lowell, although they were hindered as were other groups before them by a lack of money. Even though there was a permanent priest starting in 1895, services had to be held in a variety of halls not really suited to the purpose. Not until 1906 could the Greek community finance a proper church building. Designed by a Boston Irish architect dispatched to

---

*The black population of Lowell is small, estimated at between fifteen hundred and eighteen hundred persons. They live mostly in Lower Belvidere, and in the area around Central and Lawrence Streets. There are two black churches, both Protestant, the Pentecostal Church and the African Methodist Church. A women's association, the Black Genesis Foundation, is in 1976 the leading active community organization.

Holy Trinity Greek Orthodox Church. Photograph by A.L. Eno, Jr.

Istanbul to study the style, this church, Holy Trinity, was a statement by the Greeks of their culture. It was in the Byzantine style, complete with decorated interior and topped by a large glittering golden dome, fronted by two smaller ones. Like St. Anne's Episcopal Church, Holy Trinity seems, much more than the neo-Gothic Roman Catholic churches, to be an authentic part of the old world transferred to Lowell. It summons up the atmosphere of the eastern Mediterranean even when there is only the wan, North American winter sun to reflect off its cream colored bricks and golden domes.

Construction of the church building turned out to be only a first hurdle; at least twice in its early history Holy Trinity Church barely escaped financial disaster. In 1920 parishioners prevented a mortgage foreclosure by taking an emergency collection. During the Great Depression in 1934 only the intercession of Christos Laganas, a successful shoe manufacturer, saved the church when it found itself in a similar situation. The second crisis may have come about because in 1924 and 1928 a large part of the congregation withdrew, leaving Holy Trinity with a reduced membership just as the economy broke down.

Like the Polish religious community, the Greek one also split. In 1923 Holy Trinity Chrch refused to abandon the Julian calendar for the Gregorian as the church in Greece and the American archdiocese had directed. The bad feeling created in the congregation by this was exacerbated a year later when the community split over the deep feelings unleashed by a political crisis in Greece. The supporters of Prime Minister Venizelos could no longer get along with Lowell's pro-monarchical Greeks, and consequently the Greek Orthodox religious community divided. The new Church of the Transfiguration was the result. Yet another schism occurred in 1928 and produced St. George's Church. Like the Irish who sent money to Sinn Fein and like the Poles who supported the movement for Polish independence, the Greeks were more emigrants than immigrants. The situation in the homeland was at once more real and more important to them than affairs in their adopted land.

Beginning with the Irish, the priests, at least for the first generation and usually into the second, were born in the home country. In order to be accepted they needed to speak the language and hold in common with parishioners the familiar customs, traditions, and prejudices. The original need of the immigrants to base the ethnic island on the national religion dictated this. As long as the priests were foreign-born, community leadership stayed strongly tied to the fatherland. Each recruit was a political and cultural refreshment, a check on the tendency to alter or abandon custom. The priest also had to function as an intermediary between his parishioners and civil authorities or employers. He was often the first person to acquire status outside the ethnic community. This was frequently a burden, but a Father John Mahoney or a Father Garin managed it. They became acknowledged leaders in the city.

From the churches sprang the benevolent societies, whose prototype was the Hibernian Moralizing and Relief Socety of 1833. The French-Canadians began with the Union St. Joseph, and followed it after 1889 with the larger Corporation des Membres de l'Association Catholique. The Poles set up their Spojnia and Polish-American Club. While the Greeks in 1894 founded the Washington-Acropolis with the aim of preserving their religion and tradition, they tended to set up their benevolent societies in order to cater to regional loyalties. The Portuguese-American Club came closer to the Irish and French-Canadian model by drawing a community-wide membership. So too did the Jewish Twenty-five Cent Society, which provided its membership with a doctor. The Jews also operated the Workmen's Circle which paid the unemployed person ten dollars a month. As rent in the decade after 1900 averaged $1.25 a week, this sum provided subsistence for the out-of-work. Lowell's newest immigrants run a Spanish-American Center, and UNITAS, a federally funded association. Both try to help the newcomer find jobs and housing.* UNITAS works under the leadership of an Oblate priest, Father Daniel Crahen, who also has sponsored the establishment of a credit union and a used clothing and furniture store.

These organizations offered (and, in some cases, continue to offer) the immigrant a cushion against loneliness, and often against disaster or destitution. They were mostly mutual-aid societies providing relief, group insurance, and a meeting place. They were, like the church, a place where the respectable strands of community life came together, and where successful laymen, like Hugh Cummiskey or J. Henri Guillet, found scope for social leadership. The societies sponsored dinners, fêtes, plays, picnics, and parades, where the immigrants could indulge

---

*The Spanish-speaking minority (Colombian, Mexican, Cuban, but largely Puerto Rican) is Lowell's most rapidly growing population. It numbers around eight thousand. This immigration has taken place over the last fifteen years.

their nationalism on celebration days held to honor patron saints or national heroes like St. Patrick, St. Jean Baptiste, and Casimir Pulaski. In time, the societies multiplied and specialized to serve fractions of the community, but they always tended to maintain their ethnic exclusivity.

For the male immigrant worker, there existed other meeting places besides churches and social clubs. The most idiosyncratic and characteristic example was the Greek coffee house, a village social institution transplanted to Lowell. Strung out along Market Street, the coffee houses numbered about thirty at the height of their popularity, which interestingly enough came only after Greek women had arrived in large numbers and home life had been regularized. Individual houses tended to be frequented by people from a small region of Greece. In the coffee house the immigrant could sit for hours on end, drinking the favored sweet, strong, black coffee, talking in the native language about politics (usually Greek), playing cards, or reading newspapers. The single room was simply set up with chairs around small tables. The place was warm in winter; in summer the entire operation moved to the sidewalk. For the young, single, and poor Greek, the coffee house was one of the few alternatives to the saloon or the brothel for recreation. While the Reverend George Kenngott in his sociological study of immigration in Lowell, primly alludes to "sexual vice" among the unmarried Greeks, arrests for drunkenness among them were relatively few in number, so the coffee house was partly successful as a sobering social institution. Ethnic attitudes toward alcohol are pointed up nicely by the reaction of Lowell's Irish police to the first coffee houses. They could not believe that these were not saloons in disguise and raided them often, finding neither liquor nor gamblers. It took some time before the police could be persuaded that Greek males could gather together to drink only coffee and talk politics for hours.

The more universal male meeting place was the saloon. In ethnic neighborhoods it served as an unofficial social club. If the Acre of early Lowell resembled the Irish districts of nineteenth-century Boston, saloons were numerous and small, run by single families in one room of their tenements. There is evidence to suggest that wives ran the saloons while husbands worked at outside jobs like laboring (although in at least one case the husband was a lawyer). As new groups of immigrants staked out their territory in the city they either set up saloons or frequented

Greek coffee house patrons, 1914. Photograph courtesy of Mr. and Mrs. C. Koumoutseas.

and came to monopolize established ones.* All the nationalities
appear in the police-court records of arrests for drunkenness,
some (like the Irish) in higher percentages than others (like the
English). This disproportion in the records may reflect economic
differences, such as the ability to afford bottled liquor, or
possession of a pleasant home in which to drink and a wife who
tolerated alcohol in the house. Perhaps it just expressed ethnic
custom: in some cultures drinking was to be done among people
outside the home. In any event the statistics show that
drunkenness was the ubiquitous scourge of working class
families in Lowell in the same way it has always been when
poverty dominated life. Before prohibition, beer to take home
was sold by the bucket, and rye whiskey was cheap. Kenngott
wrote that patronage of saloons was largely limited to young and
unmarried men because wages were so low that the married man
could not afford to drink. He could not, of course; but he did. As
a result temperance movements flourished. From time to time
priests administered the "pledge" to the Irish in the city.
French-Canadian women posted "La croix tempérance," a black
cross, on their walls, and tried to keep alcohol out of the house.
"No licence" appeared on the ballot often in the nineteenth
century, backed by moralistic prohibition supporters.† For the
nineteenth and early twentieth centuries, Kenngott found
evidence that alcoholism was the chief reason for husbands
deserting or failing to support their families. The husband and
father who drank up and gambled away his wages before he
reached home every week was no more rare in Lowell than in
any other industrial city in the world.

Sometimes an ethnic island created a unique institution in
Lowell. Such was Tsagaroulis' drug store. Many of the Greek
immigrants could give no set address to their families back
home, and the U.S. Post Office found it difficult to deliver letters
on which only the city name seemed legible to the postman. The
drug store became a sub-post office, a kind of *poste-restante* or
general delivery, for the immigrants. The store became a community center, a check-in point for the immigrants; it performed
a useful, necessary service, as long as the native language remained the primary tongue of the immigrants and their families.

*This process is at work today in the bars on Central and Charles Streets, where
Spanish-speaking and black patrons have eased out an earlier clientele.

†Probably the real reason for placing it on the ballot was political. See Chapter
XI.

Language, except in the case of the Irish, defined the ethnic community and reinforced it. There was a close link between religion, nationality, and language. Maintenance of all three retarded assimilation and preserved the ethnic island. The various church schools aided in this effort, as did the understandable reluctance of people to abandon the language in which they had learned to think and in which they invested much patriotic love of the homeland. The French-Canadian Club Richelieu still fines its members twenty-five cents for every slip into English. The ethnic communities preserved their languages in a number of ways.

Newspapers in the native tongue were a consequence of the establishment of fairly large immigrant groups. The French-Canadians had at least twenty-two: *L'Etoile* (1886-1957), a weekly at first, then a daily, was the most successful. The rest tended to be short-lived and of less frequent issue. Foreign language dailies usually had too small a circulation to make them business successes. The Greeks, who also had twenty-two different newspapers at various times, supported only weeklies or monthlies. Other nationalities' efforts at publication were more modest. The Poles had literary societies, and men who corresponded with newspapers back home, reporting on the lives of the immigrants to Lowell. There were French-Canadian, Polish, and Greek writers, poets, and novelists; Irish and French-Canadian song writers. Plays in the native language were performed for most nationalities. The urge to preserve the language started a minor cultural movement in the first two generations of Lowell's immigrants, and was the main reason each group set up its own schools.

In the end the responsibility for maintaining the language fell on the family, the basic unit of the ethnic community. In the first two generations children spoke French, or Greek, or Armenian, or Polish at home, and sometimes parents forbade the use of English. Yet the line could not be held. The state of Massachusetts, after 1901, required any minor not competent in English to attend an evening school to learn the language in order to obtain a work permit. Not every family could pay tuition for the ethnic elementary schools, and some groups like the Greeks and Poles could not afford to build their own high schools. In all these cases economic necessity insured that the children would be forced to learn English. For most nationalities then, the exclusivity of the ethnic community could not extend to

the children. Sometimes practicality alone dictated that children
would become bilingual. It was not uncommon for a mother with
no English to take her child with her when shopping. The child
translated and kept her from being cheated. Gradually the old
language became the second language because it was a handicap
not to speak English. By the time television came along the
supremacy of the native tongue had been broken. And television,
the most powerful acculturator ever developed, insured by its
selling of levelled values and homogenized taste that the non-
English languages would lose their currency.

Sentimental attachment to the old languages remains among
all the ethnic groups. Even in the third generation children still
learn French, or Polish, or Greek, or Lebanese, often in order to
talk to their grandparents. Poles at their holidays try to keep the
language alive by encouraging small children to recite patriotic
poems. Yet there are some signs that the third may be the last
bilingual generation as intermarriage and acculturation take
place and the ethnic community dissolves.

There was an exception to this pattern of jealous maintenance
of the old language. The Jews, who unlike most ethnic groups
were anxious to assimilate, quickly picked up English. After
1900 the community even encouraged women to put aside
housework to take night classes in English at the Lincoln School.
They sent their children to public school and had them learn
Hebrew at the synagogue in the afternoons. The children, especially the eldest child, became the invaluable authority on
American ways for the parents. The acculturation of the children
which other ethnic groups regretted and tried to prevent, the
Jews encouraged. They took advice from the eldest child on how
to dress, what goods to buy, or what first names to give their later
children. The first-born acquired an authority and place in the
family not found in Jewish communities in Europe.

Among the foreign-language communities maintenance of a
national cuisine was a mark of the ethnic island. The practice
began as a natural consequence of coming to a foreign land.
There is nothing, except for language, which so continually
reminds the immigrant of his submersion in an alien environment as daily contact with strange food. What the traveller seeks
out, the immigrant avoids. Whenever possible, people cooked
and ate the familiar food. Because American stores could not
supply the unusual foods needed by ethnic cooks, Greeks, Poles,
Jews, Portuguese, French-Canadians set up grocery stores,
delicatessens, butcher shops, and bakeries. In a way they

followed the lead of the Irish, who fifty years before began to make a place for themselves in the middle class by becoming victuallers and purveyors to the city. The demands of the national cooking produced, in the case of the Greeks and Poles, supporting farms in the "countryside" in Dracut. The Greeks opened restaurants, some of which have developed a clientele drawn widely from outside the ethnic community.

After the first generation, the immigrants saw in their cooking one way of passing on their national traditions to their children and grandchildren. As the ethnic island lost its isolation, as pressures toward conformity with the American style of life grew and the younger generations moved into the larger community, the ethnic cuisine became more and more restricted to the holiday ritual. It was not that the traditional cooking was abandoned, but that the specialties of the cuisine came to be associated with festivals, when special menus were followed. These holidays were times of reaffirmation, of playing out old customs, when the extended family reinforced its links by a resort to ritual. On Christmas Eve the family feast for the Poles followed a pattern of symbolic acts. It began with all the diners breaking and eating a wafer together, and a solemn mutual embracing of all present, before the meal made up of traditional Polish foods—kielbasa, babka, pierogi, borcht, potatoes, cabbage, and fish—was eaten. The other nationalities placed similar emphasis on the importance of holidays to the family and community. Greek, French-Canadian, Syrian, and Armenian women began the preparation of food days ahead of time. Even in periods of depression and unemployment they made the greatest effort to provide something special to eat, at least at Christmas. The effort was required by tradition, and was habitual. People were scarcely conscious of the cementing social purpose behind the tradition. The celebration alone counted.

The most important protection of the ethnic community's integrity was the marriage of its members to people within the community, even if it meant recruiting a husband or wife in the homeland. Lists of marriages made by the earliest Irish inhabitants show very few out of the community. This pattern seems to have been followed by all the groups subsequently entering Lowell with the exception of the Greeks, who arrived in the beginning without women. A few, therefore, intermarried with other groups. When women began to arrive from Greece in numbers, intermarriage slowed down, but for the men at least, did not cease. Marriage outside the Greek community did not begin for women until the 1940s, and even then was the cause of scandal in the family. In most groups opposition to exogamy was deeply rooted. Religious and national prejudices covered up what was really fear of the outsider. There was no good reason why a Polish man and Irish woman should not marry. But they tended not to, well into the third generation. The prejudicial feelings must be seen therefore as expressions of a behavior pattern by which the community protected its integrity. There is no doubt that intermarriage was the principal solvent of the isolation of the ethnic island.

The first generations resisted assimilation by keeping to the old ways, yet they quickly obtained citizenship. For those who spoke a foreign language, this required that they learn enough English to pass the citizenship test. The French-Canadians set up a series of organizations, among which were the Naturalization Club in 1885, l'Union Franco-Américaine in 1895, the Pawtucketville Social Club in 1897, the Club des Citoyens Américains (CCA) in 1898, and then, just after the city charter change of 1911, they brought all these efforts together in the Permanent Committee on Naturalization, which added a woman's section in 1922 after the passage of the Nineteenth Amendment. This progression demonstrates nicely the political motivation which lay, at least in part, behind naturalization for the French-Canadians. Their numbers grew rapidly after 1885, and they could expect to contest at the polls Irish and Yankee control of the city. A political motive is not so easily discerned among the early Poles, Portuguese, Jewish or Greek immigrants who sought naturalization, and who attended language and citizenship classes at the International Institute. Many of these people, like the Poles, were deeply nationalistic, but they became Americans. Except for Jews from Russia and Lithuania, naturalization was almost a cosmetic process. Americanization tended to cease after the swearing-in ceremony, and few went on to learn any more English. A Greek once explained why: though there were many different nationalities in the mills, they spoke little and seldom mixed after work. Instead they went home into the ethnic isolation of their own communities. In the clubs, saloons, and coffee houses, the serious conversations were about affairs in the homeland; America and Lowell seemed unimportant. What need was there to learn a foreign language? The self-sufficiency of the ethnic community counteracted any pull

toward assimilation created by the English-speaking outside
world.

For the immigrants the "new world" as it was realized in
Lowell was often a deep disappointment. The city was crowded,
noisy, and dirty. Early prints of Lowell made it look bucolic, but
they never showed the Paddy Camp Lands. By the time of the
Civil War, Lowell was a typical nineteenth century industrial
city, complete with slums and soot. A Pole remembers arguing
with a train conductor who directed him off at the Middlesex
Street depot that this dirty place could not be Lowell. So convinced was he of the mistake that he tried to get back on the
train, only to be forced off by the conductor. It was disillusioning that "new" and "young" when applied to this country and
city did not mean "better."

In the beginning the mills built housing only for the young,
Yankee women they employed. Gradually the Irish replaced
their tent city with more permanent housing and the area
became a neighborhood, Lowell's Irish section, the Acre. Given
its start as a shantytown, the Acre never could become in the
nineteenth and early twentieth centuries anything better than a
slum. The wooden tenement houses, built close together,
showed no design for life: sun and air reached only a few of the
rooms. Generations of tubercular people spat on the floors and
left a killing bequest to those who followed them into the buildings. There was no attention to sanitation and well into the
twentieth century many of the buildings had no sewerage except
"vaults" which seldom were cleaned and often overflowed. In
the tiny yards, in the alleys, in the streets, junk and garbage
collected. A typical slum, the Acre was infested with disease,
misery, and death. The buildings had been inadequate to begin
with and did not age well. By the time the Greeks took over the
eastern—and oldest—end, the houses in the Acre were by all
standards uninhabitable. The underpaid Greeks had no choice
but to live there, as close to the mills as possible, while many
Irish moved to the better sections of town, opened up by the
network of streetcar lines. Thus the Acre served two nationalities
consecutively as the location of their ethnic island.

The French-Canadian section, Little Canada, began less haphazardly than did the Acre. It was built on a piece of open land
directly northwest of the mills, which was owned by the Locks &
Canals Company and used by the city as a dump. The company
let out the land to people—usually French-Canadians—who

Two companies have had comprehensive histories published about them: *The Saco-Lowell Shops* by George S. Gibb, and the Lowell Manufacturing Company in *Broadlooms and Businessmen: A History of the Bigelow-Sanford Carpet Company*, by John S. Ewing and Nancy P. Norton.

CHAPTER VIII

There are several excellent contemporary sources of information both by and about the female operatives of Lowell. *The Lowell Offering* has been reprinted. The columns of *The Voice of Industry* present the anti-establishment view. Harriet H. Robinson wrote two valuable memoirs: *Early Factory Labor in New England* and *Loom and Spindle*. Many visitors to Lowell mentioned the mill girls; the Rev. William Scorseby of Bradford, England, wrote a full-length volume about them which, although highly favorable to the corporate management, nevertheless contains much of interest to the twentieth century student: *American Factories and Their Female Operatives*. The Rev. Henry A. Miles wrote a similar full-length study: *Lowell as It Was and as It Is*. *Corporations and Operatives* by "A Citizen of Lowell" contains many interesting details.

The best general history of the Lowell factory operatives is *The Golden Threads: New England's Mill Girls and Magnates*, by Hannah Josephson. Although the author surveys the entire New England textile industry of the pre-Civil War era, she focuses primarily on Lowell. Written almost thirty years ago, the book reads very well today even in a time of newly aroused feminist consciousness.

An important survey of the early American labor movement is *The Industrial Worker* by Norman O. Ware. Madeleine B. Stern devotes a chapter to Sarah G. Bagley in *We the Women: Career Firsts of Nineteenth Century America*. Lise Vogel, in *Women of Spirit, Women of Action: Mill Workers of Nineteenth Century New England* (forthcoming) has drawn a moving and sensitive group portrait of the Yankee mill women, using material from their own letters, speeches, and journalism.

CHAPTER IX

The events leading up to the Civil War are well treated by Professor Thomas H. O'Connor in his excellent *Lords of the Loom*. On George Thompson's visit, see the dramatic report by Z. E. Stone in II ORC 112.

The military history of the war is comprehensively treated in *Butler's Book* (and any other biography of Ben Butler). The New Orleans occupation is the subject of a biography by James Parton, *General Butler in New Orleans.*

William Schouler, the state adjutant general during the war, published *A History of Massachusetts in the Civil War*, a detailed report, not only of the battles, but also of Governor Andrew's war-time administration.

A *Historical Sketch of the Old Sixth Regiment* was written by its chaplain, John W. Hanson. The Baltimore view of the events of April 19, 1861 was written by its mayor, George W. Brown, in *Baltimore and the 19th of April, 1861.*

The fascinating and moving story of the two sons of Judge Josiah G. Abbott, both of whom were killed during the war, is told in *The Abbotts of Lowell, Mass. in the Civil War* by William Greene Roelker.

Both the Butler and Gustavus Fox correspondence have been published. For more on Fox, see article by Alfred Gilman in II ORC 33.

CHAPTER X

The most important works concerning the decline of the textile industry are James C. Ayer's *Some of the Usages and Abuses in the Management of Our Manufacturing Corporations* and Erastus B. Bigelow's *Remarks on the Depressed Condition of Manufactures.* The anonymous *Corporations and Operatives* also rebuts the rosy views of the founders and early visitors.

Norman Ware's *The Industrial Worker, 1840–1860* is an excellent treatment of the labor story during those years. Margaret T. Parker's *Lowell: A Study of Industrial Development* discusses the closing down of the textile industry.

On J. C. Ayer, see Cowley's *Reminiscences of James Cook Ayer*, and James H. Young's *The Toadstool Millionaires.*

CHAPTER XI

The best primary sources on Lowell politics are the Lowell newspapers collected on microfilm at the city library, the fascinating *Butler's Book*, oral interviews at the University of Lowell Alumni Library, and scrapbooks on the career of Woodbury F. Howard in the possession of the Lowell Historical Society.

In addition to the general histories of the city, the most useful discussions of the politics of the nineteenth century are: D. Hamilton Hurd, *History of Middlesex County;* Trades and Labor Council, *Lowell: A City of Spindles;* George O'Dwyer, *The Irish Catholic Genesis of Lowell;* John P. Robinson, "The Melvin Suits," II ORC 201 and Howard P. Nash, Jr., *Stormy Petrel: The Life and Times of General Benjamin F. Butler, 1818–1893.*

Most useful on the politics of the twentieth century are: Margaret T. Parker, *Lowell: A Study of Industrial Development;* George Kenngott, *The Record of a City: A Social Survey of Lowell, Massachusetts;* Mary Blewett, "Urban Progressivism and Ethnic Politics: The Irish Capture of Lowell, Massachusetts, 1890–1911" (unpublished); Carol Matyka, "The Politics of Liquor Licenses in Lowell, 1906–1909" (unpublished); Milton Cummings, Jr., *Congress and the Electorate: Elections for the U.S. Household and the President, 1920–1964* (1966); *Current Biography,* 1942 (on Edith Nourse Rogers) and the obituary of Rogers, *New York Times,* Sept. 11, 1960.

CHAPTER XII

Much of the episodal, illustrative material in this chapter comes from oral history interviews done by members of the Lowell Historical Society, the Human Services Corporation, and students working with the Department of History and Political Science of the University of Lowell. The author would like to acknowledge his special indebtedness to Jane Leczynski, Mary Anne Roux, Dale Nyder, David Baskin, and Lewis Karabatsos for their research on ethnic groups.

There is one very useful book (*The Record of a City* by George Kenngott) which covers the classic period of immigration, 1890–1910. A little prim in tone, the book nonetheless is valuable social history. Kenngott relied heavily on statistical data, and his book would be very fashionable had it been written today.

Two major ethnic groups are treated in George F. O'Dwyer, *The Irish Catholic Genesis of Lowell,* and Richard Santerre, *The Franco-Americans of Lowell, Massachusetts.*

CHAPTER XIII

Besides the works cited in the chapter, the best sources for a general view of the intellectual life of early Lowell are Harriet

Robinson's *Loom and Spindle* and Lucy Larcom's *A New England Girlhood*.

There are many biographies of Whistler, but, understandably, none stresses the Lowell years. Charles E. Jarvis' *Visions of Kerouac* concentrates on the Lowell aspects of Kerouac's life and work. There is a lengthy and informative chapter on Sarah G. Bagley in *We The Women* by Madeleine B. Stern. For James B. Francis, see paper by William E. Worthen in V ORC 227. On Whistler *père*, see memoir by George L. Vose in III ORC 334. Frederick W. Coburn has written an excellent monograph on Thomas Bayley Lawson, which is published by the Essex Institute. Coburn also wrote a series of articles on Poe and Lowell in the *Lowell Courier-Citizen* (January 20, 27; February 3, 10, 1941). Mrs. Jane Ermina Locke's daughter wrote a memoir of her mother in IV ORC 259.

The popular literature of Lowell is well treated in an unpublished paper by Professor Warren French entitled *Mysteries of Lowell*.

The Butler literature is plentiful, but neither *Butler's Book* nor any published biography concentrates on Butler's legal career.

An excellent series of biographies of the early Lowell doctors by Dr. D. N. Patterson appears in II ORC 329.

CHAPTER XIV

Most of the travelers referred to in the text wrote their own reports of their visit. In addition to these, the dramatic story of George Thompson's visit to Lowell is well treated by Z. E. Stone in II ORC 112. Lincoln's visit is described by Judge Hadley in I LHSC 368. The visit and demonstration of the telephone by Alexander Graham Bell is discussed in an article by Z. E. Stone in V ORC 165.

Bibliography

BIBLIOGRAPHY

Abbott, Edith. *Women in Industry*. New York: D. Appleton and Company, 1910. Reprint: Arno Press, 1969.

Addison, Daniel D. *Lucy Larcom; Life, Letters, and Diary*. Cambridge: Riverside Press, 1894.

Aiken, John. *Labor and Wages, At Home and Abroad; in a series of newspaper articles*. Lowell: D. Bixby and Company, 1849.

Album Souvenir et Historique de la Paroisse Saint Joseph de Lowell, Massachusetts. Lowell: 1916.

Allen, Hervey. *Israfel; The Life and Times of Edgar Allan Poe*. New York: Rinehart, 1934.

Allen, Wilkes. *History of Chelmsford*. Haverhill: P. N. Green, 1820. Reprint: Chelmsford Revolutionary War Bicentennial Celebrations Commission, 1974.

Amaron, Calvin E. *The Evangelization of the French Canadians of New England*. Lowell: Campbell and Hanscom, 1885.

———. *Inspection of Public and Private Schools*. Springfield, MA: Le Citoyen Franco-Américain, 1890.

Ames, Blanche Ames. *Adelbert Ames, 1835–1933; General, Senator, Governor*. New York: Argosy-Antiquarian Ltd., 1964.

Andrews, John B. and W. D. P. Bliss. *Report on the Condition of Women and Child Wage-Earners in the United States*. Vol. X. *History of Women in Trade Unions*. Washington: Government Printing Office, 1911. Reprint: Arno Press, 1974.

Annual Statistics of Manufacturing in Lowell and Neighboring Towns. Lowell: Vox Populi Press, 1835–1882.

Appleton, Nathan. *Introduction of the Power Loom, and Origin of Lowell*. Printed for the Proprietors of the Locks & Canals on Merrimack River. Lowell: Penhallow, 1858.

———. *Memoir of the Hon. Abbott Lawrence*. Boston: J. H. Eastburn's Press, 1856.

"Argus." *Norton; or, The Lights and Shades of a Factory Village Wherein are Developed Some of the Secret Incidents in the History of Lowell*. Lowell: Vox Populi Press, 1849.

Ayer, Frederick. *Reminiscences of Frederick Ayer*. Boston: Private Printing, 1923. Reprint: Redwood Press, 1971.

Ayer, Frederick F. *Bell and Wing*. New York: G. P. Putnam's Sons, 1911.

Ayer, James Cook. *Some of the Uses and Abuses in the Management of Our Manufacturing Corporations*. Lowell: C. M. Langley, 1863.

Bagnall, William R. *The Textile Industries of the United States*. Cambridge: Riverside Press, 1893.

Baines, Edward. *History of the Cotton Manufacture in Great Britain*. London: H. Fisher, R. Fisher, and P. Jackson, 1835. Reprint: Kelley, 1966.

Baird, Robert H. *The American Cotton Spinner, and Managers' and Carders' Guide: A Practical Treatise on Cotton Spinning*. Philadelphia: Hart, 1851.

Ball, Benjamin W. *The Merrimack River, Hellenics, and Other Poems*. New York: G. P. Putnam's Sons, 1892.

Barber, John W. *Historical Collections, Being a General Collection of Interesting Facts, Traditions, Biographical Sketches, Anecdotes, etc. Relating to the History and Antiquities of Every Town in Massachusetts, with Geographical Descriptions, Illustrated by 200 Engravings.* Worcester: Dorr, Howland and Company, 1839.

Bartlett, Elisha. *A Vindication of the Character and Condition of the Females Employed in the Lowell Mills against the Charges Contained in the Boston Times and the Boston Quarterly Review.* Lowell: Huntress, 1841. Reprint: Arno Press, 1975.

Batchelder, Samuel. *Introduction and Early Progress of the Cotton Manufacture in the United States.* Boston: Little, Brown and Company, 1863. Reprint: Kelley, 1972.

Bender, Thomas. *Toward An Urban Vision, Ideas and Institutions in Nineteenth Century America.* Lexington, KY: University Press of Kentucky, 1975.

Bennett, Whitman. *Whittier, Bard of Freedom.* Chapel Hill: University of North Carolina Press, 1941. Reprint: Kennikat Press, 1972.

Bigelow, Erastus B. *Remarks on the Depressed Condition of Manufactures in Massachusetts, with Suggestions as to Its Cause and Its Remedy.* Boston: Little, Brown and Company, 1858.

Bishop, John L. *A History of American Manufactures from 1608–1860.* 3 vols. Philadelphia: Edward Young and Company, 1868. Reprint: Johnson Reprint Corp., 1967.

Blanchard, Rev. Amos. *An Address Delivered at the Consecration of the Lowell Cemetery, June 20, 1841.* Lowell: L. Huntress, 1841.

Bland, T. A. *Life of Benjamin F. Butler.* Boston: Lee and Shepard, 1879.

[Bradbury, Osgood.] *Mysteries of Lowell.* Boston: 1844.

Bradford, Gamaliel. *Damaged Souls; Discredited Figures in American History.* Boston: Houghton Mifflin, 1923. Reprint: Kennikat, 1969.

Bradlee, Francis. *The Boston and Lowell Railroad.* Salem, MA: Essex Institute, 1921.

Brandeis, Louis D., and Josephine Goldmark. *Women in Industry.* New York: The National Consumers' League, 1908. Reprint: Arno Press, 1969.

Bremer, Fredrika. *The Homes of the New World.* 2 vols. New York: Harper and Brothers, 1868. Reprint: Negro Universities Press, 1968.

Brown, George W. *Baltimore and the 19th of April, 1861.* Baltimore: Johns Hopkins University, 1887.

Burgess, Thomas. *Greeks in America.* Boston: Sherman, French and Company, 1913. Reprint: Arno Press, 1970.

Burgy, J. Herbert. *The New England Cotton Textile Industry.* Baltimore: Waverly Press, Inc., 1932.

Butler, Benjamin Franklin. *Butler's Book.* Boston: A. M. Thayer and Company, 1892.

_____ . Private and Official Correspondence of Gen. Benjamin F. Butler, April 1860 to March 1868. 5 vols. Norwood, MA: Plimpton Press, 1917.

_____ . *Record of Benjamin F. Butler, compiled from original sources.* Boston: 1883.

_____ . *Record of Benjamin F. Butler since His Election as Governor of Massachusetts.* Boston: 1883.

Caverly, Robert B. *The Eagle, Arlington, and Other Poems.* 2 vols. Dover, NH: F. W. B. Printing, 1871.

———. *History of the Indian Wars of New England, with Eliot the Apostle Fifty Years in the Midst of Them.* Boston: James H. Earle, 1882.

———. *The Merrimac and Its Incidents; An Epic Poem.* Boston: Innes and Niles, 1866.

Chambers, William. *Things as They are in America.* London: W. and R. Chambers, 1857. Reprint: Negro Universities Press, 1968.

Charters, Ann. *Kerouac, A Biography.* San Francisco: Straight Arrow Books, 1973. Reissue: Warner Paperback, 1974.

Chevalier, Michael. *Society, Manners, and Politics in the United States; Letters on North America.* Boston: Weeks, Jordan and Company, 1839. Reprint: Kelley, 1966.

Chronicle of Textile Machinery, 1824–1924. Issued to Commemorate the 100th Anniversary of the Saco-Lowell Shops, 1924.

Clark, Victor S. *History of Manufactures in the United States.* 3 vols. New York: McGraw-Hill Company, Inc., 1929. Reprint: Peter Smith, 1949.

Clarke, Mary Stetson. *The Old Middlesex Canal.* Melrose, MA: Hilltop Press, 1974.

Cobden, Richard. *American Diaries,* ed. by Elizabeth H. Cawley. Princeton: 1952. Reprint: Greenwood, 1975.

Coburn, Frederick W. *History of Lowell and Its People.* 3 vols. New York: Lewis Historical Society, 1920.

———. *Moses Greeley Parker, M.D.* Lowell: 1921.

———. *Thomas Bayley Lawson; Portrait Painter of Newburyport and Lowell.* Salem, MA: Newcomb and Gauss Company, 1947.

Coburn, Silas R. *History of Dracut, Massachusetts.* Lowell: Courier-Citizen, 1922.

Colburn, Warren. *Intellectual Arithmetic, upon the Inductive Method of Instruction.* Boston: 1833.

Cole, Donald B. *Immigrant City, Lawrence, Massachusetts; 1845–1921.* Chapel Hill: University of North Carolina Press, 1963.

Commons, John R., and associates, editors. *A Documentary History of American Industrial Society.* 10 vols. 2nd ed. New York: Russell and Russell, 1958.

———. *History of Labour in the United States.* 4 vols. New York: Macmillan Company, 1921–1935. Reprint: Kelley, 1966.

Conklin, Edwin P. *Middlesex County and Its People.* 4 vols. New York: Lewis Historical Society, 1927.

Contributions of the Lowell Historical Society, 2 vols. Lowell: Butterfield Printing Company, 1913–1926.

Contributions to the Old Residents' Historical Association, Lowell, Massachusetts, 6 vols. Lowell: 1879–1904.

Coolidge, John P. *Mill and Mansion: A Study of Architecture and Society in Lowell, Massachusetts, 1820–1865.* New York: Columbia University Press, 1942. Reissued: Russell and Russell, 1967.

Copeland, Melvin T. *The Cotton Manufacturing Industry of the United States.* Cambridge: Harvard University Press, 1912. Reprint: Kelley, 1966.

Corporations and Operatives: Being an Exposition of the Conditions of Factory Operatives and a Review of the "Vindication" by Elisha Bartlett, M.D., by a citizen of Lowell. Lowell: Samuel J. Varney, 1843. Reprint: Arno Press, 1975.

Correspondence between Nathan Appleton and John A. Lowell in Relation to the Early History of the City of Lowell. Boston: Eastburn Press, 1848.

Courier-Citizen Company. *Illustrated History of Lowell, Massachusetts and Vicinity.* Lowell: Courier-Citizen Company, 1897.

Cowley, Charles. *A Handbook of Business in Lowell, with a history of the city.* Lowell: E. D. Green, 1856.

_____ . *Illustrated History of Lowell.* Boston: Lee and Shepard, 1868.

_____ . *Memories of the Indians and Pioneers of the Region of Lowell.* Lowell: Stone and Huse, 1862.

_____ . *Reminiscences of James C. Ayer and the Town of Ayer.* Lowell: Penhallow Printing Company, 1879.

Crockett, David. *The Life of David Crockett.* New York: A. L. Burt Company, 1902.

Cummings, Ariel Ivers. *The Factory Girl; or, Gardez La Coeur.* Lowell: J. E. Short and Company, 1847.

Curtis, Harriot F. *Jessie's Flirtations.* New York: Harper and Brothers, 1846.

_____ . *Kate in Search of a Husband.* New York: 1843.

Curtis, Josiah. *Brief Remarks on the Hygiene of Massachusetts, more particularly of the Cities of Boston and Lowell.* Philadelphia, 1849.

Dana, Samuel L. *A Muck Manual For Farmers.* New York: C. M. Saxton and Barker and Company, 1860.

Dedicatory Exercises at the New Court House, Lowell, Massachusetts. Sept. 12, 1898.

Dickens, Charles. *American Notes for General Circulation.* New York: Harper and Brothers, 1842. Reprint: Penguin, 1972.

Dickinson, C. A. *In Memory of William Kittredge.* Boston: Rockwell and Churchill, 1887.

Drake, Samuel A. *History of Middlesex County, Massachusetts.* 2 vols. Boston: Estes and Lauriat, 1880.

Easy Catechism for Elastic Consciences; Comprising the Creed, Articles of Faith, Covenant, Signs and Tokens of the Incorporated Sabbath-Labor-Christians of Lowell. Lowell: 1847.

Eddy, Caleb. *Historical Sketch of the Middlesex Canal.* Boston: 1843.

Eddy, Daniel C. *Lectures to Young Ladies.* Lowell: B. C. Sargeant, 1848.

Edson, Theodore. *An Address Delivered at the Opening of the Colburn Grammar School, in Lowell, December 13, 1848.* Lowell: James Atkinson, 1849.

_____ . *Historical Discourse on the Occasion of the Fiftieth Anniversary of the First Introduction of Stated Public Worship into the Village of East Chelmsford, now the City of Lowell.* Lowell: Marden and Rowell, 1874.

_____ . *Memoir of Warren Colburn.* Boston: Brown, Taggard and Chase, 1856.

_____ . *Sermons.* Lowell: S. W. Huse and Company, 1891.

Eliot, John. *The Indian Primer*. Edinburgh: Andrew Elliot, 1880. Fac-
simile: Xerox University Microfilm, 1975.

Eno, Arthur L. *Les Avocats Franco-Américains de Lowell, Massachusetts, 1886–1936*. Lowell: 1936.

Ewing, John S., and Nancy P. Norton. *Broadlooms and Businessmen;
A History of the Bigelow-Sanford Carpet Company*. Cambridge:
Harvard University Press, 1955.

*Exercises of the 50th Anniversary Commemorative of the Incorporation
of the City of Lowell, Thursday, April 1, 1886*. Lowell: 1886.

*Exercises of the 75th Anniversary of the Incorporation of the Town of
Lowell*. Lowell: 1901.

The Factory Detective; or The Mystery of the Merrimack Mills. New
York: Norman L. Munro, 1886.

Factory Life As It Is; by an Operative. Factory Tract No. 1. Lowell:
1845.

Fairchild, Henry Pratt. *Greek Immigration to the United States*. New
Haven: Yale University Press, 1911.

Farley, Harriet. *Happy Hours at Hazel Nook; or, Cottage Stories*. Boston: Dayton and Wentworth Company, 1854.

————. *Operatives' Reply to Hon. Jere. Clemens; Being a Sketch of
Factory Life and Factory Enterprise and a Brief History of Manufacturing by Machinery*. Lowell: S. J. Varney, 1850.

Fielden, John. *Curse of the Factory System*. London: A. Corbett, 1836.
2nd. London: Cass, 1969.

Finch, Marianne. *An Englishwoman's Experience in America*. London:
1853. Reprint: Negro Universities Press, 1969.

Fisher, Marvin. *Workshops in the Wilderness: the European response to
American Industrialization, 1830–1860*. New York: Oxford University Press, 1967.

Flynn, Elizabeth Gurley. *I Speak My Own Piece; an autobiography of
"The Rebel Girl"*. New York: Masses and Mainstream, 1955. Reprint:
International Publishers Company, 1973.

Foner, Phillip S. *History of the Labor Movement in the United States*. 2
vols. New York: International Publishers, 1965.

Fox, Gustavus Vasa. *Confidential Correspondence of Gustavus Vasa
Fox, Assistant Secretary of the Navy, 1861–1865*. New York: Naval
Historical Society, 1920. Reprint: Books for Libraries Press, 1972.

Francis, James B. *Lowell Hydraulic Experiments*. Boston: Little, Brown
and Company, 1855.

Frazier, Arthur H. *Water Current Meters in the Smithsonian Collection
of the National Museum of History and Technology*. Washington:
Smithsonian Institution Press, 1974.

Gaylord, N. M. *Kossuth and the American Jesuits; A Lecture Delivered
in Lowell, January 4, 1852*. Lowell: Merrill and Straw, 1852.

Gibb, George S. *The Saco-Lowell Shops; Textile Machinery Building in
New England, 1813–1949*. Cambridge: Harvard University Press,
1950.

Gillon, Edmund V., Jr. *Victorian Cemetery Art*. New York: Dover, 1972.

Goode, George W. *Dan Hayes' Greatest Case or the Mystery of the
Central Bridge Fire*. Lowell: 1887.

Goodfellow, W. H. *Industrial Advantages of Lowell, Massachusetts and Environs.* Lowell: W. H. Goodfellow, 1895.

Gookin, Daniel. *Historical Collections of the Indians in New England.* Boston: Belknap and Hall, 1792. Reprint: Arno Press, 1972.

Gould, Levi S. *Ancient Middlesex; with Brief Biographical Sketches of the Men Who Have Served the County Officially since Its Settlement.* Somerville, MA: Somerville Journal Print, 1905.

Green, John O. *The Factory System, In Its Hygienic Relations.* Boston: William S. Damrell, 1846.

Greenslet, Ferris. *The Lowells and Their Seven Worlds.* Boston: Houghton Mifflin, 1946.

Gregory, Frances W. *Nathan Appleton, Merchant and Entrepreneur, 1779–1861.* Charlottesville, VA: University of Virginia, 1976.

Griffin, Sara Swan. *Little Stories about Lowell; Romances and Facts of Earlier Days.* Lowell: Butterfield Printing Company, 1928.

———. *Quaint Bits of Lowell History; A Few Interesting Stories of Earlier Days.* Lowell: Butterfield Printing Company, 1913.

Hall, Basil. *Travels in North America in the Years 1827 and 1828.* 3 vols. Edinburgh: 1829. Reprint: Arno Press, 1974.

Hammond, Matthew Brown. *The Cotton Industry: An Essay in American Economic History.* New York: Macmillan Company, 1897. Reprint: Johnson Reprint Corp., 1966.

Hanaford, Phebe A. *Women of the Century.* Boston: B. B. Russell, 1877.

Handbook for the Visiter to Lowell. Lowell: D. Bixby and Company, 1848.

Hanson, John W. *Historical Sketch of the Old Sixth Regiment of Massachusetts Volunteers during Its Three Campaigns in 1861–1864.* Boston: Lee and Shepard, 1866.

Hazen, Henry A. *History of Billerica, Massachusetts, with Genealogical Register.* Boston: A Williams and Company, 1883. Reprint, Howard A. Doyle, Cambridge, 1973.

Hedrick, Charles C. *Cotton Spinning; A Complete Working Guide to Modern Practice in the Manufacture of Cotton Yarn.* Chicago: American School of Correspondence, 1909.

Hedrick, Mary A. *Incidents of the Civil War during the Four Years of Its Progress.* Lowell: Vox Populi Press, 1888.

Hilbourne, Charlotte S. *Effie and I; or, Seven Years in a Cotton Mill: A Story of the Spindle City.* Cambridge: Allen and Farnham, 1863.

Hill, Frank P. *Lowell Illustrated; A Chronological Record of Events and Historical Sketches of the Large Manufacturing Corporations.* Lowell: Huse, Goodwin & Company, 1884.

Historical Sketch of Saint Anne's Church, Lowell, Massachusetts. Lowell: Courier-Citizen Co. 1925.

Holden, Raymond P. *The Merrimack.* New York: Rinehart, 1958.

Holzman, Robert S. *Stormy Ben Butler.* New York: Macmillan, 1954.

Hunt, G. W., ed. *Historical Sketch of the First Baptist Church, Lowell, Massachusetts, Centennial Anniversary.* Lowell: 1926.

Huntington, Elisha. *An Address on the Life, Character, and Writings of Elisha Bartlett.* Lowell: S. J. Varney, 1856.

Hurd, D. Hamilton. *History of Middlesex County, Massachusetts, with Biographical Sketches of Many of Its Pioneers and Prominent Men.* 3 vols. Philadelphia: J. W. Lewis & Co., 1890.

Indentures, Agreements, and Other Documents Concerning the Pro-prietors of the Locks & Canals on Merrimack River and Other Corpo-rations at Lowell, Massachusetts. 2 vols. Lowell: 1887–1921.

Jarvis, Charles E. *Visions of Kerouac.* Lowell: Ithaca Press, 1973.

———. *Exile.* Salonica, Greece: Nicolaide, 1965.

Johnston, James F. W. *Notes on North America, Agricultural, Economi-cal, and Social.* 2 vols. Boston: Little & Brown, 1851.

Josephine Mellen Ayer; A Memoir. New York: Knickerbocker Press, 1900.

Josephson, Hannah. *The Golden Threads; New England's Mill Girls and Magnates.* New York: Duell, 1949. Reissue: Russell and Russell, 1967.

Kasson, John F. *Civilizing the Machine: Technology and Republican Values in America 1778-1900.* New York: Grossman, 1976.

Kenngott, George F. *The Record of a City; A Social Survey of Lowell, Massachusetts.* New York: Macmillan, 1912.

Kerouac, Jack. *The Town and the City.* New York: Harcourt, Brace & Co. 1950. Reissue: Harcourt, Brace & Jovanovich, 1970.

———. *Doctor Sax; Faust Part Three.* New York: Grove Press, 1959. Reissue: Ballantine, 1973.

———. *Maggie Cassidy.* New York: Avon, 1959.

———. *Visions of Gerard.* New York: Farrar, Straus, 1963.

Kerr, Malcolm. *Manufacturing.* New York: Ronald Press Company, 1928.

Kimball, Gilman. *Report of the Lowell Hospital from 1840 to 1849.* Lowell: 1849.

Kossuth in New England; A Full Account of the Hungarian Governor's Visit to Massachusetts. Boston: John P. Jewett and Company, 1852.

The Ladies' Pearl; a monthly magazine embellished with engravings and original music. Lowell: E. A. Rice, 1840–1843.

Lankton, Larry, and Patrick Malone. *The Power Canals of Lowell, Massachusetts.* Lowell: Human Services Corp., 1973.

Larcom, Lucy. *An Idyl of Work.* Boston: James Osgood and Company, 1875. Reprint: Greenwood, 1970.

———. *A New England Girlhood; outlined from memory.* Boston: Houghton Mifflin, 1889. Reprint: Peter Smith, 1973.

———. *Poems.* Boston: Fields, Osgood and Company, 1869.

Lawrence, Abbott. *Letters from the Hon. Abbott Lawrence to the Hon. William C. Rives, of Virginia.* Boston: Eastburn's Press, 1846.

Lawrence, William. *Life of Amos A. Lawrence; with Extracts from His Diary and Correspondence.* Boston: Houghton Mifflin and Company, 1888.

Lawrence, William R. *Extracts from the Diary and Correspondence of the Late Amos Lawrence.* Boston: Gould & Lincoln, 1855.

Life of Luther C. Ladd; the First Martyr that Fell a Sacrifice to His Country in the City of Baltimore, on the 19th of April, 1861. Concord, MA: P. B. Cogswell, printers, 1862.

Lights and Shadows of Factory Life in New England; by a Factory Girl. New York: J. Winchester, 1843.

Locke, Jane E. *Miscellaneous Poems.* Boston: Otis, Broaders and Com-pany, 1842.

Lord, Robert H., et al. *History of the Archdiocese of Boston.* 3 vols. New York: Sheed and Ward, 1944.

Loubat, James F. *Narrative of the Mission to Russia, in 1866 of the Hon. Gustavus V. Fox.* New York: D. Appleton and Company, 1873.

Lowell an Early American Industrial Community; by the Department of English and History at Massachusetts Institute of Technology. Cambridge: M.I.T., 1950.

Lowell and Suburban Street Railway Company. *Scenes Along the Routes.* Lowell: June, 1896.

Lowell Board of Trade. *Yearbook of the Lowell Board of Trade.* 1911–1912.

Lowell, Chelmsford, Graniteville, Forge Village, Dracut, Collinsville of Today, Their Commerce, Trade and Industries, Descriptive and Historical. Lowell: Daily Citizen, 1893.

Lowell Institution for Savings. *At the Meeting of the Waters; A Sketch of Lowell Life from the Discovery of the Merrimack to the Present Day.* Lowell: 1929.

Lowell, James Russell. *The Biglow Papers.* Boston: Houghton Mifflin, 1885. Reprint: AMS, 1973.

The Lowell Magazine; devoted to the commercial and civic interests of Lowell, Massachusetts. Lowell: 1909–1910.

Lowell Morning Mail. *City of Lowell, Massachusetts, Its Commercial and Financial Resources; Souvenir of Lowell Morning Mail.* Lowell: 1890.

The Lowell Offering; prepared by females employed in the mills. Lowell: 1840–1845. Reprint: Greenwood, 1970.

Lowell: Past, Present and Prospective, 1891. Lowell: Citizen Newspaper Company, 1891.

Lowell Technological Institute. *Alexander Goodlet Cumnock; 1834–1919.* Lowell. n.d.

Lowell Trades and Labor Council. *Lowell; A City of Spindles.* Lowell: 1900.

Lynch, P. J. *Souvenir History of St. John's Hospital;* written for the quarter-centennial celebration of the founding of the institution. Lowell: Morning Mail Print, 1892.

Marryat, Frederick. *A Diary in America.* London: 1839. Reprint: Greenwood, 1973.

Martineau, Harriet, ed. *Mind Amongst the Spindles.* Boston: Jordan, Swift and Wiley, 1845.

————. *Society in America.* New York: Saunders and Otley, 1837. Reprint: AMS, 1966.

Massachusetts House of Representatives. *Report of a Committee in Response to a Petition by Robert B. Caverly Accusing Lowell Manufacturing Companies of "Unduly Influencing" . . . the Citizens of Said City in the Exercise of Their Elective Franchise.* Boston: May 4, 1852.

McGouldrick, Paul F. *New England Textiles in the Nineteenth Century; Profits and Investments.* Cambridge: Harvard University Press, 1968.

Meader, J. W. *The Merrimack River; Its Sources and Its Tributaries.* Boston: B. B. Russell, 1869.

Memorial Services for Eli Wait Hoyt, Sunday, February 20, 1887. Lowell: Morning Mail Company, 1887.

Meserve, H. C. *Lowell–An Industrial Dream Come True*. Boston: National Association of Cotton Manufacturers, 1923.

The Middlesex Hearthstone. Lowell: Middlesex Hearthstone Co., 1895–1896.

Miles, Henry A. *Lowell As It Was and As It Is*. Lowell: Powers, Bagley and Dayton, 1845. Reprint: Arno Press, 1972.

Montgomery, James. *Practical Detail of the Cotton Manufacture of the United States of America Contrasted and Compared with that of Great Britain*. Glasgow: John Niven, 1840. Reprint: Johnson Reprint Corp., 1968.

Murray, Charles A. *Travels in North America during the Years 1834, 1835, 1836*. 2 vols. New York: Harper and Brothers, 1839.

Nash, Howard P. *Stormy Petrel: The Life and Times of General Benjamin F. Butler, 1818–1893*. Rutherford, NJ: Fairleigh Dickinson University Press, 1969.

Nelson Colonial Department Store. *Lowell Illustrated; A Souvenir of the Textile Metropolis of Modern Industrial New England, and of the Great Nelson Colonial Department Store*. Lowell: 1907.

Nesmith, James E. *The Life and Work of Frederic Thomas Greenhalge, Governor of Massachusetts*. Boston: Roberts Brothers, 1897.

The New England Offering; a magazine of industry, written by females who live by their labor. Lowell: Harriet Farley, April, 1848-March, 1850. Reprint: Greenwood, 1970.

The New Moon. Lowell: C. I. Hood and Company, 1881–1885.

Nickerson, Jan. *Bright Promise*. New York: Funk and Wagnalls Company, 1965.

O'Connell, William Cardinal. *Recollections of Seventy Years*. Boston: Houghton Mifflin, 1934.

O'Connor, Thomas H. *Lords of the Loom: The Cotton Whigs and the Coming of the Civil War*. New York: Scribner, 1968.

O'Dwyer, George F. *The Irish Catholic Genesis of Lowell*. Lowell: Sullivan Brothers, 1920.

The Operatives Magazine; published by an association of females. Lowell: William Schouler, April, 1841-May, 1842.

Owen, Frank N. *Fire Service of Lowell; A Souvenir Presented to the Appreciative Public of the City of Spindles*. Lowell: Lowell Firemen's Fund Association, 1888.

Parker, Margaret Terrell. *Lowell: A Study of Industrial Development*. New York: Macmillan, 1940. Reprint: Kennikat Press, 1970.

Parton, James. *General Butler in New Orleans; History of the Administration of the Department of the Gulf in the Year 1862*. New York: Mason Brothers, 1864.

Patterson, David N. *Reminiscences of the Early Physicians of Lowell and Vicinity*. Lowell: Morning Mail Print, 1899.

Pennell, Elizabeth R., and Joseph Pennell. *The Life of James McNeill Whistler*. 2 vols. Philadelphia: J. B. Lippincott Company, 1908. Reprint: AMS, 1973.

Perry, Albert. *Whistler's Father*. Indianapolis: The Bobbs-Merrill Company, 1939.

Pictorial Lowell. Lowell: Thomas E. Lawler, n.d.

Pollard, John A. *John Greenleaf Whittier, Friend of Man*. Boston: Houghton Mifflin, 1949. Reprint: Archon Books, 1969.

Pomeroy, Marcus M. *Life and Public Service of Benjamin F. Butler, Major-General in the Army and Leader of the Republican Party.* New York: 1868.

Proceedings in the City of Lowell at the Centennial Observance of the Incorporation of the Town of Lowell, Massachusetts, March 1, 1926. Lowell: 1926.

Proceedings in the City of Lowell at the Semi-Centennial Celebration of the Incorporation of the Town of Lowell, Massachusetts, March 1, 1876. Lowell: 1876.

Proposal for the New City Hall and Memorial Building. Lowell: 1890.

Pulsifer, Mrs. Nathan. *Wheel and Spindle; An Historical Pageant of the Lowell Textile Industry, 1836–1936.* Lowell: M. G. Wight and Company, 1936.

Rankin, J. E. *The Battle Not Man's but God's.* Lowell: Stone and Huse, 1863.

Record of Massachusetts Volunteers; 1861–1865. 2 vols. Boston: Wright and Potter, printers, 1868.

Report of the Ministry-at-Large in Lowell to the Missionary Society Connected with the South Parish. Lowell: 1845–1868.

A Review of "The Necessity of Sabbath Labor" on Corporations, by a Citizen of Lowell. Lowell: Published by the author, 1847.

Roberts, Christopher. *The Middlesex Canal, 1793–1860.* Cambridge: Harvard University Press, 1938.

Robinson, Harriet Hanson. *Early Factory Labor in New England.* Boston: Wright and Potter Printing Company, 1883.

———. *Loom and Spindle; or, Life Among the Early Mill Girls.* New York: Thomas Y. Crowell and Company, 1898. Reprint: Press Pacifica, 1976.

———. *Massachusetts in the Woman Suffrage Movement; A General, Political, Legal, and Legislative History, from 1774 to 1881.* Boston: Roberts Brothers, 1881.

Robinson, William S. *The Salary Grab.* Boston: Lee and Shepard, 1873.

———. *"Warrington" Pen Portraits.* Boston: Lee & Shepard, 1877.

Roelker, William G. *The Abbotts of Lowell, Massachusetts in the Civil War.* Lowell: 1941.

The Rosebud. Lowell: Oliver Sheple, 1832–1833.

Saint Joseph's Hospital. *One Hundreth Anniversary Celebration of St. Joseph's Hospital.* Lowell: 1940.

Saloutos, Theodore. *The Greeks in the United States.* Cambridge: Harvard University Press, 1964.

Santerre, Richard. *Bibliographie des Imprimés Franco-Américains Parus à Lowell, Massachusetts, de 1837 à 1968.* Manchester, NH: Ballard Frères, 1969.

———. *The Franco-Americans of Lowell, Massachusetts.* Lowell: Franco-American Day Committee, 1972.

Sarmiento's Travels in the United States in 1847. Tr. by Michael A. Rockland. Princeton, NJ: Princeton University Press, 1970.

Schouler, William. *A History of Massachusetts in the Civil War.* 2 vols. Boston: E. P. Dutton, 1868.

Scoresby, William. *American Factories and Their Female Operatives.* Boston: Ticknor, 1845. Reprint: Burt Franklin, 1968.

Shadwell, Arthur. *Industrial Efficiency; A Comparative Study of Industrial Life in England, Germany, and America.* New York: Longmans, Green and Company, 1906.

Stern, Madeleine B. *We the Women; Career Firsts of Nineteenth Century America.* New York: Schulte Publ. Company, 1963.

Struik, Dirk J. *Yankee Science in the Making.* Boston: Little, Brown, 1948. Revised: Collier Books, 1962.

Sumner, Helen L. *Report on Condition of Woman and Child Wage-Earners in the United States.* Vol. IX: *History of Women in Industry in the United States.* Washington: Government Printing Office, 1910. Reprint: Arno Press, 1974.

Tharp, Louise H. *The Appletons of Beacon Hill.* Boston: Little, Brown, 1973.

Thompson, William T., *Major Jones' Sketches of Travels.* Philadelphia: Peterson and Bros., 1848.

Thoreau, Henry David. *A Week on the Concord and Merrimack Rivers.* New York: G. P. Putnam, 1849.

Trefousse, Hans L. *Ben Butler; The South Called Him Beast.* New York: Twayne Publ., 1957. Reprint: Octagon, 1974.

Trollope, Anthony. *North America.* 2 vols. New York: Harper and Brothers, 1862. Reprint: Kelley, 1970.

Tryon, Warren S., ed. *A Mirror for Americans: Life and Manners in the United States, 1790–1870, As Recorded by American Travelers.* 3 vols. Chicago: University of Chicago Press, 1952.

Van Slyck, J.D. *New England Manufacturers and Manufactories.* 2 vols. Boston: Van Slyck and Company, 1879.

Varnum, Atkinson C. History of Pawtucket Church and Society. Lowell: Morning Mail Print, 1888.

Views of Lowell and Vicinity. Portland, ME: L. H. Nelson Company, 1904.

Vital Records of Lowell, Massachusetts to the End of the Year 1849. 4 vols. Salem, MA: The Essex Institute, 1930.

Voice of Industry. Lowell and Worcester: May, 1845-May, 1848.

Vose, George L. *A Sketch of the Life and Works of George W. Whistler, Civil Engineer.* Boston: Lee and Shepard, 1887.

Walton, Perry. *The Story of Textiles.* Boston: Walton Advertising and Printing, 1925.

Ware, Caroline F. *The Early New England Cotton Manufacture, A Study in Industrial Beginnings.* Boston: Houghton Mifflin, 1931. Reprint: Johnson Reprint Corp., 1966.

Ware, Norman. *The Industrial Worker, 1840–1860; The Reaction of American Industrial Society to the Advance of the Industrial Revolution.* Boston: Houghton Mifflin, 1924. Reprint: Quadrangle Books, 1964.

Waters, Rev. Wilson. *History of Chelmsford, Massachusetts.* Lowell: Courier-Citizen, 1917.

Wayman, Dorothy G. *Cardinal O'Connell of Boston: A Biography of William Henry O'Connell, 1895–1944.* New York: Farrar, Straus & Young, 1955.

Webber, Samuel. *Manual Power for Machines, Shafts, and Belts; with the History of Cotton Manufacture in the United States.* New York: D. Appleton and Company, 1879.

Webster, Prentiss, ed. *The Story of the City Hall Commission, Including the Exercises at the Laying of the Corner Stones and the Dedication of the City Hall and Memorial Hall.* Lowell: Citizen Newspaper Company, 1894.

West, Richard S., Jr. *Lincoln's Scapegoat General; A Life of Benjamin F. Butler, 1818-1893.* Boston: Houghton Mifflin, 1965.

Whistler, James A. M. *The Gentle Art of Making Enemies.* New York: G. P. Putnam's sons, 1890. Reprint: Dover, 1967.

White, George S. *Memoir of Samuel Slater; The Father of American Manufactures. Connected with a History of the Rise and Progress of the Cotton Manufacture in England and America.* Philadelphia: 1836. Reprint: Kelley, 1967.

Whittier, John G. *Snow Bound; A Winter Idyl.* Boston: Ticknor and Fields, 1867.

_____. *The Stranger in Lowell.* Boston: Waite, Pierce and Company, 1845.

Winthrop, Robert C. *Memoir of the Hon. Nathan Appleton;* prepared agreeably to a resolution of the Massachusetts Historical Society. Boston: John Wilson and Son, 1861.

Women of Lowell. New York: Arno Press, 1974.

Woodbury, C. J. H. *Bibliography of the Cotton Manufacture.* Waltham, MA: Press of E. L. Barry, 1909.

Young, James H. *The Toadstool Millionaires; A Social History of Patent Medicines in America Before Federal Regulation.* Princeton, NJ: Princeton University Press, 1961.

Notes on Authors

NOTES ON AUTHORS

Mary H. Blewett earned her PhD. degree at the University of Missouri. Professor of History at the University of Lowell, she is currently president of the Lowell Historical Society. She is the author of "Roosevelt, Truman and the Failure to Revive the New Deal, 1944–1946." in *Harry S. Truman and the Fair Deal*, edited by A. L. Hamby.

Himself an immigrant, Peter F. Blewett received his PhD. degree from Boston College. He is Associate Professor of History at the University of Lowell, and a member of the Past and Present Society of London.

J. Frederic Burtt has done work in archaelogical sites throughout the world. A former president of the Lowell Historical Society and the New Hampshire Archaeological Society, he is Associate Professor in the Department of Mechanical Engineering at the University of Lowell.

Charles F. Carroll holds a PhD. degree from Brown University and is currently researching technology in early America. Professor of History at the University of Lowell, he is the author of *The Timber Economy of Puritan New England*.

Harry C. Dinmore settled in Lowell in the 1930s, after earning a degree in mining engineering from the University of Minnesota. He is the treasurer and a former president of the Lowell Historical Society.

Robert Dugan is reference librarian of the Beverly Public Library and previously worked at the Dracut and Lowell libraries. As a planning aide in Lowell, he served as preservation officer and liaison with the Massachusetts Historical Commission.

Arthur L. Eno, Jr., is a native of Lowell, a practicing lawyer and former president of the Lowell Historical Society.

John A. Goodwin began his teaching career in the cotton department of Lowell Textile Institute. He is now Professor in the Department of Mechanical Engineering at the University of Lowell. A former president of the Lowell Art Association and of the Lowell Historical Society, he is currently president of the Lowell Museum Corporation.

Joseph W. Lipchitz was awarded his PhD. degree by Case Western Reserve University. He is Professor of History and Political Science at the University of Lowell, and has been chairman of the Tewksbury school committee.

Nancy Zaroulis is an editor and writer.

Index